W9-AOV-002

DISCA

Praise for Our Work

"Your work is integral to our efforts and will help us meet our current and future workload by creating a new operating state that improves trust and teamwork and propels our vision to new heights."
- Donald Cromer, President, Hughes Space and Communications

"This experience is one that we will never forget and I thank you for creating such a great program."
- Edmond Haronian, Executive Vice President, New York Life Insurance

"As a result of your program people are working just as hard, but now there is trust, mutual support, openness and sensitivity. It's a different place."
- Jeanne Scott, Director of Corporate Training, Taco Bell

"I know you are well supplied with accolades for your work, so I won't belabor it, but suffice it to say you are masters at your craft."
- Cor Westerhoff, Deputy Government Programs, Loral Space Systems

"Your work exposed me to more concise, contemporary improvement skills than I have ever seen presented in one place at one time."
- Boyd Willat, Founder of Day Runner and
President of Willat Writing Instruments

"During the last 15 years and especially during my tenure as Director of Human Resources for The International Division, I have used a wide variety of consulting and training services, but none have been more impactful than your work."
- Jerry LoPorto, GIA Manager, Digital/Compaq

"I am awed by your ability and desire to impact lives. What a career to have."
- Rhodes Robinson, President of Environmental Services Inc.

"This strategic planning and team development work resulted in a major breakthrough and led to a winning team effort."
- Gary Johnson, HR & IPD Implementation Manager, TRW

Praise for *Say Yes to Change*

"In a world as technologically advanced as ours, it is easy to get overwhelmed by change. Yet change, as George & Sedena Cappannelli remind us in this book, is not only inevitable but valuable. The unique insights and practical tools they share with us can help us—as executive teams and as individuals to live more expansive, empowered and successful lives."
- Brewster Shaw, US Astronaut and
Boeing's Director of The Manned Flight & Space Exploration

"In these turbulent times we are all faced with dramatic changes. Our ability to accept change, to deal with it consciously and with the kind of optimism, positive attitude and confidence that George & Sedena Cappannelli discuss in this book may well be one of the most important abilities we can develop. That, of course, and our constant focus on love which in the end is the most important antidote we have against the fear that limits us."
- Gerald Jampolski, Author of Love Is Letting Go of Fear

"You hear a lot about change in corporate America these days. In boardrooms and coffee rooms people are aware that the pace of technology and the challenges of a global economic marketplace make incredible demands on us all. So no matter what your role or level of responsibility, the ideas and suggestions for dealing with change that George & Sedena present in this book can make a real difference in your life—both professional and personal—by helping you to make change one of your best allies."
- Cody Plott, President, Pebble Beach Resort
Former Executive VP Hyatt International

"In *Say Yes to Change*, the authors present realistic ways to handle career challenges, new primary relationships, personal issues and much more."
- Publishers Weekly

"This inspiring book is filled with motivational exercises to move you forward step by step to a place where you can enthusiastically make successful changes."
- NAPRA ReView

"Real answers for individuals and a world—in crisis."
- Radio-TV Interview Report

Authenticity

Simple Strategies
for Greater Meaning and Purpose
at Work and at Home

GEORGE & SEDENA CAPPANNELLI

1700 Madison Road   Cincinnati, Ohio 45206

Authenticity
Simple Strategies
for Greater Meaning and Purpose
at Work and at Home

© 2004 by Emmis Books
www.emmisbooks.com

ALL RIGHTS RESERVED under
International and Pan-American Copyright Conventions.

Library of Congress control number: 2004105792

ISBN 1-57860-000-0

Edited by Jack Heffron
Cover and interior designed by Stephen Sullivan

PRINTED IN THE UNITED STATES OF AMERICA

Measure your individual and organizational authenticity quotient today.
Visit: www.Authenticity.cc

For information on corporate consulting and training, motivational and
inspirational talks and other special seminars and programs presented by
George and Sedena Cappannelli, visit them at www.Authenticity.cc,
www.InformationandTraining.com and www.AboutLifeInc.com.

Providing innovative solutions in Business Strategy, Technology,
Process Improvement and People Skills
The Information & Training Company (480) 837-5758

*The secret of health for both mind and body is not
to mourn for the past, worry about the future, or anticipate troubles,
but to live in this moment wisely and earnestly.*
⊰ Buddha ⊱

CONTENTS

◆

First Things

Welcome to *Authenticity*. You may be someone who leads a large organization, operates a small business or is self-employed. You may be a stay-at-home mom or dad, a senior citizen, a member of a team at work or on a playing field, or a volunteer in your community. You may be responsible for the well being of your family or of a loved one, at the beginning of your career or ready to retire, or you may simply be doing what you can to deal with the many challenges and opportunities that come up in your life each day.

If you have opened this book you probably have days on which you feel your life is reasonably successful and others on which you sense you somehow stepped off the path and lost touch with your direction and purpose. In this complex world of rapidly changing rules and roles it's easy to lose sight of what you value most—a life of real meaning and genuine satisfaction, the life, in fact, you were born to live.

Authenticity is for those of us who deal with the rising pressures and demands of modern life each day at work, at home, and in the world at large. It is for those of us who sometimes find ourselves repeating the same costly mistakes over and over again—not out of laziness, ill will or incapacity, but because we do not take time to explore some of the limiting beliefs and less-than-effective strategies that prevent us from living engaged, rewarding lives.

These limiting beliefs can run the gamut from personal and professional goals, our sense of entitlement, worthiness and our own abilities, to our views on success and failure, happiness, health and freedom, aging and death. These limiting beliefs can be about our careers, our relationships with ourselves, with those who we hold most dear and with that Higher Power we call God or Spirit or Oneness. No matter what the subject, the beliefs we hold and the strategies we practice either expand our potential to live authentic lives or keep us circling around in lives and careers that lack the personal meaning our hearts call us to express.

Authenticity is designed to help you determine if you have lost touch with your sense of meaning and purpose, why it matters and where to find it again. You will do this by examining your beliefs as well as your life and career strategies. You will learn how to move past beliefs that limit you, especially those that create some of the emotional drama that distracts you from experiencing the kind of joy and inner peace you know it is your right as a human being to experience.

So if you sometimes sense that your life is a gift you have not yet fully unwrapped, the concepts and suggestions offered in these pages can help. If, from time to time, you lose touch with your sense of passion, clarity, energy or enthusiasm, then this is a good place to begin finding it again. If you are in the second half of life and worry that the best part of your life may be over, then this book has some terrific gifts for you. If your dreams sometimes get tarnished in your interaction with this topsy-turvy world, if you want to raise your level of commitment in your life, or if you do not want to squander any more of your precious opportunities, then read on.

YOUR PART

We want to be clear at the beginning, however, that this is not one of those soft and fuzzy books that promise you the moon and suggest you can have it effortlessly and immediately. In our experience, finding greater meaning and purpose requires a good deal more than that. It requires a deep willingness to do a number of things differently: express more compassion and honesty for ourselves and others; examine our beliefs and replace those that no longer work; explore some of the challenging and disturbing topics we often avoid; eliminate some of our habitual behaviors; and, above all, practice some of the essential skills we already know and are not practicing and learn some of the lessons we did not learn in school, at church or at home.

Finding greater meaning and purpose is a life-long job. It is also the job you were born to do. The search is not easy, but it is the most valuable thing you can do, and you have the courage and skill to do it. Like every person on this Earth, you have a unique gift to share that has never been shared before and never will be again in quite the same manner, and this gift can benefit all of us. So even if you do not yet know your gift or how to share it, please know that this book can serve you.

OUR PART

In writing these pages we have done our best to avoid the "chewing-gum answers" and "feel-good strategies" that tend to evaporate almost as soon as the page is turned or the speaker has left the podium. We also hold too much respect for you to sugarcoat our message. Frankly, we think the world already has far too much polite information that does not advance our lives. As a result, we hope these words will motivate, prompt and, at times, even prod you into a more meaningful dialogue with yourself. Through this important dialogue you will discover the most direct path to the life you came here to lead.

We come to writing this book from worlds that have presented us with a number of different experiences and challenges. In some of these roles we have learned from our own mistakes and in others we have been graced to work with world leaders, successful people from various professional and academic disciplines and some of the best organizations in the world. This group includes Golda Meir, Desmond Tutu, Lech Walesa, Mother Teresa, U.S. Senate and Presidential Candidates, Hollywood personalities, artists, athletes and thousands of people who attend our talks and programs.

We have worked with leading companies, such as Boeing, Disney, PepsiCo, Sun Microsystems, TRW, Digital/Compac, Oracle, *The Los Angeles Times* and others. We have worked with government agencies and national associations such as The U.S. Army, The U.S. Navy, NASA, NOAA, the Department of Defense and the U.S. Forest Service. Taken together this experience has driven home one primary and essential point: *It is not only desirable, but also essential to discover and live authentic lives.*

Those who seek to create greater meaning and purpose live fuller, longer, more joyful, healthier and more rewarding lives. They learn and contribute the fruits of this learning to others. They add significantly to the quality and grace of the lives of everyone they touch.

Oprah Winfrey, who is a living example of this ability to add quality and grace to the lives of those she touches, said it this way: "What we are all striving for is authenticity, a spirit-to-spirit connection." Linda Ronstadt, whose music has touched so many of us, tells other musicians and entertainers, "Don't worry about being original. Focus on being authentic and all the rest will follow."

Our experience has made it clear to us that those who have the courage to seek their destiny often reach more evolved levels of consciousness while those who do not end up leading lives far more constricted and far less rewarding. Of course, to be successful in our search for greater meaning and purpose we have go against the tide, because most of us emerge from our formative years and education ill equipped to lead uplifting, unique and authentic lives. Indeed, while our minds may be filled with information, our emotions, our spiritual intelligence and our unique talents have remained largely undernourished.

As a result, far too many of us don't know how to love fully and joyfully, to balance our emotions and to communicate constructively with ourselves and with others. We do not know how to build consensus, establish collaboration, develop teamwork, craft truly aligned visions, identify and live by fundamental values, and create practical strategies for our lives and our careers. Nor do many of us know how to build sane lives that balance our physical, emotional, intellectual and spiritual needs.

Many of us also do not know how to identify ways to best serve our families, our organizations or our communities. Nor do we know how to create constructive rules of social engagement, or contribute to harmonious global systems. Far too few of us know how to listen, observe, communicate, share, inquire, meditate, love, and of special importance, find comfort in the silence from which all true wisdom comes.

This understanding—along with more clumsy life experiences than either of us cares to remember—constitutes the primary reason we began our own search to live more aligned and authentic lives. As a result, *Authenticity* is a personal book. Though it pokes at a number of institutions and social practices, it is not intended as a critique of these institutions or a criticism of those who work within them.

From our perspective, if there is any criticism or accountability for the troubled state of our world today, it must be spread equally across all of our shoulders.

Our primary goal is to approach the subject of societal and organizational change by focusing on individual change. Our intention is to be inspirational and provocative, to talk with you and not at you. We invite you into our personal lives and the lives of some of the people we have been privileged to work with in the hope that you, in turn, will feel encouraged to dig more deeply into your own life and to share the fruits of your exploration with those around you. Our purpose is to offer some alternative perspectives, skills and insights that may encourage you to examine your beliefs, identify some of their limitations and experiment with new strategies that can lead you to a more meaningful and authentic life.

USING THIS BOOK

As you read, give yourself time to digest some of the ideas, wrestle with some of the larger and more controversial subjects. We also suggest that you experiment with the recommendations.

Though maximum value can be gained by reading the chapters in order, this material can also be read in any order. You can turn to whatever chapter most applies to a current challenge. You can also use *Authenticity* as a source of guidance by randomly opening the book and using that topic or the daily reflection as a theme for practice that day.

Authenticity combines the masculine and feminine points of view, a combination we find lacking in this world in which men and women often find themselves on opposite sides of many issues. Indeed, this understanding is one of the reasons we have come together in marriage and why we have chosen to work jointly on a series of books.

It has also been clear to us from the beginning of this project that if we are going to speak on the topic of authenticity we have to live it more fully ourselves. As a result, during the writing of this book we have had to learn more about the differences in our individual beliefs and alternate roles we play in our relationship. You will find some of these lessons captured here through the sharing of some of our personal strengths and frailties as well as those we have encountered in our interactions with others. We have tried to be candid about some of the places where we have struggled and others where we have managed to break through to new levels of harmony.

Finally, we have done our best to deal with some of life's more controversial topics and sensitive issues: love, death, personal addiction, original sin and God. You might find the exploration disturbing, at times. Or you might find it enlightening or liberating. Whatever your response, know that we do not claim to have an exclusive corner on truth. We offer our beliefs with the utmost respect for your beliefs. We use some images and concepts that are designed to assist you in allowing aspects of the mystery to disclose themselves to you in less direct ways.

We express our deepest gratitude to the thousands of men and women who have had the courage to share their hard-won wisdom with us. Our heartfelt thanks and appreciation also to Jack Heffron, Richard Hunt, Howard Cohen and Steve Sullivan at Emmis Books and to Cricket Pechstein, our agent, who have assisted us in giving birth to this book. Finally, of course, we dedicate *Authenticity* to you and trust you will find it a useful and inspiring book about some shifts in perception, belief and behavior you can experiment with to bring greater meaning and purpose into your life.

George & Sedena Cappannelli

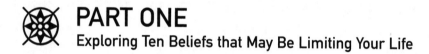

PART ONE
Exploring Ten Beliefs that May Be Limiting Your Life

Authenticity Is...

It is not because things are difficult that we do not dare.
It is because we do not dare that things are difficult.

--◄[Seneca]►--

Authentic from the Latin, *authenticus*, and the Greek, *authentikos*, means "worthy of acceptance, authoritative, trustworthy, not imaginary, false or imitation, conforming to an original." Synonyms include: genuine, veritable, unique, sincere, original, bona fide.

Quite a word! Quite a range of connotations and synonyms! As we set out on our journey to bring greater meaning and purpose into our lives and our careers, let's begin by talking about the essential role authenticity plays in our lives and in the lives of those with whom we are privileged to work.

In our lives authenticity serves as a signpost pointing toward a way of being in the world that offers greater alignment of body, mind, emotions and spirit. It informs our search to perform meaningful work and to live in accordance with the fundamental principles or core values that issue from our souls. It assists us in our quest to discover why we are here and to honor the gift of our life and the mystery that we call God. For us, "authenticity" means seeking to live in harmony with life. It means having respect for the earth and all life forms that reside here. It means closing the gap between the values we hold and the way we demonstrate these values every day through our thoughts, words, intentions and actions.

Authenticity does not mean perfection or moral or ethical superiority or self-righteousness. In fact, there is no place in our definition for arrogance, for holding ourselves separate or for judging others. It is not about trying to be right, affecting a holier-than-thou attitude, being sanctimonious or pretending that we know what is right for anyone else. And it is certainly not about trying to "have it all together."

In our experience, living authentically is an inside-out job. It is about having the courage to take risks and the willingness to make mistakes, to admit our shortcomings and to learn from them. It is about owning our vulnerability, accepting our humanness and acknowledging our interdependence on others. It is about going to the edge, not in search of personal gain—although that may result—but in search of what is best and highest, what is original and unique.

Authenticity is not about seeking the approval of others or dancing to the tune of public recognition. It is about being honest with ourselves, curious about life, willing to experience the discomfort of being a work in progress and staying true to our deepest personal values as we search to discover what we are here on this earth to experience and express.

In defining authenticity in this way we do not mean to imply that we are able to live authentically in every moment or that we have mastered the physical, emotional, mental and spiritual aspects of our lives sufficiently to demonstrate true alignment in all areas or at all times. Instead, we are saying that this extraordinary word helps us to remember that our lives and our careers become more sane, joyful, and meaningful when we have the courage to seek alignment with purpose and to measure that alignment against the contribution our purpose makes to the elevation and advancement of others.

To illustrate how this works, let us take you back a number of years in our lives. At the time, George was running a foundation in Los Angeles that honored individuals whose lives demonstrated "personal integrity." One of the recipients of that year's International Integrity Award was Stevie Wonder. During his acceptance speech at a gala at The Beverly Hilton Hotel in Beverly Hills, he talked about how authenticity and its cousin, integrity, helped him to measure his own alignment. To paraphrase Stevie Wonder's remarks: "When I first learned about this award, I was going to refuse it. I didn't believe I had demonstrated enough personal integrity to warrant the honor. But the more I thought about it the more I realized that if I accepted this award it would serve as a reminder, a kind of signpost that could help keep me honest and help me to bring more personal integrity into my life."

Zusya of Hanepoli is reputed to have said it this way: "In the other world they will not ask me, 'Why were you not Moses? They will ask me, 'Why were you not Zusya?'" In our opinion, Zusya and Stevie Wonder were both talking about their search for greater authenticity.

This search for authenticity is not new or limited to the famous. It also is not easy. Indeed, we find that it is not only challenging but also requires a willingness to experiment with some strategies very different from those we were introduced to earlier in our lives. In fact, living a life of greater meaning and purpose often requires that we turn 180 degrees and face a direction different from the one recommended to us in our early instruction.

What do we mean? From the beginning we were both taught to look outside of ourselves to other people and sources for the rules, guidance, approval, confirmation, permission and authority that made up our lives. In short, we were led to believe that life is supposed to be outer-directed and outer-authenticated.

We learned that everything, even our connection with God, was to be accessed through intermediaries—parents, preachers, teachers and coaches being the most predominant. We were also led to believe that the information and experiences we needed most were to be found in places of worship that were sacred like churches and temples, formal places of learning such as schools, and places of knowledge that were quiet, such as libraries. Above all, we were taught that these places were different from the places where we lived and played.

This formal training went on for years. Perhaps this is true in your life too. Perhaps the primary institutions that helped to shape you—family, church, schools and local community organizations—also promoted the belief that wisdom is an outside-in process.

Education, at least in the form we were introduced to, was about taking things in and reciting them back as precisely as possible. In fact, our grades improved or dropped based on just how precisely we did this. As a result, we learned that if we wanted to be successful in school we needed to value outside opinion more than our own inner messages and to delegate our sovereignty to the outside world. Was it like that for you?

Of course, when we were little we needed a reasonable amount of this outside-in stuff. Our species, it seems, comes to this planet ill prepared to meet the primary needs of life, which is one of the reasons we have longer gestation and development periods than most other species. Eventually, however, most of us get big enough to leave a lot of this outside stuff behind. But here is where the ripple comes in. In our experience, even when most of us no longer need all of this outside support, we continue to function as if we did. Yes, having been trained to look to other people and institutions outside ourselves for authentication and validation, most of us continue to get our rules, guidance, approval, permission and authority from someone or something outside us.

We believe this outside-in education is extremely debilitating. In fact, we believe that it is the principal reason so many of us live emotionally and spiritually immature lives and build such emotionally and spiritually immature worlds. We also believe it is the reason few of us ever truly develop enough self-validation and self-actualization to lead original and authentic lives.

Anne Morrow Lindbergh, the author of *The Gift from the Sea*, appears to agree. She said, "The most exhausting thing in the world is to be insincere." From our perspective exhaustion comes from being out of touch with our truth and our connection to our selves. In short, low energy, lack of passion, low self-esteem and low confidence issue from leading inauthentic lives.

TAKING BACK OUR SOVEREIGNTY

After years of experiencing the direct impact this "exhaustion" that Anne Morrow Lindbergh refers to has in our own lives and in the lives of the thousands of folks in the companies, government agencies and non-profits we are privileged to work with, we believe it is time, long overdue time, to change this pattern. How? By exploring a different set of strategies and practicing a deeper, truer set of values. We believe it is time to begin living lives that are not so obsessively focused on "outside" experiences and "other" sources for validation. In short, it is time to move beyond our dependence on other people's opinions, our own worldly status and our possessions as ways of measuring our success. Instead, we need to start focusing on achieving real emotional maturity, greater intellectual discernment, much deeper heart connection and, above all, true spiritual cooperation and alignment with the mystery that is life. We believe, in fact, that it is time to reinvest greater meaning and purpose in our own lives. We believe it is time to recommit to choosing values over possessions and relationships over tasks, not as a form of rebellion against the world, but as way of finally discovering and making peace with what is important.

Indeed, if we are ever to create a life for ourselves that is in balance with nature and in harmony with the needs of all of the species that reside here, if we are ever going to create sane, sustainable and successful economic, social, and political systems, all of us must take responsibility for our own lives. We must start living lives based on adherence to core values that we identify, experiment with and come to own. In this way, and only in this way, will we ever have the opportunity to experience that essential difference between what Carl Jung has called, "believing and knowing."

This life, this very moment, can and must be our opportunity to start holding ourselves accountable for emotional and spiritual maturity. It is our opinion that this can and must be our time to start singing the song of our own souls rather than parroting the canned 'muzak' of contemporary fads and superficial accomplishments.

This life can be our time to learn how to gain access to our own primary wisdom through communion with ourselves and to take better advantage of the opportunities, experiences and people that make up our lives whether the world approves of efforts or not. This is the real trick to being not only conscious members of humanity, but also authentic ones. When we no longer look to or wait for the world or any-one else to give us permission to live out our destinies, we can actually discover them. When we finally summon the courage to follow the unique beat of our own drum, we have the chance to discover our per-sonal connection with the primal and original rhythm we call God. On the day we choose to become the true "author and composer" of our destiny, there will be no more excuses. No more exits. No more time outs. No more disharmony and disease.

When this locus of control shifts from an outer-directed focus to an inward one, there will be no more room for pretending. No more reason to hang out on the sidelines. No more treating life as if it were a rehearsal. This does not mean that life has to be an endless drudgery of hard work and emotionally wrenching self-explorations. The truth is that the longer we walk on this path of "authenticity" the more we are discovering that our lives and our careers become wonderful adventures, more rewarding, friendly, joyful and relaxed trips from one great desti-nation of self-discovery to another.

From this vantage point, our lives and our work offer us endless opportunities to discover and explore the unknown. Our lives then become more about experimenting with new skills and options, more about living closer to the edge than in the middle, more about disclos-ing who we are than about hiding or pretending or avoiding. They become more about truth and maturity and solutions, than about blame and criticism or just getting by; more about gratitude, acceptance of the mysteries that we may never fully understand, and about celebrating the diversity and opportunities that are present each day. Life and work can then become more about "being" rather than "doing" and finally, about greater alignment between ourselves and God with no space in between.

HOW DO WE KNOW IF WE ARE LEADING AUTHENTIC LIVES?

We wish we could give you a simple answer to this question, but we can't. Our experience leads us to believe that authenticity is a person-al matter that each of us must ultimately discover in a personal way. After thousands of experiences in our personal lives and years of work in the fields of individual and organizational change, we can only conclude that each of us must answer this question in a different way based on slightly different standards.

At the same time, we do have ways to measure the degree of authenticity in our personal lives and in the work we do in the world. We will ask you some of the questions we ask ourselves:

- Are you currently experiencing areas in your life—at work and at home—where you feel there is less meaning and purpose than you would like there to be?
- Have you allowed what you do as work in the world to become ordinary, habitual and more about financial security than about learning?
- Are the contributions you make at work about gaining recognition and status or about adding genuine value?
- Are your personal relationships about getting what you want and satisfying your personal needs or are they about giving, serving and supporting others as well as yourself?
- Are you listening more to the world around you, your friends, colleagues at work and society at large or are you being faithful to the prompts that issue from your "inner voice"?
- Are you taking responsibility for your wants and needs or are you delegating the responsibility for the fulfillment of your longings to others?
- Are you looking to the outside world for your values or are you inner-directed?
- Are the things you do every day contributing to improving the quality of life for yourself and others, elevating their spirits, assisting them to empower their dreams or are the things you do keeping you and the world running in place?

In short, are you committed to bringing greater meaning and purpose into your life and the lives of people around you?

A VALUABLE REMINDER

In his autobiography titled *Memories, Dreams, Reflections*, Carl Jung describes a visit he made to the Southwestern United States. On that trip, Jung spent time with the Hopi Indians. From his first moments in their presence, he sensed something special about the tribe. He did not identify, however, what produced the unusual quality of character and deportment until he gained the trust of the chief of the tribe. Then he learned that the Hopi believed their job was to help the sun cross the sky each day.

Imagine his amazement! He was, a sophisticated European, educated in some of the best schools, cultured and well respected by his peers, a man of science from a species that considers itself at the apogee of the evolutionary tree. Some people in his culture called the Indians "savages," and yet while he and many of his colleagues and patients were still searching for meaning and purpose in their lives the Hopi already had tremendous meaning and purpose. They knew that their job was to help the sun cross the sky each day.

Talk about purpose and meaning! Talk about nobility, honor and respect! The Hopi's belief in their own purpose is large enough for most of us to hang the picture of our entire lives on. In fact, this single belief gave the Hopi something to measure each thought, word, intention and action against. By comparison, what do most of us who live in this so-called sophisticated world of ours use to measure our days against? What special task or function gives meaning and purpose to our lives?

Not everyone can help the sun cross the sky. That job is already taken. But surely we all can admit there are some other positive, uplifting and constructive things we can do in our lives. Perhaps it is not our job to change the world, invent new social systems or run for public office, but all of us can learn to share love more generously, provide greater support, strength and example for our children, execute our jobs with greater honor and a truer commitment to excellence. Perhaps all of us are not fated to lead revolutions in consciousness or invent new products or services, but we can deal with the people in our lives at work and at home with more respect and trust. We can identify our fears and learn to befriend them, reach across the chasms of prejudice and hate and express new levels of cooperation, understanding and collaboration. Perhaps it is not our task in this life to draft new legislation, break the world's speed record or hit 100 home runs in a single season, but we can develop our own unique talents, master our challenges, overcome our dysfunctions and contribute to the healing of our lives and in that way contribute to the healing of this planet and its species. These are just a few of the things we can do to find greater meaning and purpose even if the Hopi's already have that other important job.

So if you are looking for greater purpose and meaning in your life, perhaps it is time to start listening less to the noise of the world around you and more to your own wisdom. In this way you will discover a number of other ways to touch and elevate your own heart and the hearts of others. Perhaps you will find other ways to support yourself and to assist those you interact with to have greater compassion and consciousness. Perhaps in this way everything that you do and each person that you encounter will be a little bit better as a result of your interaction with them.

We have found that when we do these and other things we are able, at the end of each day, to say, "I've done my best today." So we recommend this practice to you. Perhaps if you are able to do this more and more each day, you will begin to contribute more of that unique spark that's never been contributed in the same way before because there has never before been anyone here quite like you. Perhaps this is what the search for "authenticity" is all about.

TODAY'S REFLECTION

I have the opportunity today to take some new and different steps to bring greater authenticity into my life. Today I have the chance to seek greater alignment between me, my values and my destiny. The question is—What will I chose to do today and every day for the rest of my life?

The Only Game in Town

*An Egyptian legend suggests that at the moment of our death,
our lives are reviewed and our goodness evaluated.*

*This evaluation is accomplished by placing our heart on one side
of the Scales of Justice—and the Feather of Truth on the other.*

*If the scales balance we are judged to have lived a good life
and are allowed to pass into the afterlife. If the scales do not
balance we must return to earth again for yet another try.*

*Imagine how innocent, how pure, open and true the heart
must be to balance a feather.*

There are not many among us who have hearts that are pure and weightless enough to balance the "Feather of Truth." Therefore, most of us do not have another precious moment to waste avoiding the critical things we have to learn and practice—things about life, intimacy, communication, emotional intelligence, awareness, honor, love, respect and, most especially, about the purpose and meaning of our lives. And if this is true for each of us as individuals then it is equally true for all of us as members of families, as leaders and employees in various companies and organizations and as members of local, regional, national and global communities.

Does it really matter that our hearts are not pure and weightless enough to balance a feather? We certainly think it does! In fact, we believe it is time to admit, out loud and once and for all, what so many of us have longed to admit for some time—that we do not want to settle for lives that are dogged by the sense of incompleteness and frustration that comes from not expressing our originality and authenticity.

In short, we believe it's time to say "Yes" rather than "No" to our wisdom, our energies, our talents, our opportunities, and above all, to those prompts and longings that issue from the depths of our hearts. It's time to make friends again with ourselves, to turn toward rather than away from the things that trouble us and to remember how important it is to do and be what we have come here to do and to be.

This is the path that we have chosen to walk and one that many of the people we have been privileged to know and work with are also walking. Through their example and courage they have taught us that to lead a life of real meaning and value we must face our fears and accept the lessons life offers us. World leaders, CEOs, astronauts, athletes, artists, statesman, spiritual leaders and just plain folks, all echoing the same thing—authenticity is worth its weight in gold.

HOW AND NOT WHY

In this scientifically sophisticated and technologically advanced age that constantly trumpets its own accomplishments, it is sometimes easy to miss this message and to be seduced into assuming that our progress in mastering some aspects of the physical universe assures us equal progress in mastering life's ordinary challenges. Indeed, many of us assume that in a world as advanced as this one, our schools and universities, our churches, families and community organizations must be providing us with strategies that allow us to live life more productively, joyfully and successfully. We certainly must be living more effectively, sanely and authentically than our parents or their parents before them.

But, of course, that is not the case, is it? Although our schools and universities have become larger and more complex, our religious institutions more diverse, and our media more abundant with information on more subjects than any of us could ever absorb in a lifetime, neither these institutions nor these sources appear to be doing a very good job of preparing us to live our lives as intelligently or organically as our best and highest inner promptings tell us we can.

Although the word "education"—which comes from the Latin root *educare* - means to 'call forth from within,' our schools and universities, our religious institutions and even our families do not appear to be delivering on this promise. They prepare us to meet the qualifications for a particular career or job and to be reasonably polite, law-abiding members of society. For the most part, however, they do not teach us how to access our inner wisdom or how to develop and sustain meaningful, lasting relationships, create sane systems or maintain and heal our bodies, minds and emotions. They do not teach us how to access the both sides of our brains or how to lead spiritually evolved lives. They do not encourage us to go beyond thinking and doing to 'being," beyond believing to knowing, and beyond hoping to actually experiencing a direct and meaningful relationship with ourselves and with God. In short, for all the razzle dazzle about advancements, our society does not prepare us to live lives that are in alignment with the underlying wisdom and harmony of the universe.

We could, of course, spend a great deal of our time trying to identify why we did not learn some of these primary lessons, but in truth the "why," even if we were lucky enough to locate it, is nowhere near as important as solving the real conundrum which is "how."

So let's explore how we can get from the places that confuse us and obscure our search to those where greater skill and willingness and a life of quality and alignment with our soul's purpose are to be found. It is, we believe, the only game in town worth playing.

EFFECTIVENESS BEGINS WITH COMMITMENT

The Chinese say "the journey of a thousand miles begins beneath one's feet." Our personal life experience verifies this fact. We have found that our willingness to accept where we are and what is going on in every moment, coupled with our willingness to work on the things that need our attention, have proven to be the difference between discovering real purpose and meaning in our lives and losing sight of our path.

This message has also made itself apparent many times in our personal relationship. And let's face it—these are rather perilous times for personal relationships. The changing gender roles and rules make it very challenging to navigate the turbulent waters. As a result, there are many times when issues, differences of opinion and disagreements arise. After a reasonable amount of pain and a lot of confusion and disappointment, we have finally begun to realize that each time one of these disagreements arises we have a choice. We can pretend these differences are not present, or we can choose to be present and deal with whatever has come up, including recognizing that we may not be able to agree. In the face of our disagreement—or perhaps we should say, especially during moments of disagreement—we can be responsible in our communication and committed to holding up our end of our partnership. In this way we access more of our authenticity.

In writing this book we have faced a number of these same challenges. This manuscript has had a number of different iterations and has hit both obstacles and snags. The framing of the original manuscript was George's task, but the shaping and tuning of it was something we both needed to be involved in. And as you can image, this is where "stuck" sometime showed up. Pretending "stuck" was not happening would not have done either of us or the book any good. Instead, we had to admit our differences and that often meant finding new ways to communicate, collaborate, to be truthful and, of particular consequence, respectful.

You probably have similar experiences in your life. Perhaps they show up in your interactions at work, or maybe these challenges appear more often in your personal relationships. No matter where they turn up, however, when you find yourself in the middle of a disagreement you may feel as though you have somehow stepped off the path and do not know how to find your way back.

Instead of following the sage advice of Native American scouts who suggest that when we are lost, we should stop, perhaps you, like us, try to forge ahead and in the process end up missing the path or turning away from rather than toward the reality of your situation. Perhaps you also find that eventually, no matter how hard it is to face reality, you must ultimately come to terms with the fact that you are lost. But don't feel upset. The desire to avoid facing reality is as true for large multi-national organizations as for us as individuals. It is as relevant for nation states as for families.

Another example of how we sometimes avoid the things that challenge us also comes from our personal lives. Both Sedena and I have lost our parents. If you have lost someone dear to you, you know that dealing with the loss of someone you love is never easy. In our case we have each lost one parent to the ravages of Alzheimers. Not an easy passage, we can assure you. As a result, at various times and in different ways we found ourselves dealing with a lot of fear, sadness and a sense of helplessness from the ravages of this disease. It also brought up enormous vulnerability that at times threatened to overwhelm us. Still, no matter how much we wanted to deny what was happening, no matter how difficult it was to face the slow fading away of parents we loved, in the end, if we wanted to honor our parents and the lives they had lived, as well as the enormous contributions they had made to our lives, we had to turn toward the reality and accept it. It was the only way we could mourn for them and allow our sad and troubled hearts to heal.

In other instances, there are challenges and issues that arise between us as business partners as well as marriage partners. Places where we have expectations of each other that go unmet. Places where we disappoint each other. Places where the stress of being alive and in a relationship at this confusing time has triggered anger, frustration, denial or withdrawal. And yet, no matter how deep the denial, no matter how great the desire to withdraw or how great the differences that seem to separate us, we eventually have to turn toward each other and toward whatever pain or disappointment we have been avoiding.

Our professional experience validates the fact that these same lessons apply between colleagues at work, members of volunteer organizations, fellow students, strategic partners, nation states and more. To succeed we must face our challenges honestly, compassionately and directly. Only in this way can we hope to find true alignment and authenticity.

With this understanding in mind, we invite you to take an important next step on the road to greater meaning and purpose. We invite you to make an agreement with yourself, to admit out loud or in writing that there is no way you will ever accomplish anything of true and lasting value without making a deep commitment to bring greater meaning and purpose into your life.

So right now, in the quiet of your own space or on the pages of your journal, acknowledge that, at the very least during the time you spend reading this book, you will be willing to turn toward rather than away from the things that scare, confuse and trouble you. You will be willing to learn the things you need to learn in order to fulfill your destiny.

TODAY'S REFLECTION

My commitment to learn more about my self, my life and my world in each moment is a deep and true commitment. It is a commitment to my authentic self and to my freedom, joy and true fulfillment. It is my way of saying—This is my life and I will honor it by living courageously.

◆

A Most Critical Ingredient

When you are inspired by some great purpose, some extraordinary project,
all your thoughts break their bonds; your mind transcends limitations,
your consciousness expands in every direction, and you find yourself in a new,
great and wonderful world. Dormant forces, faculties and talents
become alive, and you discover yourself to be a greater person by far
than you ever dreamed yourself to be.

⊰ Patanjali ⊱

In those hauntingly quiet or sometimes turbulent moments before you get up in the morning, or especially late at night when you lie there waiting for sleep, do you ever question the value and purpose of your life?

Most of us do, of course, even if we do not openly talk about it. In fact, even when we are up to our ears in all of the usual daily distractions we use to avoid paying attention to our inner thoughts, we cannot completely drown out that "still small inner voice," the one that keeps prompting and encouraging us to keep faith with ourselves, to remember that life lived without meaning, without purpose, without a sense of service and contribution is a life lacking in value. It is not an authentic life.

If your inner voice sounds at all like ours, it probably reminds you that a life spent obsessively or compulsively playing the Acquisition Game or the Money and Security Game, the Sports or Hobbies Game, the Political Game, the Business Game, the I'm Okay Game, the Sexual Attraction Game, the Let Me Entertain You Game, the I'm Important Game or even the Social Cause Game may get you some attention and recognition. It may help you pass the time, give you a sense of importance or cause you to feel like you are making some progress, but for an increasing number of us, it isn't all that satisfying, is it? Why? We believe that even though they occupy us and give us the sense that we are "doing something," underneath all the hustle and bustle these pursuits do not speak to or represent that essential part of us that longs for something truer and deeper that is not always easily defined but once encountered can be called authentic.

In our case, our "inner voices" tell us that to move beyond the sense of restlessness, incompleteness and exhaustion—and to satisfy our deepest longings—we must avoid using any of these games as preoccupations and distractions. Instead, we must take the necessary risks that come with moving into the unknown. When we honor our inner voices we move closer to our authentic selves. When we deny them, we often end up in a lot of muck and mire.

TRYING DOESN'T DO IT!

Of course, honoring our inner voices isn't always easy. In fact, because dissatisfaction and restlessness are not pleasant experiences, when these uncomfortable feelings arise our tendency sometimes is to turn away from them. We do this in hundreds of ways, from outright avoidance to doing whatever we are doing harder, faster or more frequently. Yes, instead of acknowledging and befriending the restlessness, instead of trying to learn why dissatisfaction is trying to get our attention, we tend to get even busier or do something we hope will change our mood or our situation, anything except feel the depth of the dissatisfaction and restlessness.

Perhaps you recognize this tendency. You might have also done your best to avoid or silence these feelings, assuming they are the result of some inadequacy, incompetence or dysfunction that you do not want to admit to or do not know how to overcome. And, of course, this deduction, faulty though it may be, in turn may prompt you, as it does us, to immerse yourself in other "games" or to look for one of those quick-fix formulas that someone claims will relieve your discomfort and alleviate the problem without your having to break a sweat.

Our world today is certainly full of these ready-made, one-size-fits-all formulas and quick-fix solutions. Bookstores and drugstores loaded with prepackaged formulas and strategies that promise effortless relief. Exercise machines that exercise for you, medicines that will take away your pain and only leave you with ten or twenty side effects. Electrical stimulators and remedies designed to shrink your problems or, at the very least, make you more beautiful and thinner, which by implication, will make you sought after, admired, and free of problems.

Strangely enough, however, even with all of these "games," all of these quick-fix remedies and effortless strategies, many of us still find that a lot of our uncomfortable feelings keep hanging around. We also find that our attempts to avoid them results in an increase rather than a decrease of the dilemmas and dysfunctions that distract us and the confusions and frustrations that confound us.

Are we suggesting that all of these formulas and remedies are flawed, that all of the "games of life" are worthless or ineffective? No. While some of these remedies are, indeed, little more than sleights of hand and placebos created for the gullible and the undisciplined, other remedies and "games" are truly helpful. They offer content, some genuine opportunities to learn and some strategies that are sound and that can make a difference in the quality and value of our lives.

THE CRITICAL INGREDIENT

There is a common quality about all of these remedies and strategies, the fraudulent as well as the excellent: In order to discover if they work, we must be willing to invest energy and effort in them.

Thus, no matter what strategy or method you select, for change to occur you must apply some elbow grease. This involves a willingness to change some of your beliefs and practices. You must be willing to experiment and risk in order to discover your own unique and specific solutions to the challenges you face. This hands-on element is a critical ingredient. As Seneca tells us, "It is not because things are difficult that we do not dare. It is because we do not dare that things are difficult."

As you take your next steps on this path, keep these examples in mind. Over the course of our careers we both have had the privilege

of working with some remarkable people who have demonstrat
power of this ingredient. In particular, there are two people Georg
has worked with whose lives have touched many of us and who have
been special symbols and living examples to him of the willingness to
dare and courage to be authentic.

In the late 1960s and early 1970s I (George) was part of team
that was asked by the government of Israel to create a more balanced
public image for that country. The assignment, of course, arose during a time of great unrest and turbulence in the Middle East. I had the
privilege of working with and for a number of leading figures, including Golda Meir. Talk about a person of courage, a person willing to be
authentic. There was no pretense in her. No affectation. No time for
small talk or the superficial. She was direct, powerful, and of singular
purpose. There was a deep commitment to her truth and to her cause,
and as a result, I believe the state of Israel and people all over the world
owe her a debt of gratitude for her authenticity.

Later in my life I had the privilege of running a foundation dedicated to promoting personal integrity, which we mentioned earlier in
the book. During my tenure I was instrumental in creating and presenting International Integrity awards to a host of remarkable men
and women. Desmond Tutu remains one of the most memorable.

Early one morning I was riding in the back of a town car with
Bishop Tutu as we made our way to a television studio in Burbank
for a West Coast feed to *The Today Show*. It was very early. We were
both tired, but I noticed that he was his usual cheerful self, and so I
asked him how he could remain so cheerful and upbeat in the face
of such turmoil and suffering in his country. I still remember the
look he gave me before answering. It was a thoughtful look, full of
caring and understanding.

"I have no other acceptable choice," he said in that clipped, dis-
tinctly upbeat tone that is his signature. "I must remain open, curious
and cheerful or else I will not be of use to my people. I have no other
choice because I also know that our cause is just and that we must seek
to understand the white people in South Africa, to realize that if we
were in their shoes we would be afraid too."

In the years that followed, Bishop Tutu and Nelson Mandela, who later was released from jail, went on to craft the concept of restorative justice in South Africa. I often think about that morning and am deeply grateful for the insights he offered and for the gift of his authenticity he shared with me. I am also grateful for the invaluable lesson in leadership, the kind of leadership that is hard won and therefore of particular relevance.

ANOTHER STEP IN THE DANCE

Keeping in mind the gifts of courage, humility and authenticity that Golda Meir and Bishop Tutu have given the world, consider another fundamental premise on which much of the work in this book is based: everything we have in our lives is the direct result of how we have lived our lives up until now. Our lives at this moment are the sum total of what we believe, what we have valued, what we know and do not know, what we have placed our attention on and what we have been willing to risk to follow our hearts' callings.

If you are willing to accept this premise—that your life and your career are a direct expression of the kind of person you have been "practicing" up until this moment—then it must follow that for your life and your career to be different, more fulfilling and authentic, you will have to begin allowing and expressing a different kind of "person." If you are responsible for your life, you will have to live more responsibly and that will mean accepting the fact that the primary reason you are alive is to learn, to practice, and to awaken to your next level of consciousness.

Using this concept as your guide, your life and your work can become opportunities to improve your skills and to experiment with new opportunities, to let go of what does not work and to replace it with what does, and to apply your creativity and experience your gratitude. Most especially, your life and your work are chances to practice a higher and more meaningful game. And if you can agree on this much, then perhaps you can also agree that from this perspective life and work are not really mysteries or complicated puzzles that some obscure and impersonal God has designed to test you. Life and work not games that you need to constantly analyze and try to figure. Instead, life and work are processes of discovery, and the earth is a large school. A giant one, no doubt. A challenging one, most certainly. But a school in which we have the opportunity to take whatever courses we require or desire and in which we have the opportunity to learn and to practice how to live our lives and express our dreams more fully, more joyfully and more meaningfully.

BEYOND THE GAMES AND OTHER PREOCCUPATIONS

If you are willing to test this premise, you will no longer find it necessary to expend so much of your precious time and effort focusing so exclusively and obsessively on acquiring more money, security, status or recognition. In fact, the acquisition of these things may become far less important than learning how to express and become who and what your soul calls you to be.

Does this mean that you will have to give up your material comfort? Not necessarily, but maybe. Maybe Dag Hamerskjold, former Secretary General of the United Nations, was right when he asked, "Dare the man whose life offers him the opportunity to discover his true destiny refuse this simply because he is unwilling to give up everything else?"

You can, of course, dismiss this approach and go back to pretending that your life and your work are very difficult, requiring you to sacrifice your deepest longings in order to gain material comfort or advantage. You can go back to preoccupying yourself with more of those compulsive "games" we identified earlier. You can also pretend that you are not sad or frustrated by the absence of meaning in your daily life or by the anxiety this absence of meaning in your work produces. In short, you can go on doing whatever you were doing before you opened this book, but you already know how that story ends. As the old saying goes, "if you always do what you have always done, you will always get what you have always gotten." That is what too many of us have done for too long. Therefore, when the time comes for us to place our hearts on that Scale of Justice, there is a damn good chance we will find that it does not balance the Feather of Truth and that we will have to come back again and again to this school called the "Earth."

TODAY'S REFLECTION

The meaning and value of my life and my work can be found in the way I choose to live each moment. So the question I will ask today and every day is—How am I living this moment? Can I live this moment more joyfully, move lovingly, more authentically aligned with my purpose for being alive?

This School Called Earth

Seek above all, for a game worth playing. Such is the advice of the oracle of modern man. Having found the game, play it with intensity...play as if your life and sanity depended on it. Follow the example of the French Existentialists and flourish a banner bearing the word "Engagement." Though nothing means anything and all roads are marked "No Exit," yet move as if your movement had some purpose. If life does not seem to offer a game worth playing, then invent one. For it must be clear, to even the most clouded intelligence, that any game is better than no game.

-⟨ Robert de Ropp ⟩-

Far too many of us spend too much time rushing around believing there is something important to do and that our job is to discover this something and to get it done within the limited period of time called our lives so that we will be considered successful and important. As a result of this belief, and the fact that a number of us have not yet found this "something to do," our rushing around generally involves a lot of stress, effort and energy and a good deal of pressure and anxiety. Often this stress is compounded by the guilt we feel about not yet finding our "something to do."

In our own professional lives we work with thousands of executives—good, talented, well-intentioned men and women who are often so captured by this dynamic and driven by the need to succeed within systems that are becoming more and more devoid of spirit that they often end up forcing themselves as well as those below them to sacrifice much that is dear. In fact, what used to be described as a dys-

...tion called "workaholism" now appears to have become both the norm and an acceptable and rewarded strategy for getting to the top in our highly competitive, pressurized world. Of course, the fact that this strategy is also becoming a socially acceptable way of abdicating our sovereignty and denying our authentic selves is not discussed often or openly in most boardrooms or government chambers.

There are, of course, some notable exceptions to this new rule. For example, a few years ago we were in the office of the president of one of our nation's leading aerospace companies at the end of the workday. As we were wrapping up the meeting, our client looked closely at a rather substantial pile of folders in his "in" basket and then seemed to make a decision not to take any of them with him. We noticed that his briefcase was empty when he closed it and mentioned this fact. He smiled. "Yes, I do my best not to take my work home anymore unless it is absolutely essential. I used to do it. Hell, for years I used to fill my briefcase and then another, a spare I kept over in that closet. But I've changed my strategy. I no longer believe working myself to death helps me or the people I'm responsible for. So now when I go home, I try to spend some quality time with my wife and with the kids when they are in town. I've also gotten into the habit of giving the problems of the day a little rest and allowing my intuition and creativity to work on them. The result is I find I can do a better job of doing what I'm supposed to do, lead this company."

A few minutes later as we rode down in the elevator, we noticed a number people carrying a lot of work and worry home. Exchanging glances with our client, it was clear that we were all thinking about our earlier conversation. A few minutes later, we stopped to talk about how we could communicate to folks at other levels of the company the importance of maintaining their balance. We talked about how to convince them that sometimes putting down their bags and spending time with their children, their husbands and wives and, most especially with themselves, might prove to be the quickest and most productive way to do their jobs.

ABOUT BEING

The same thing can be said about "being." Most of us believe we are supposed to "be" someone and that in order to "be" this someone we have to become someone other than who we now are. And naturally, as in the case of not finding our "something to do" and not becoming this other "someone" fast enough or well enough, we get to feel not only badly, but unworthy.

Our description of this cycle of belief and reaction may sound a little exaggerated, but far too many of us spend far too much of the precious gift of our lives laboring under this odd and limiting belief. Beliefs about "doing" and "having" are very prevalent. They are also misleading and debilitating. They contribute immensely to the amount of frenzy and fanaticism, frustration and dissatisfaction that many of us have come to accept as unavoidable components in our lives today. This issue is, in fact, one we encounter again and again in many of the organizations and groups we coach, and its impact is enormous. Low productivity, declining profitability and loss of personal efficacy, physical and emotional disease, addictions, divorce, and of course, lost opportunities are just some of the prices we pay when we deny our authentic selves.

A large number of us are caught in this strange paradox. On the one hand we want peace, joy and contentment, and on the other we are goaded by pressures and beliefs that suggest that we need to get ahead, to make more, be more, accumulate more and compete more. And the more of this frenzy and obsessive behavior we feel within ourselves and observe in the world around us, the more both of us wonder what would happen if everyone admitted that these beliefs are erroneous, limiting and, in many cases, downright stupid. We wonder what our world would be like if everyone listened to the wisdom of the following story.

"Why are you rushing so much?" the teacher asked. "I'm rushing after my livelihood," the man answered. "And how do you know that your livelihood is running on before you?" asked the teacher. "Perhaps it is behind you, and all you need to do is stand still."

NG ASSUMPTIONS LEAD TO WRONG ACTIONS

So what if our assumptions about "doing," "having" and "becoming" are wrong? What if it doesn't matter so much what we choose to do as an occupation, avocation or even a pastime as much as it matters how we do what we choose to do? What happens to all of our frenzy and fanaticism? What happens to all the trying, struggling, anxiety and frustration if what we do neither justifies nor defines who we are? What if the only thing that is truly important is that we give ourselves something to do that is not harmful to others and instead contributes to their well being and that through this "doing" we give ourselves the opportunity to learn how to be more aligned with our authentic selves? What if this is what truly matters and not all of the accumulating and accomplishing, the trying and the hoping? What if this is the way that we actually get to experience the real purpose of our lives and demonstrate the truth of who we are?

If the purpose of life is not so much an issue of what we do—so long as we do something that is not harmful—and if what we do does not define who we are, then perhaps we should be paying attention to something else. Perhaps life really is not so much about what we do, but how we do it. Perhaps life is a process in which everything we do reflects back to us what we already know and have mastered and what we still have to learn. In short, perhaps life is not about doing, but about authentic "being." It's not about what we have, but about attitudes, beliefs and values that we demonstrate in life, while we do whatever it is that we choose or are called upon to do.

NOT THE DESTINATION BUT THE JOURNEY

This is not a new point of view, of course. Many teachers and spiritual and secular leaders have been saying this for a very long time. In tongues and languages too numerous to name, they have told us that it is not the result, but the process, not the destination but the journey, not the "done," but the manner of the doing that counts.

Investigate it for yourself. Use your own life experience as the testing ground and find out if your joy lies in the realm of having or doing or being. For us it is becoming increasingly clear that if we enjoy the doing while we are doing it, if we put care and excellence into whatever the task or process is, then the finished object or product or process has love and excellence in it. And the next thing we do will build upon this foundation and momentum, and it will also have care and excellence in it.

Could it be that simple? We think so. We think it's time to stop spending so much of time focusing on the result rather than being present in each moment of actual doing. It's time to stop long enough in the process of doing things to acknowledge and celebrate the various steps along the way. It's time to move beyond our obsession with getting things done as quickly and cheaply as possible and to avoid jumping unconsciously right into the next task and then the next without debriefing our experience, identifying lessons learned and saluting what we did well. No wonder we all feel such pressure. No wonder our hearts and souls have such little breathing room. So much sound and fury. So much frenzy.

What's the alternative? Authenticity! Yours. Ours. Everyone's. Indeed, if we have the courage to examine our beliefs and pay attention to our habitual patterns, if we are willing to learn to be present, to focus on and take pleasure in each thing we do, then we could well discover that our lives and our careers stop being pressure cookers and a series of endless "have to's," and instead become opportunities to experience an enormous amount of pleasure, joy and true self-actualization.

This is what we want. What about you?

TODAY'S REFLECTION

Today I choose to stop focusing on what I have done and what I think I still need to do and start focusing on what is happening right now and who I am demonstrating in this moment. Today I choose to honor the what (the task) and the how (the process) by doing each thing I do in my life with love, attention, awareness and excellence. Today I will also honor myself and everyone I come in contact with by remembering that my primary job is to be authentic.

◆

The Secret Is in the Basics

You see things and say, "Why?" But I dream things
that never were and say, "Why not?"
⋅≺[George Bernard Shaw]≻⋅

When we both look closely and with the perspective that time sometimes gives us at the events in our own lives, we find that no matter how challenging any one period, event or relationship may have been, the challenge or problem we faced resulted primarily from something we forgot to do, something we chose not to do, or something we had not yet learned how to do.

For example, when we compare notes about earlier periods in our lives, we both admit there were many times when it was our own confusion or sadness, anxiety or anger, fear or not knowing that contributed to the end of a relationship, a job opportunity, a project and more. In some instances we left the experience feeling we might not ever find that kind of person or that kind of opportunity again. Of course, with the passage of time and the understanding that the challenges within those relationships or jobs had resulted largely from things we had not yet learned or from our unwillingness or inability to do things that needed doing, we were able to enter the next relationship or tackle the next project. In short, in time we came to appreciate that what we called our "failures" were really not failures at all, but instead they were steps on the way to getting better at life.

This personal experience coupled with the st
over a number of years with the folks we have wo
our contention that the Earth is a large, remarka
we are given the opportunity each day to learn how
successfully, more authentically and more lovingly. This awareness also
confirms another of our experiences: until we complete or master a
subject or lesson in this school, that subject or lesson will keep presenting itself over and over again in our lives.

Pause for a moment and test this hypothesis against your own
life experience. Do you also find that no matter how difficult, troublesome or painful a period, specific event or relationship is or has
been in your life, at least some portion of that trouble or pain can be
traced to something that you had not yet learned or something you
had left undone? Do you also notice that the lesson or challenge present in that circumstance keeps presenting itself again and again in
your life in a variety of different forms and disguises until you learn it?

Reflect on one such experience in your own life. Having a specific example in mind will make this subject much more personal and
real. Indeed, no matter how brief the reflection, you will find that it
will help you to integrate your understanding.

THE PERSISTENCE OF THE UNLEARNED

Unlearned lessons and incomplete actions keep hanging around until
we learn the lesson, complete the action or declare that the lesson or
action is no longer something we need to learn or to do.

As a way of testing this point, ask yourself if any of the same
unlearned lessons or incomplete actions that obstructed you in your
last job, your last primary relationship, in a friendship or even in one
of your leisure time activities is showing up in a current one. And
don't stop there. Identify some of the basic rules of life among the
things that remain undone and unlearned—rules about social skills,
grammar, spelling, communication, honesty, intimacy, fairness, trust,
and so on. In fact, do this little exercise on paper or in a journal.

As you do this exercise, consider how many times these
unlearned rules have come up in your life recently. Perhaps some of

umber of times in a single project at work or in a
And when they do, what do you say? What do you
pact or cost do these repetitive occurrences have

In our experience, they cost us significant amounts of time, effectiveness, energy, focus, creativity, self-confidence and self-worth. We find, in fact, that these unlearned rules and incomplete actions contribute enormously to our not being very effective, compassionate, successful, and of course, authentic.

A case in point. We are both strong willed and opinionated, and both of us are accustomed to getting our way. Naturally, when we bring these qualities and expectations into our relationship we can be almost certain of a few things—argument, disharmony, hurt feelings and break down in communication between us. For us it has been necessary to learn new ways to communicate and new ways to cooperate. Getting to this place requires greater compassion for ourselves and each other and greater patience—two qualities we find are essential if we want to be more authentic and successful.

On the professional side we often come across companies that have low profitability and poor customer service. Though these are serious problems, they are only the symptoms of deeper issues. The leaders often claim they do not know what is causing the problems, but just by walking around, observing daily procedures and talking to the folks who do the work reveals the presence of habitual practices, outmoded thinking, ineffective policies and procedures and a lack of commitment to excellence. When the leadership is open and receptive to making some changes, these problems are usually easy to solve. When the leadership is resistant to change or obsessively focused on the bottom line, however, the problems not only persist, but increase substantially over time.

Do these or other examples ring a bell in your world? How many times each day or week does one of your incomplete actions or unlearned rules embarrass or limit you, your family or your organization? How many times do you find yourself reacting to that experience by avoiding the rule or by pretending that knowing that rule is not important or even that you already know how to do it or handle it? How many times each week do you react by trying to push the responsibility for some unlearned rule or incomplete action off on someone else? Or do you erect one of those complicated justifications for doing or not doing whatever needs doing or learning in the same old unconscious and ineffective way?

THE UNAVOIDABLE PRICE OF AVOIDANCE

If you find that some of what we are saying applies to you, please know that we are not passing judgment or suggesting that you should be harsh on yourself. Instead, we are asking you to become more honest with yourself so that you can discover how you actually feel about this type of behavior. Does it cause you to feel more or less than successful? Does it raise or lower your self-confidence? And what about your self-esteem, your energy, passion and the commitment you bring to your life? Do your habitual behaviors advance or retard your dreams?

In our own lives we find that our limited and habitual behaviors definitely retard our ability to manifest our dreams. Our unlearned and incomplete lessons limit our lives. In fact, as a result of our encounters with some of our unlearned rules, we often find ourselves feeling badly and saying things like, "Oh, I'm not very good at that!" or "I can't do that!" or "It doesn't matter!"

We also find that when one of these unlearned rules shows up, like a scratch on a CD that causes a skip each time we play it, we sometimes get annoyed at the unlearned thing or at the person who reminds us of the lesson we have not learned. Sometimes we get mad at each other or at a member of our family or a friend or colleague who happens to be around when the unlearned lesson or incomplete action presents itself. Sometimes we also get mad at the action or the job we are asked to do that discloses the unlearned lesson. Sometimes we get mad at 'the system' for making the lesson necessary. And, of course, when there is no one else left to get made at we get mad at God for creating such an awkward, clumsy world or such an awkward, clumsy or incomplete us.

Does this sound familiar? If you do any of this, do you also find yourself losing touch with what you feel and, equally consequential, with what others feel? If you do, then perhaps there are times when you also sense that this habit of avoiding and denying what you need to learn results in greater feelings of separation from yourself and others, a reduced level of energy and enthusiasm for the things you do, a lack of self-respect and sometimes, eventually, depression and despair. These are, after all, some of the automatic prices all of us pay when we know we are cheating on ourselves, when we know we are breaking some of the fundamental agreements we have made to take advantage of what the poet Mary Oliver calls, "this one wild and precious thing called your life."

A DIFFERENT CHOICE

But what if life does not have to be lived this way? What if life is not something that happens to us but something we choose? What if all that we define as our lives—the quality, the content, the experiences, the relationships, the limits as well as the opportunities—are really the result of what we have learned and not learned, what we have done and not done?

Consider the implications of this perspective. If life is something we choose based on what we know and don't know, do and do not do, then at some level we must be more in charge of our lives than we sometimes are willing to admit. Or stated another way, what if all that happens to us is the result of the choices we have made or not made and the things we have learned or not learned in previous moments of our lives? What if the ball is really in our court?

We know you have heard it before, but please take a moment now to think about it again. Clearly, it is a message that is available to us in all of the great books of the world. And while some may choose to interpret it as a cause for sadness or regret, it can actually be the source of enormous joy. We can be the authors of our own destinies. We no longer have to live our lives as passive recipients of the pain and discomfort that result from incomplete past actions and unlearned lessons. We no longer have to feel victimized by lives that seem to happen to us. Instead, we can admit that our lives are the result of what we have learned and done and that the sooner we get to new learning and new doing, the sooner our experience of life will also become new.

As obvious as this premise may be or as often as you have heard it, in our experience it is one of the most revolutionary concepts in our search for authenticity. Why revolutionary? Because with this admission each of us can decide that the next time one of these unlearned rules comes up, the next time we face one of those incomplete actions or undone things, we can do something about it. We can go to a dictionary or to the web or to a relative or friend and explore an answer. We can seek out someone's guidance or ask for their support in our getting it done. We can experiment with new behaviors, try different approaches or methods. We can take a class or hire a coach or a professional. In short, we can roll up our sleeves, take the time and energy to finish whatever remains unfinished, identify whatever fear or concern may be in our way, and learn whatever there is to learn. In this way we get to uncover more originality and uniqueness in our lives.

A LITTLE SWEAT EQUITY

Is this easy to do? Yes, in some ways, and in other ways it may be one of the hardest things you ever do. Breaking old habits, changing patterns of response, and learning to do things differently can be challenging. You will face resistance—your own and sometimes the resistance that comes from others who do not want you to change. Still, easy or hard, challenging or not, the fact remains that if you do not want to continue feeling badly about any aspect of your life, if you do not want to continue to pay the automatic prices exacted by the lessons you have not yet learned and the things you have left undone, you must be willing to take your life in your own hands and live it fully and courageously.

So our recommendation is simple. Start today to identify the things you know that limit you and the things you still have to complete. Then put some of that courage and humility to the task of learning or finishing them. You do not, of course, have to do them all at once. You do not even have to tackle the hard ones first. Just pick one and get it done or learned. Then pick another and so on until the unlearned have been learned and the undone are done or declared complete. We guarantee you will find greater freedom, energy and authentic alignment. These are the automatic rewards you will reap for keeping your agreements with yourself and for taking responsibility in your life.

Remember that the tallest building in the world is built one level at a time. The longest novel is written one word at a time. The most complex symphony or scientific formula comes into being one note, one symbol at a time. Yes, "the journey of a thousand miles" begins with one step and then another. So start rewriting your life story today. No matter how many other starts you have made, no matter whether you have judged them to be false or real, take a step today, an authentic step and keep stepping toward a remarkable, unique you.

Follow this recommendation and we believe you will discover that beyond the things that remain unlearned and undone is a new and greater sense of self, a new opportunity, a new and authentic experience of your life. In short, beyond the habitual is the new, the marvelous and the wonderful. Beyond the struggle and the avoidance is your true meaning and purpose. Beyond the feeling of being stuck and out of touch, your life can begin again. Yes, beyond the boundary of the incomplete, the denied and the unlearned lies the realm of infinite possibility and opportunity.

Will all of your suffering and challenge disappear simply because you are learning what you need to learn and doing what you need to do? Not necessarily, but one thing is clear. No matter how steep the path, no matter how challenging the course, if you take it one step at a time and if you are willing to be present each step of the way, you will know how to deal with your life and you will know what next right choice to make and that, perhaps, will be the beginning of real authenticity.

TODAY'S REFLECTION

I can significantly reduce my discomfort and dissatisfaction today by learning what I do not know and by completing what I have left incomplete. In this way, one step, one action, one lesson at a time, my life can becomes something I am proud of, something that expresses the unique, remarkable, and magnificent being that I am.

◆

The Fool's Gold of Happiness

Forget about likes and dislikes, they are of no consequence.
Just do what must be done. This may not be happiness,
but it is greatness.

⊸[George Bernard Shaw]⊶

Is happiness important to you? Until recently it has been very close to the top of the list of goals for us. In fact, we have spent a substantial portion of our lives searching for this illusive, glittering, tempting thing called "happiness." And we have conducted our search with varying degrees of fervor, ranging from casual interest to obsession. Indeed, at times, happiness has not only been our goal, but the state or condition to which we felt we were entitled.

Consequently when we woke up on any particular day and "happiness" wasn't present or, worse yet, the probability of it showing up in that relationship, job, or life circumstance was growing dim, we often concluded that something was seriously wrong with the relationship, the job, the life circumstance or—or as a last resort—with us. Conversely, each time we started a new relationship, got a new job or a new friend, moved into a new house or were introduced to a new opportunity, we were inclined to assume that "this" was it. This new person, situation, or thing was going to be our key to happiness.

You are probably familiar with this story line. Most of us know that as time passes the new job often becomes more ordinary or less interesting, the new love sometimes becomes a little or a lot more tarnished, and the new friendship, house or strategy begins to show some of the same old challenges and problems we encountered in the last one.

If this is your experience, you also know that once this realization sets in, you experience another condition called "unhappiness" or "disappointment." In fact, a large number of us live lives in which we alternate between these poles and suffer disappointments from the appointments we make with happiness.

EXPLANATIONS AND RATIONALES

We can't speak for you, but in our case when happiness started to show some of its other faces, we would often tell ourselves that our disappointment or unhappiness must have something to do with our new love or with the new job or our new boss. Maybe there was something about the new home we hadn't noticed when we moved in or maybe the new strategy or game plan at work wasn't so fool proof after all. Last but not least, when disappointment or unhappiness showed up and we could find no other reason, we would sometimes blame it on fate or bad karma or God and of course, eventually, after numerous attempts in that old game of Pin the Tail on the Donkey, we would once again direct our attention back to ourselves.

Understandable, of course. Disappointment and unhappiness are not easy things to stomach. And most of us have had more than our share of both, haven't we? The truth is most of our hearts are sore from the disappointments we have experienced in our lives and, of course, most of us keep forgetting that here on this Earth where duality is the rule our search for happiness guarantees that this opposite state will and must be present as well.

But, of course, when we are in the heat and hustle of the daily "dance of life" it is easy to forget this fact. Easy to forget what Buddha called the Dharma and so we eventually come full circle to blaming our unhappiness or disappointment on ourselves. We decide there must be some psychological wound or cause, some childhood drama, early betrayal or loss that is at the root of our unhappiness. After all, that's what our psychologists tell us.

After numerous hours of therapy and countless excursions to

seminars, workshops and programs, however, we both began to realize, each in our own way and with different timing, that this search to
discover why we were unhappy or why we suffered so much disappointment was no more productive than our previous attempts at
finding happiness or placing blame on others or fate or God. While
this search for a "why" did provide us with some new perspectives on
ourselves and our world and a few new tools to practice, we began to
notice that all of that digging around in our past did not really do
much to enhance our ability to live in the present.

Eventually we also got the point that there probably was not a
single cause or root problem that once identified would make us
whole, immune to disappointment and therefore happy. In short, we
realized that even if we managed to identify the "why" we were still left
with the biggest question of all. How do we lead lives that are joyful
and authentic?

AN INVALID GOAL

It was in pursuit of the answer to the "how" that we both finally
began to consider the possibility that it might not be fate or a flawed
partner or even a flawed us that was at issue, but rather that the goal
of happiness itself might not be as valid as we first thought. That is
when we started to make real progress. That was the moment when
"happiness" began to look a lot less like real gold and a lot more like
"fool's gold."

Happiness gives the appearance of being the real thing. It
sparkles and glitters. It seems tangible and so tantalizingly attainable.
And so available. In fact, one need only look at an evening of television or spend an hour perusing the pages of a contemporary maga-
zine to see how many things promise "happiness." There are trips to
magical destinations, shiny cars and beautiful clothes, expensive jew-
elry and makeovers, elegant houses, trim and sexy bodies and sensu-
ous foods. The message is clear. If we buy more, possess more, use
this or that product we will become thin or rich or powerful or successful or independent or strong or talented and, in turn, we will be
admired, respected, sexually satisfied and, of course, happy.

Would that it were so simple! Would that it were even true! But it is not, is it? Money, power, fame, and beauty may, at times, seem to make our lives a little easier or provide us with some of the opportunities or experiences we desire for a while. They even can be temporary fixes to some of the challenges and pains of life. In the end, however, these elements, possessions and experiences only magnify and amplify what is already present within us. No matter how special or seductive these objects or experiences may be, in the end they only forestall the disappointment for a while.

This is the message we eventually got. We finally realized that our search for happiness could offer us only temporary relief from the pain and confusion of life. Our search could only provide us with the illusion of security or safety or satisfaction, because our possessions and experiences could not permanently hide what was deeper and undeniably true—we were afraid. We were afraid of change, afraid of impermanence, afraid ultimately of death and the mysterious doorway that it represents.

Our experience showed us that whenever we put happiness to the most accurate of all tests, time and truth, we found we did not have what we thought we had. We also found that whatever our latest and seemingly most important key to happiness was, it did not open any of the doors we hoped it would and, in some instances, it did not open any doors at all.

MISSED CLUES

Of course, for a long time this awareness did not deter either of us from going on with our search. In fact, we went from one job to the next, one relationship to the next, one scheme to get rich or thin or buff or wonderful or successful to the next. We went right on to the next lifestyle, career, therapist, or spiritual practice, always in search of the mother lode, always willing to put our faith in happiness.

Along the way, of course, that "still small inner voice" kept prodding us. Sometimes in a whisper. Sometimes in a roar. "Happiness isn't the answer!" it said. "You are chasing an illusion," it whispered. But we chose not to listen, at least for as long as we could. Only when it dawned on us that our lives were passing and that we were still not doing what our hearts kept telling us we were supposed to do, only when it became obvious that we might actually die without ever having fully lived that we got serious about examining this thing called "happiness."

Maybe you have had one or more of these moments in your life too. Maybe one of your primary relationships was in serious jeopardy again, or perhaps a health issue prompted your "inner voice" to speak. Perhaps the loss of a job or a financial setback or the death of someone close triggered the message.

No matter what causes the prompt, however, in moments like this some of us finally realize that as long as we continue to pursue an illusion true peace and satisfaction will always elude us. In these moments some of us decide that as long as we continue to seek a reason to be happy, we will set ourselves up for a lifetime of unmet wishes, revolving disappointments and unfulfilled expectations. Indeed, in these moments some of us come to understand the old Sufi expression, "No sooner is there happiness than there is unhappiness."

IF NOT HAPPINESS, WHAT?

But if "happiness" isn't the goal, what is? For each of us, of course, the answer is a little or a lot different. What matters is that you answer this question for yourself. In our case, our search to answer the question has allowed us to see that we don't want happiness. What we have been looking for all along is the real gold, the stuff that is underneath the fool's gold. What we have been looking for is an experience that happiness is designed to bring us—the real gold called "grace, acceptance, joy and peace." For us, this is the real bottom line.

What we have been seeking is an authentic experience that is much larger and more boundless, much more encompassing than happiness. Of course, if it is much larger and more boundless, it must contain both the positive and negative, both happiness and unhappiness, both pain and pleasure. And that is the key. We now realize that we must be willing to accept both sides of the coin to be able to spend the currency called joy or peace. We must be willing to accept that life will have its ups and downs, its time of ease and lightness and its times of struggle and darkness. That is the unalterable truth about life, and there is a great sense of peace and even joy in accepting this fact. Of course, it is also true that to deny this fact is like trying to start a car with just the positive or negative charge from a battery.

Only when we accept the opposites—truly, deeply accept them—do we ever have a chance to move past the fool's gold to the truly precious stuff. That is what we believe Carl Jung meant when he talked about the difference between "believing" and "knowing." To believe is to rely on the experience of others. To know is to have a direct experience of our own truth. In this way, and only in this way, can we ever come to understand that if God is present in all things, then all things—including happiness and unhappiness—must be God.

At this stage of our journey together, pause and take a look at the role "happiness" plays in your life. Take your next step into greater authenticity and discover if "happiness" is truly the object of your search or if there are other, deeper and more valuable states worthy of your attention. Is it possible that if you give up the search for fool's gold and begin to dig for the real vein of your true wealth you might discover that it is not only possible to find, but also much closer than you ever imagined?

For us, there is no higher calling, no finer use for our lives. We found, in fact, that once we made this level of commitment another important piece of the puzzle fell into place. Obvious to some, perhaps, certainly available in thousands of spiritual and religious texts, the message, once again, is simple. The object, end state, goal or whatever you choose to call it, is not nearly as consequential as the process. Or said another way—the real gold is in the doing and not in the "done."

Our key to better living is found in the way we live. One moment at a time. One choice at a time. One thought, action, word and breath at a time.

THE INNER DOORWAY

We believe what so many wise men and women throughout the ages have been telling us. As so many have said, "God puts all of the real secrets where most of us never think to look... right in front of us, right inside of us; right in the heart of the matter." He/She/It puts the answers to our greatest desires and most sacred prayers right here in every moment and all we have to do to receive them is to be present.

Where else could such a treasure be hidden? We know it sounds too easy, but that is the way it is. And the history of this planet is a testimony to this truth. History—with all of its stops and starts and false paths—is proof that the secret to life lies in how we live each moment, not in what we possess or build or seek outside of ourselves.

That's why we believe it's time, as the rabbit told Alice, to say "No" to those recalcitrant, outer-directed voices that keep counseling us to go for the glitter. It's time to give up the complaining, the resisting and the restlessness of the search that always ends in disappointment. It's time to accept that the Earth is our place to learn and that like it or not, if we do not learn we are going to have to keep repeating the same painful lessons over and over again until we do.

It's time to listen to the wisdom of our souls. After all, they have been guiding us and calling to us long before we were even in the womb. Yes, we believe it's time to step into our authenticity. What do you believe?

Clearly the choice is yours. And you get to make that choice every moment of your life. The best choice you can make is to stop looking out there for something to make you happy. Forget the "fool's gold" called happiness and go after the real vein called "grace, joy and authenticity." After all, you are going to go through life anyway. The only question is whether you want to go through life laughing or crying. Finding or seeking. Full or empty. We have opted for the laughter and the finding and the grace and joy and the knowing that sustain us when all the outside pleasures and pains pass away.

TODAY'S REFLECTION

I am willing to give up searching for the fool's gold called Happiness so that I can inherit the real gold—inner peace, grace, joy, freedom and God! Today I commit to making different choices, to being more present and to saying Yes to myself and to the wonder of being authentic more often!

Who Is (Really) in Charge?

*In a world where death is the hunter, my friend, there's no room
for doubts and regrets. There's only time for decision.*

◄ Carlos Castaneda ►

Based on even a casual glimpse at the history of this planet, it is clear
that a lot of us dream of, fantasize about and strive to be in charge.

This conclusion is reinforced through our work with hundreds
of organizations in both the public and private sectors and with the
thousands of people who attend our seminars. It is also based on times
too numerous to mention in our own lives when we discover this
desire to be in charge.

For most of us, being in charge conjures up images of control
and power, control over the things that do or could happen to us and
power over external events, other people and especially over our own
lives and careers. And if we are really truthful with ourselves, most of
us want this kind of power, don't we? It gives us a sense of security—
perhaps a false sense, but a sense nonetheless. In fact, most of us want
things to be just the way we want them to be. The fantasy seems to be
that if we could do what we want we would have what we want. The
fantasy seems to be that if we were in charge of this project or that
team, this person or that decision everything would be much better.
Most of us, in fact, seem to believe that if we were the "boss" or the
"leader," things would be different and, of course, by different we
mean more effective than they are now. Most of us, that is, except

those who are already bosses and leaders. Leaders do not labor under any such illusion. They already know how difficult it is to be in charge and how, most of the time, we really can't control anything. In fact, a number of management gurus and students of leadership, including people such as Peter Drucker, suggest that we cannot control or manage anyone except ourselves and even that is a pretty daunting, if not impossible task most days.

Still a number of us who are not in charge tend to cling to our illusion about control. If we were only in charge, we reason, we could fix, or not have to participate in, the stuff that upsets us. Of course, those already in charge have a different perspective. They understand that being the "boss" tends to bring experience to us faster and in larger chunks.

Here are a couple of examples of how folks who are in charge feel about their responsibilities. As part of our long-term strategic work with one of our client companies, we were coaching one of this multinational's rising young stars who had, about a year before, been given the task of re-organizing one of the company's most important divisions. The division comprised approximately twelve thousand employees and he had, in fact, done such an impressive job that he was under consideration for a new one.

During a conversation with him we were discussing this possibility and he suddenly stopped in mid-sentence. "My God," he said, "I just realized that if this assignment comes through I'll be responsible for twice the number of people that I now have in my current division."

From the look on his face, it was clear that the burden of leadership had made itself felt in a whole new way. Later, when we began discussing the specifics of the assignment and some of the things he might be required to do, he also admitted it was clear that to be successful in this new job he would have to significantly alter his leadership strategy. The challenge, however, was that he was not sure what these changes should be.

After a few coaching sessions during which we asked him to examine various aspects of his leadership style that worked well and others that did not produce the kind of results he wanted, he came to understand that to be successful he would have to demonstrate even greater trust in his subordinates, further empower his line directors and force decision-making and accountability much further down throughout the organization. He also realized that he would have to provide more in-depth training, support and encouragement to a new cadre of leaders at all levels of the organization. In short, he would have to create a vision-driven, values-based organization that celebrated innovation, accountability and authenticity at all levels. That moment was a kind of satori for him, a moment of awakening when the mantle of leadership, of being in charge, took on new weight and meaning.

A second example comes from an encounter with Mother Teresa. The occasion was a talk she was about to give in New York City. Prior to her going on stage there was a private ceremony backstage in which she was given an award for personal integrity.

After the ceremony concluded, she moved off to the side and mentioned to her assistant that she was feeling a little tired and hoped she would have the energy to do a good job during her talk. Her assistant, a young nun, turned to her and said, "Don't worry, Mother. Remember God never gives us anything we can't handle."

Mother Teresa smiled at her and said, "Yes, Sister, but sometimes I wish He didn't have so much confidence in me."

INTERNALS VS. EXTERNALS

Since this subject of being in charge has a great deal to do with our ability to be authentic in our lives, it deserves a deeper look. Let's begin with what being in charge means and how the meaning we assign to this concept can lead us to a less effective and limited life and career or to more productive, empowered and fulfilling ones.

Like many who have walked this path before us, we both spent a good deal of time earlier in our lives struggling to be in charge. Like the wolf in "The Three Little Pigs," we huffed and puffed and tried to blow the house down—or at least blow it in the direction we wanted. But after a great deal of effort and not all that much success, we have been forced to admit that being in charge has a lot less to do with external rank, position or privilege, a lot less to do with who has the final word, and a lot more to do with our own attitudes and beliefs. Being in charge has much less to do with having authority over other people or external circumstances or events and much more to do with our having responsibility for and dominion over ourselves. Of course, we forget this lesson a number of times each day, especially in our relationship, where many of the issues that are present between men and women in our contemporary world arise, but our forgetfulness does not invalidate the lesson itself.

This personal experience, complemented by the lessons our work has given us, has made it clear that being in charge has a great deal to do with three little words and the very large concept they describe. The words are *create, promote* and *allow.* They form the backbone of a concept that suggests that everything in our lives is the result of something we have created by a specific action, promoted by some other type of action or allowed to come into existence by the absence of an action or by some other means. We have found that our relationship to these three words and this concept dramatically influences our ability to lead authentic, empowered lives.

For a long time, we found this concept objectionable and were quick to point out all the exceptions. Natural weather phenomena, for example, tragic losses, mass plagues, new diseases, and physical afflictions and disabilities are clear exceptions to this rule. "Certainly we have no responsibility for these," we were quick to say.

We have changed our tune. Though we cannot offer, at least not within the space of these few pages, irrefutable scientific proof, our experience now leads us to believe that all of us—individually and collectively—do create, promote and allow even these phenomena or what the insurance industry calls "acts of God."

We believe, in fact, that this has been true throughout history, and that it is especially true in this age when our news media can spin a story from one end of the planet to another in just minutes. Indeed, we believe that just as NASA's scientists are finding that the density of population and the amount of building mass in an urban area can affect the temperature and weather in that area, we believe that negative stories, thoughts, beliefs and attitudes that we hold collectively affect the way we feel and think and these, in turn, affect the balance of nature. Furthermore, we also believe that it is our individual and collective responsibility to acknowledge this relationship and to begin working toward positive change.

ENERGY FOLLOWS THOUGHT

While we do not pretend to be physicists, we are sufficiently experienced in the connection between thought and physical manifestation to know that a change in our thoughts affects our mood, our energy level and our state of health. If positive thought can, at the very least, affect our mood and if laughter and positive envisioning can contribute to our healing, it certainly follows that negative thoughts can bring about negative or unhealthy physical and emotional states and even destructive environmental experiences.

Furthermore, if thought can move objects or bend them—as studies executed at a number of reputable universities and institutes have clearly shown—it seems not only possible, but probable that millions of minds focused on negative emotions or beliefs can create a fissure in the earth, a forest fire, a flood or even a war.

Because the Earth and the heavens are composed of the same basic "stuff" that makes up our own bodies—electromagnetic energy —it seems reasonable to conclude a change in the frequency of our collective thought can change the frequency of our collective vibration and this in turn could affect the earth and heavens in the same way that a change in our "mood" can cause us or someone we are in relationship with to react or reflect that change back to us.

MORE OBVIOUS CONNECTIONS

When we explore the "promote and allow" parts of this concept and apply them to the external, global equation, the connection between our thoughts and beliefs and the effects they produce may be a little easier to swallow. How many times, for example, have we received a warning about some change we need to make in our use of the environment, such as clear-cutting timber without regard to erosion, over-planting fields without regard to resting the soil or dumping toxic waste in our landfills or streams without concern for its impact on groundwater?

Today, the scientific community as a whole is finally admitting what some members have been saying for decades, that we are destroying our natural resources at an alarming and perhaps irreversible rate. The pollution of our water, the wholesale destruction of forests, the elimination of species critical to the food chain, the putrification of the air that sustains us, the overheating of the atmosphere that protects us, and the abusing of the soil that feeds us is not only unconscionable, but in the end, will have a detrimental impact on every living organism on this planet. Many of us are aware of this situation, and yet many of us, far too many, pretend we are not creating, promoting or allowing the future catastrophes and tragedies that will certainly visit themselves upon future generations as a result of our failure to honor our natural environment.

We will not belabor this point, but lest you think we are limiting the discussion to environmental concerns, consider the same cause-and-effect relationship in the private sector, when financial malfeasance triggers a crisis in public confidence, or the long term impact on the stability of a community when police or political corruption surfaces. Consider the result we, as a nation, will inherit when those who we allow to pass through school without learning many essential lessons and disciplines come of age in our society.

OUR ATTITUDES AND BELIEFS

For the moment, however, let's focus closer to home. Let's explore the possibility that even if we do not create the rain or snow, there is something happening inside of us—our attitudes, beliefs and feelings—and in this domain we can be much more in charge than we are willing to admit.

For example, when it rains we can choose to complain and moan because we cannot go on the picnic or take that trip, or we can say, "I think I'll use today to rest or read or fix that door, spend time with a friend or do any of the thousands of things rain is perfect for." In short, we can fight against the obvious or we can use it to our advantage.

Most of us have had this experience at least once in a while. We see that it is raining or snowing and use the opportunity to redirect our attention to ourselves or to something else we can do. And so even if you do not believe you have dominion over the rain or snow, perhaps you are willing to admit you have dominion over what you choose to do with yourself in relation to these weather occurrences.

Many of the wise ones who have walked on this Earth have told us that all things are interconnected and interdependent, that everything is a part of God, and that the inner realms hold the secrets most of us search in vain to find in the outer world. Again and again, in sacred texts and Holy Scriptures we have been told we are here to learn and to practice gaining dominion over the one thing that we can have dominion over and that is our selves. We have been told that our primary job in this and in every other lifetime is to learn how to live our lives in a state of trust, innocence and peace, because trust, innocence and peace are the keys to the authentic life we all seek.

TRUST, INNOCENCE AND SURRENDER

Trust, innocence and surrender may be called by other names—bliss, completion, wisdom, joy, satisfaction, success, wholeness, love, God, or even our old friend, happiness. No matter what name we apply, however, it is innocence, trust and surrender that give us the courage to remain in the present moment long enough to see through the illusions and discover the truth about ourselves and our lives and our false beliefs about control. It is trust, innocence and surrender that allow us to be curious and inventive, unique, and above all, that enable us to live in harmony with the forces in our world and to experience life with a sense of fullness and contentment, the kind of fullness and contentment these books of wisdom have told us is the reason we are here and the key to the door we are seeking to open.

When we are struggling constantly to be in charge, we are living in a state of tension and distraction. And when we are tense and distracted, we are not present. And when we are not present we forfeit our ability to have dominion over ourselves because life only happens in the present. Only in the present can we practice choice and responsibility.

Only in the present can we discover what we want, what we feel and what we can do. Only in the present can we exercise the power that is our divine right. Only in the present can we be authentic.

So please take another look at the strategies you live by. Ask yourself if this constant quest to be in charge is assisting you or limiting you. Ask yourself what all of this effort is creating, promoting or allowing. Ask yourself if the beliefs and attitudes you hold about life, learning, responsibility, success, freedom, abundance and more are shaping your destiny, your growth and your family's well-being. If you find that all of this struggling to be in charge is creating, promoting or allowing a positive, uplifting and constructive destiny then, by all means, keep doing what you are doing. If, however, you find these beliefs and practices do not result in the kind of life you want, then be ruthless in discarding them. Before you throw them out, however, do something more with them. Take the time to identify them, observe them, understand the purpose they may have served in your life and then, when you are ready, replace them with more positive, ennobling and uplifting beliefs and attitudes.

TODAY'S REFLECTION

I accept responsibility for my life and its lessons. I am aware that as the author of my life I create, promote or allow all that happens to me. So today I will make a commitment to become a responsible "author" of my life. Today I will accept that it is my decision whether my story is a tragedy or a love story, a horror story or an extravagant Broadway musical that celebrates my life.

◆

Hope Is a Thing with Thorns

In the midst of winter,
I discovered within myself an endless summer.
⋅⊰ Albert Camus ⊱⋅

In her remarkable book *When Things Fall Apart*, Pema Chodron explores the Tibetan phrase ye tang che. She translates it to mean "totally tired out or totally fed up" and suggests that this condition of hopelessness is "the beginning of the beginning." She writes, "Without giving up hope that there is a better way to be, that there is someone better to be—we will never relax with where we are or with who we are."

For those of us who have been schooled in the West and who rely strongly on hope, this concept can be a little shocking. After all, hope is the thing that keeps most of us going, isn't it? Hope is as American as apple pie, ice cream and Starbucks. Hope is the belief that there is something different, better, more acceptable than whatever we may be experiencing in the moment. Hope is the promise of something new and more gratifying. Hope really is the Starbucks of emotion. It promises good taste. It looks good and sounds good and, of course, you meet the nicest people in line waiting for it.

THE FALSE FLAVOR OF HOPE

Over time, however, hope shows us another side. Like coffee, it can get us addicted to false stimulation. And so the more we evaluate the role hope has played in our own lives, the more certain we are that, like "happiness," hope has been one of the beliefs that not only blocks our access to authenticity, but in the end, has been a serious retardant to our well being.

There is a story that Hermann Hesse, the German novelist, tells in one of his autobiographical writings that may help illustrate what we mean. Hesse tells us that for a number of years he had a fantasy about a summer house, a place he might someday own where he could get away from the heat and experience the quiet and beauty of nature. The fantasy began quite innocently, of course, the way most fantasies do. It was just a comforting image to use when things got a little cramped or awkward. As those of us who have fantasies know, however, they are tricky devils that after a while tend to have a life and energy of their own.

In Hesse's case, his fantasy grew in proportion to the amount of time he invested in it. In fact, he began to notice that when he found something troubling or challenging, he would go to this summer house in his mind for comfort and reprieve. One day, however, as he was visiting this fantasy he realized that if he kept holding on to this idealized cottage and using it as a diversion when things got difficult in his world, he would continue to avoid the challenges, and equally important, that he would never realize his dream of actually owning this summer house. For Hesse, this realization was important enough to record it in his writings.

We both have our own "summer houses." One of them is very much like Hesse's. Since moving to the high desert of Arizona, we have wanted a place in the mountains away from the summer heat. Of course, our "summer houses" are not limited to this single manifestation. We also have held hopes for greater success in our careers, for enough wealth to provide us with stability and financial independence. We have held hopes for good health, for joy and peace, and travel. We have held hope for less tangible, but perhaps more meaningful things—a life of genuine loving, a direct knowledge and communion with God, spiritual enlightenment, and more. Yes, hope has played a large part in our lives.

And yet, the more we explore this illusive and deeply rooted thing called hope, the more we realize that hope is one of the ways we have of going away from the present moment and into some future state that we want to believe will be better, different, and easier than whatever condition or experience constitutes our current reality.

Seems rather natural, doesn't it? And what's wrong with having these diversions? Nothing is wrong with them, if we use them appropriately and consciously. They can be limiting and harmful, however, if we end up needing them, like morning coffee, to get us started. Those of us who truly want to live lives of meaning and purpose must leave behind the "summer houses" in our minds and go out in search of the real things.

There is something else we notice about hope and this is the really troubling part. Hope, like happiness and approval and other qualities in this world of duality, must, by its very nature, bring its opposite along with it. Hope sets us up for hopelessness. And we are not talking about the conscious, freedom-producing kind of giving up of hope Chodron mentions but instead the unavoidable opposite condition that is heavy and negative and that is inextricably linked to hope. Up to down, in to out, hope is tied to hopelessness and to a range of other emotions that are equally debilitating—fear, doubt, anxiety, and despair, to name just a few.

GOALS AND HOPE

There is a positive side of hope, but we do not think it is called hope. We think it's called "trust," "surrender" and a lot of other things that keep us aligned with the natural order of life. There is a natural, neutral state, a deep faith in the appropriateness and possibility of each opportunity, person and event that occurs in the present. And if we are open and trusting enough to accept the lesson offered to us, we will live a far more relaxed and authentic life all the time.

As for goals, it's terrific, even important, to have them. But goals are tricky. Like hope, goals have some real thorns. When we view them as future possibilities—like Hesse's summer house—they are just as destructive and, in some cases, more so. Goals projected into the future set us up for disappointment because when we create goals as future possibilities we keep them hanging off in the distance. They become something we might someday invest real energy in, and this future state precludes their realization. They are like a carrot hung out in front of a donkey, always a little out of reach, always designed to get the poor animal to take one more step and then another, but never hung quite close enough to be attained. Goals viewed and worked with in this way are mental diversions.

THE UP SIDE OF GOAL SETTING

Goals can be powerful when they are experienced as real and tangible in each present moment. In other words, let's say we want our "summer house." As long as we do what Hesse did, using it as a mental fantasy, a someday kind of thing, we probably will never have it. Why? As Lester Levenson, the founder of the Sedona Institute, often said, "You can't want and have something at the same time because wanting and having occupy the same space in consciousness."

So how do you manifest your goals? And how do you maintain optimism about your goals without falling into the trap of hope and expectation? Let's take the summer house a little further. If we really want our house in the mountains, we can use any number of present moments to set our goals. We can spend these present moments—as often as we want to—actually living in the mental images as if they were occurring right now. We do this by bringing the image of the summer house alive in as much vivid detail as possible. What style is the house? Is it one story or two? How many square feet? What kind of materials? What color? What type of environment is the house set in—on a lake, beside a stream, adjacent to fields, near a forest? Is the house isolated or near a town or village? How much land is around the house? What does it cost? What kind of unexpected and delightful surprises are associated with it—wildlife or brilliant fields of wild flowers or extraordinary views? These are all valuable parts of our "summer house" that we can experience in every present moment we choose to devote to it.

Each of the aspects involves real and tangible details. And each time we experience one of them, our summer house gets more real and specific. For our purposes, the more real this goal gets—the more we can see it, walk around it, hear the sounds, smell the smells and feel the feelings—the more quickly and certainly it manifests. Real in this moment, real in the next.

MAKING GOALS REAL

There are, of course, other things we can do. We can consciously designate some present moments to review actual drawings and to analyze our timetable. We can spend others doing very specific and tangible things like arranging financing, talking to financial planners about the use of other assets and establishing relationships with real estate agents. We can visit alternate sites in different areas. Yes, in addition to the experiences of setting and envisioning our goals in present moments, we can do other things in other present moments.

So what would your life or your work be like if you gave up hope that it might someday be better? Would it would be more real and eventually much more satisfying? The answer is "yes." Without the distraction of hope you would experience your life and work in the present. For some of us most of the time and for all of us some of the time, this is an uncomfortable thought. After all, your life and work probably include things, events, people and activities that are distasteful, painful, and unwanted. Other aspects of your life might be vague, confused, or terrifying. Your career might feel as if it is on hold or at a dead end. But when you let go of the hope that it will be better or different and experience it as it is right now you can begin from a base of reality your "journey of a thousand miles" toward greater meaning and purpose.

When you do let go, you begin something extraordinary—the possibility for real change. You take your next step toward greater authenticity. Your life and work in the world, without the false drug of hope, might make you uncomfortable at first, but it will be the moment, maybe the first moment in a long time, that you actually have a chance to live your dream more fully.

This approach, although a little painful, is not only effective, but quite remarkable. In fact, it is quite revolutionary. As the same character in Chinese writing can stand for crisis or opportunity, so the present moment, as uncomfortable as it sometimes is, can be a doorway to possibility.

Eckhart Tolle, whose book *The Power of Now* is helping millions of people to wake up to new levels of consciousness, says, "Every challenge, each scenario contains a disguised opportunity for salvation. At every stage of the dysfunctional process freedom from unconsciousness is possible." He also tells us that sometimes—through the loss of job or career opportunity, the death of a loved one, an accident or some other tragedy—holes are torn in the fabric of our lives and if we are awake, "the winds of grace blow through these holes."

So instead of leaning on hope like an old crutch or allowing it to set you up for disappointment, regret, loss and despair, begin to learn to live without it. If you stay in the present and are willing to experience your discomforts and start living your goals and mental fantasies as real, you will soon begin to have the life you want. In fact, in our experience it is the only way you will actually begin to experience the things that you now are "hoping" you might experience one day.

TODAY'S REFLECTION

Hope is contributing to my hopelessness. Hope is holding my life off in the distance as a future possibility. Today I commit to giving up hope and to living right where I am, no matter how uncomfortable or challenging the conditions of my life may feel at first. Today, with kindness and compassion for myself, I will live each present moment fully and discover the difference between hope and TRUST.

Everybody's Got a Jones

Sow a thought...reap an act.
Sow an act...reap a habit.
Sow a habit...reap a character.
Sow a character...reap a destiny.
◦▹[Chinese Proverb]◃◦

There is an old story about a couple who come home one evening to find that their house has been robbed and everything they value is gone. As they survey the damage the wife turns to the husband and says, "It's all our fault. If you had checked to make sure the doors and windows were locked before we left this would never have happened."

Several neighbors who come to see what has happened also have their opinions. "You did not lock the back gate," says one. "I could see it swinging open from my window."

"Why didn't you have an alarm?" asks a second. "You could have prevented this."

Finally, the man whose house has been robbed has had quite enough and says, "Wait a minute. I am not the only one to blame."

"Who else should we blame?" the wife asks.

The husband replies, "What about the thieves?"

Blame has always been common in our culture. Over the course of our professional careers, however, we have seen a dramatic increase in this practice within many companies and government agencies. The tendency to blame has become so prevalent it is almost an epidemic. In both private and public sector organizations an enormous amount of energy is expended trying to identify who to blame for a problem. The same epidemic is prevalent in our public arena. The media's first and most fervent efforts are to find a culprit—the heck with identifying the root cause or exploring real solutions. It doesn't seem to matter that the same event will occur again and again with different faces and under different circumstances. No one seems to have time to find real, sustainable solutions. Things are too complex, we are told. We are too busy, others say. And of course, we *are* too busy—placing blame on others and then keeping our heads down until we get the next job offer or accept an early retirement buyout.

We have also noticed that in playing this blame game, a large number of us seem to spend our time alternating between being preoccupied with the limitations of others (blaming others) and paying attention to our own limitations (blaming ourselves). The former we call *resentment* and the latter we call *guilt*.

Guilt, of course, is a learned response. Contrary to what some religions claim, we do not believe that we come into this life carrying it. Instead, we believe we are taught how to feel guilty by well-meaning parents, teachers and preachers, who introduce us to the fine art of making negative judgments about what they call our deficiencies and sins. Selfishness, greed, insensitivity, anger and hostility are just a few of the characteristics we are taught to call negative and that give rise to our feelings of guilt. Resentment, on the other hand, is what we are taught to feel when we turn a critical eye on others and criticize, judge and blame these habits and imperfections in them.

As we will discuss in greater detail in the chapter entitled, "The Mirror Complex," psychological studies suggest that the less able or inclined we are to deal with our own limitations, the more inclined we are to project these imperfections onto the world around us. The degree to which we focus on the flaws and limitations of others is in direct proportion to the degree to which we avoid dealing with our own flaws and limitations. Stated another way, the greater our sense of guilt, the more express resentment in the form of criticism and blame for the imperfections others demonstrate.

Regrettably, we both admit to this tendency. Perhaps you also find yourself avoiding some of your own issues and limitations by paying a lot of attention to those exhibited by others. Needless to say, this pastime invariably takes us away from being present and authentic and from our ability to be accepting, caring and compassionate. These qualities are essential if we truly want to live a life of meaning and purpose.

HABITUAL THOUGHTS, HABITUAL ACTIONS, PREDICTABLE RESULTS

Whether or not we are trapped in the cycle of guilt or of resentment, one truth is abundantly clear: the things we most often criticize are things we call "habits."

During this part of our conversation, we are going to substitute the word "jones" for the word "habit." The term "jones" comes from street vernacular and is used to describe the habits that afflict "junkies"—which is another street term. We elect to use these terms rather than the more politically correct terms "addiction" or "substance abuser" because these terms are not pretty or polite, and we do not want this to be a polite conversation. We want to talk to you about something that greatly affects our ability to lead authentic lives.

THE ROOT OF THE MATTER

The tendency of avoiding our own problems, frailties and flaws by "projecting" them onto others and then judging these "others" harshly comes primarily from our fears. Most of us are afraid that if we are flawed we will not be acceptable. If we have limitations or imperfections we might be judged by some "they" as unacceptable and unlovable.

Many of us also are afraid that if we admit we are less than perfect we will have to deal with the feelings associated with these limitations and with the imperfections themselves. And here's the real rub: if we avoid admitting our imperfections and project them onto other people, we can avoid admitting that at some level we are not so different from those folks we turn away from on the street. We might have to admit that we are "junkies," that we have at least one and perhaps more than one "jones."

Ask yourself if there is any truth to what we are saying. In our case, a little self-reflection verifies there is a lot of truth to it. When we see someone wandering around on the streets with dirt on their face, torn clothing and stains on their pants, we sometimes feel pity and other times, levels of fear and disgust. Sometimes they prompt us to be of assistance and, at others, to go straight past compassion to condemnation. But no matter how we feel, our willingness to recognize and accept them increases our compassion for others and for our own limitations as well. In short, this willingness to feel our feelings and own our own joneses somehow changes us.

In today's urban landscape, we have plenty of opportunities to examine our feelings, because these sights are common. What about you? Do these sights and experiences motivate you to reach out, turn away, avoid, pity, condescend or feel true compassion?

A LOOK INTO THE MIRROR OF LIFE

By comparison, what happens inside of you when you raise your own voice in anger, when you become impatient with someone at work or at home, when you verbally or perhaps even physically abuse your child, a colleague or someone else you say you care about? What do you feel when you have a third or fourth glass of wine and then drive home, endangering others on the road? What do you feel after a second or third piece of chocolate cake when you're concerned about gaining weight? What occurs when you respond sarcastically or indifferently to a friend or a loved one, light up another cigarette, or criticize someone who works with you for making a mistake?

What do you feel or avoid feeling when you turn away from a deeper intimacy with someone who loves you or when you withdraw or pout out of hurt? What do you feel when you say "no" to something that someone really needs—like your time, attention or assistance? What happens inside when you give in to lust or greed or when that part of you that wants to stuff a feeling or run away from a responsibility is more powerful than that part of you that knows better?

These questions are not designed to make you feel ashamed. As we've already discussed, there is far too much guilt in our world already. These questions are designed to invite you to be more aware, because we believe it is impossible for any of us to achieve greater authenticity if we are not willing to be honest with ourselves and to be aware of our deepest feelings. In short, we believe there are many ways in which we undercut our strength by giving in to our "jones."

Is it possible that when you are not demonstrating the best of who you are, someone more advanced on the path of self-mastery might view you in precisely the way you view that poor soul on the street? Is it possible that your habits and imperfections are as uncomfortable and painful to some people around you as the more blatant or obvious expressions of the "junkie" sometimes are to you?

PLENTY OF JONESES TO GO AROUND

We are all "junkies." Though many of us are not addicted to drugs or alcohol, many of us are emotional junkies, sexual junkies, food junkies, truth junkies, anger junkies, power junkies, security junkies, exercise junkies, religious junkies, cause junkies, work junkies, illness junkies, and so on. Everybody's got at least one "jones!"

We were introduced to the term a number of years ago. An old man who had been around the jazz scene for years saw a young friend of ours looking sad and asked him what was wrong. The young man told him he was having trouble with a woman. "I shoulda known," the old man said. "You got a jelly roll jones."

Although our young friend was feeling down, the old man's expression made him laugh. His laughter was followed almost immediately by denial: "Don't be ridiculous! She and I are having trouble, but I'm not addicted to her."

But the old man waved the denial aside. Although the young man wanted to avoid the admission, the old man repeated his phrase and it became obvious that his words were getting past the young man's defenses. No matter how much the young man wanted to avoid it, he admitted that the thought of losing his woman left him feeling very vulnerable and lost. To his credit, he also admitted that he was pretty dependent on her physical presence, on her approval, and especially on her sexual response. It was one of the ways he had come to define himself, he said, and he knew that without her he would not feel as valued or as desirable. That's when he admitted that he was addicted to this woman just as surely as other people might be addicted to drugs or alcohol. He was emotionally and physically attached. He had a "jones" and there was no denying it!

Our own lives have taught us similar lessons about ourselves and forced us to admit a number of habits and addictions that we had been excusing or denying. In fact, in our personal lives and in our work with others we have noticed how easy it is to become smug, self-righteous and superior in our less-than-authentic moments.

Oh sure, when something happens to someone else—a loss, a fall from grace or whatever, some of us feel something that approximates concern or sympathy. After all, these are socially responsible things to feel, aren't they? But at the same time, the more deeply we examine our own reactions and the more authentic we want to be, the more we have to admit that there is a rather large gap between sympathy and empathy, between concern and compassion. There is a large gap between feeling something from an altitude and being right down in the thick of it doing whatever can be done to alleviate the suffering or, at the very least, to offer support and companionship, new alternatives and a little motivation.

THE MANY FACES OF ADDICTION

Yes, life has forced both of us to take a closer look at our own addictions—our addictions to impatience and anger, to activity, to worry and doubt, to the desire for approval and acknowledgement, to material comfort and security, to certain possessions and styles of living and much more. Our lives have forced us to admit that at times we have been addicted to sex, to socially acceptable drugs like cigarettes and coffee, to blame, to resentment and gossip and to a number of other habits that have distracted us from leading more successful, empowered lives. And the more of these addictions and dependencies we have admitted, the more we also had to admit that one form of addiction is really no better or worse than another.

Sure the ravages of heroin or crack or alcohol are more blatant. And on the physical and emotional levels they are disastrous both to the abuser and to those around them. But when we examine our own addictions we have to admit that any one of our physical, emotional and mental jones is just as debilitating to ourselves, to each other and to those with whom we interacted as some of the addictions society judges as more severe.

In our cases, our joneses have not only prevented us from exercising self-mastery, they also have caused us to be insensitive to others as well as to avoid our responsibilities to ourselves and to our talents. In fact, no matter what kind of "jones" we have had, no matter to what degree we expressed them, when we look closely and honestly at them, it is apparent that when we practice any addiction we are not in possession of our own energy or our own will. We are not yet doing what we needs to be done to live a fulfilling and positive life.

Perhaps this strikes a chord with you. Perhaps, at the very least, you may be willing to admit that you have (at least) one jones. If you are, please pause here and take out a sheet of paper or your journal and make a few notes about at least one jones. We have found that this practice of admitting our frailties and vulnerabilities is very helpful and healing. In fact, even a few, timid steps along this path can allow remarkable things to happen.

Not only will it help you to stop judging the habits of others, but you will also become aware that that the time you spend judging the habits of others is time you could be spending dealing with, reducing or eliminating the hold your own jones has on you. Of equal consequence, we have found that the admission of our own frailties allows us to begin to express true love and compassion for ourselves and eventually for others.

If you are willing to experiment with this process, you will be taking some important steps toward releasing yourself and others from bondage to the joneses. As long as you judge a habit in yourself or in someone else, you hold that habit to whomever you are judging. In fact, each time you judge that habit in yourself or in someone else you are creating or expanding a negative affirmation of your own or of their limitation.

THE MIND IS SUCH A FAITHFUL ALLY

You have heard this said in a variety of ways in religious and spiritual texts:

"Be careful of what you fear, for your fear shall come upon you."

"Energy follows thought, manifestation follows energy."

"Whatever the mind can conceive of and believe in it can achieve."

"Whether you think you can or think you can't, you're right."

This same message echoes itself in many languages and cultures. When we are critical and judgmental of ourselves or others, we are creating that judgment and condemnation as a part of our own or their future. So if you want to assist yourself and anyone else who may be trapped in the limitations of a jones, then have the courage to admit what is happening. Understand that you may be projecting your fears and frailties onto them. Do your best to identify your own addictions and then feel the pain of them without denial or further entrapment. Once you do this you can begin to reduce or eliminate your addictions.

How do you do that? Begin by befriending them. Let them inform you of what they are trying to do and say in your life. Then, once you have listened, begin to work on replacing the negative "jones" with another practice.

In the beginning this "other" practice may also be a kind of jones, but so long as it is a more positive, healing action, that's okay. Better to replace anger with prayer. Drugs or drinking with yoga or some form of exercise or service work. But stay awake. Be aware that you may be depending on the new practice. Be aware and make a commitment to yourself to honor the new practice by weaning yourself of your attachment to it. In this way, you can continue to exercise or do yoga or pray without misusing these valuable new tools and turning them into new avoidances and addictions.

There are many other ways to deal with addictions—treatment centers, individual and group therapy, the 12-step programs, and alternative healing. All these approaches and more can be your allies. You also can do various kinds of inner work, including learning how to visualize yourself or another person manifesting a different kind of behavior that is far more positive and healthy. You can visualize this positive life-affirming image for yourself and for others. You can, in fact, hold that vision until you or they can hold it for themselves.

THE INCREDIBLE POWER OF SUPPORT

Failing to admit to having a jones also prevents us from being able to ask others for assistance or to be approachable to others who may need our assistance. In the former case, the jones becomes a secret that needs secreting, and so in addition to having the jones to deal with, we have the problem building a life strategy to keep it a secret. We've all been there, of course, and know how exhausting and ultimately impossible that can be.

It is also true that if we are judging someone else for having a jones, they generally are not free to come to us for assistance. Instead of being able to work together in mutual support, we all end up wandering around blind, separate, afraid and isolated, holding onto our jones and holding on to our guilt, shame and resentment, and of course, all the while pointing the finger of judgment at others.

If any part of this discussion strikes a chord with you, make a new commitment and a different choice. Begin walking on the path that leads to greater empathy and compassion for yourself and others. And in the empathy you begin to feel, notice the wisdom and pay attention to the impulses to reach out. As you admit your humanness, notice how you invite support and, in turn, become available to be of genuine assistance to others. And through this exchange of energy and support, notice how the world around you seems to become a friendly and more humane place.

You will be using your energy in constructive and lifesaving ways. Practice this kind of consciousness within yourself, with members of your family, with colleagues at work and with the world at large. Notice the difference. You might want to begin with people and circumstances that are easier, closer to you and less challenging at first. But after you begin to develop more of your compassion muscle, you can branch out to more challenging circumstances and people.

Indeed, we believe that if each of us as individuals, as members of families, as businesses and community groups, as cities, states and nations could do just this, we would finally begin to create an age that is truly golden rather than gilded, an age that is filled with love and laughter and enthusiasm, an age that is authentic and in harmony with the natural rhythms of the universe.

After all, if everybody's got a jones there must be reasons for having them. And perhaps if we take the time to understand these reasons, perhaps if we have the courage to befriend them and the skill to gain greater mastery over them, they will help us to remember that the Earth is a school and that our reason for being in this school is to learn and to practice living. And clearly one of the joys of living is learning to love ourselves; to outgrow the need for our joneses and to inherit the ability to be authentic and free.

TODAY'S REFLECTION

Whatever I have not mastered, masters me. Whatever I see as imperfect in the world around me is probably imperfect and unlearned within me. Therefore today I commit to look at myself, to own what is mine, and to inherit the power and magnificence that comes with this new level of honesty. Starting today, I agree to use the world as a mirror and accept whatever I see and judge as being present within me. Today, I will begin to accept myself and others with true compassion.

◆

Approval, the Deadliest of Games

Of this I am certain, absolutely nothing in this world
has been accomplished without passion.
⊸〔 George Wilhelm Fredrich Hegel 〕⊸

Have you ever found yourself doing something that violates one of your most important personal principles to please someone else—a boss, a friend, a colleague or a loved one? Have you ever done something that goes directly against the prompts and advice you get from that "still small voice" inside you in order to pacify someone, promote a personal gain or keep someone's attention or approval?

We certainly have. More times perhaps than either of us cares to admit, we have traded what sometimes have been small and at other times large pieces of our self-respect for someone else's attention or approval. As uncomfortable as it is to admit this, we believe that if we are to travel the path toward greater authenticity, we must look carefully and closely at this need for approval that permeates our own lives and constitutes so much of what passes as acceptable social interaction in the world around us.

And when we do look, we find ourselves concluding that the need for approval has become much more than just a part of our social fabric. It has become one of the most deadly diseases of our time. In fact, the damage and loss that result from the need for approval makes the annual carnage on our highways and the impact of other, better-known diseases look almost small by comparison.

You probably think we are exaggerating, but the need for approval is dangerous because it is so insidious. It does not screech at us from the headlines of newspapers like some of the latest epidemics, and there are no government agencies like the National Institute of Health created to do battle with its impact. Instead, this virus goes about its work unnamed, draining millions of their self-respect, self-trust and self-confidence, and crippling millions more by eroding their passion, commitment, and willingness to risk in pursuit of true meaning and purpose. It reduces our willingness to grow, to open, to be unique and to say 'Yes' to the mystery and wonder that is our life. What is particularly chilling about this disease is that the need for approval is a kind of hunger that is never satisfied, a need that can never be filled. In many ways, it is like drinking sea water. While it appears, at first, in moments of desperation, to quench our thirst, in the end it not only creates greater thirst but it kills us.

We have experienced its insidious pattern at work in our own lives and in the lives of thousands of people in the companies, organizations, associations, and local, state and national government agencies with whom we have worked. We have come to know how sometimes gross and at other times subtle this deadly a game is and the thousands of dis-guises it wears. As long as the need for approval lurks within our culture we will effectively block ourselves from experiencing lives of real joy, power, alignment and most especially true meaning and purpose. And in our book, no pun intended, nothing is any more deadly than that!

OUR EARLIEST TRAINING

Where did a disease of such proportions come from? From our earliest moments we are trained to seek and gain the approval of others. Each day millions of well-intentioned parents, teachers, religious leaders, coaches, mentors, family members and friends contribute to slowly coaxing even strong-willed children into joining the great "approval" chain. After we have learned our lesson, we begin practicing this deadly art on others. And even as children we learn that by withholding our approval from those who seek to approve of us, we can, in turn, manip-ulate them into our own version of the "approval game."

Most of us know this game well. As lovers we have demanded that others bend, weave, dance, compromise, deny, avoid and sometimes even grovel for our approval. In other instances we have denied our truth, turned away from our own desires and bartered the prompts of our conscience and soul in exchange for someone's approval.

As employees we have watched ourselves and others accept conditions and demands that are unfair, injurious to our well-being, and sometimes even illegal. At other times, we have accepted assignments that are harmful to our physical health, to the well-being of our personal relationships and to our integrity, all for the sake of a boss's approval or for his or her permission to go on accepting the same limiting and sometimes abusive conditions for a thing called job security, a raise or some other short-term gain.

More times than we even like to consider, we have witnessed ourselves and others violating a sense of personal values and decency, acting out things that are contrary to our own best interests, all in the name of a friend's or a group's, a company's or a team's approval.

FROM THE HUNGER FOR APPROVAL TO THE GIFT OF SELF-VALIDATION

As a next step in becoming more aware and authentic, of learning to create greater meaning and purpose, consider the role that approval plays in your life. Observe your desire to belong, to gain recognition or attention or companionship and ask if you are selling yourself short—or out—in return for approval. Explore whether or not you are, at least occasionally, inclined to want someone's approval so badly you are willing to subvert your core values or your spiritual well-being in order to obtain it. Discover if there is truth in a comment by Vanessa Redgrave, who said that "our integrity is so perishable in the summer months of success."

By asking these questions now and by being more aware the next time you find yourself needing approval, you will be more inclined to go to the true source of recognition and nourishment; you will go within to yourself. When you taste the deliciousness of self-validation and remember how good it feels to nourish yourself, you will stop this sometimes frenetic and almost always frustrating need and do a lot more of inward listening and confirming. When you have listened, you will know once and for all how powerful your own inner wisdom and guidance can be.

To get in touch with yourself as a true source of nourishment and approval is a gift of inestimable value.

LISTENING TO YOURSELF

There is a story about a young man who was walking along a street late one night. He noticed an older man on his hands and knees under a street light searching the ground around him. The young man approached and asked the old man what he was looking for.

"My keys," said the older man.

The young man stopped, got down on his hands and knees and began searching the ground too. After fifteen minutes he stopped and turning toward the older man asked, "When did you lose them?"

"About an hour ago," said the older man.

The young man nodded his head and went back to his search. Fifteen minutes later he stopped again. "Where exactly did you lose them?" he asked.

"Over there," said the older man pointing across the street.

The young man was incredulous. "I don't understand," he said, "if you lost them over there, why are you looking here?"

The older man answered, "The light's better over here."

The moral of the story, of course, is that even though it may seem logical at times to look for something where it seems easier to find, the fact is we must locate what we have lost where we lost it. This is especially true when it comes to approval. To truly satisfy our need for approval, we must seek it where it can be found. Though listening to yourself may not, at first, feel as satisfying or as real as listening to others, we assure you it is.

How do we know this? Because in our own personal journeys, there have been many times when we have overridden our own intuition and inner guidance and listened to some external source, some so-called expert or authority, or often just some other person who was willing to listen. Over the long run we have learned that external sources, no matter what their seeming credentials, are often no more valid (and sometimes a lot less valid) than our inner voices. In many instances, these outside sources are making up their positions, basing them on the opinion of others who may be equally arbitrary or misguided, or simply talking to gain our approval.

Approval seems so much more tangible or valuable when it comes from that attractive or powerful man or woman sitting across the table. And when an authority gives you approval it can sometimes feel pretty terrific. But let's be honest. Haven't there been a lot of times when you have wanted approval from any or all of these sources and not received it? And how many times have you gotten the approval and then immediately felt the hook or condition that was attached to it? How many times have you waited patiently for a little approval and then found that what you received was much less than you felt you deserved? How many times have you, in turn, withheld your approval? To achieve authenticity within ourselves, we must decide that our own approval is going to mean more than what we receive from others. After all, you already know that no matter what others say, if it contradicts your own experience or point of view, you will not accept it anyway. Why not admit that looking for approval from someone else is the first sign that you are out of touch and out of balance with yourself? We are not suggesting that you live your life in isolation, but rather that you seek feedback and input from others after you have at least taken the time to consult yourself. Clearly feedback from an outside source is one thing, an insatiable hunger for approval is quite another.

The next time the need for approval presents itself, turn toward yourself first. Ask yourself how you feel about whatever is going on or whatever you are doing. If you do not know how you are feel, invest a little more time and energy in observing and remaining more present. If you do not like what you feel about what is going on or what you are doing, recognize that there is something of real value to be learned. Continue to feel your feelings and observe the process until you see what you could do differently and then change the doing. If you can't change it, accept it. If you can't accept it, leave the condition or circumstance. In short, keep in touch with yourself, listen to yourself, honor yourself. Your inner wisdom is, after all, the truest form of feedback you will ever get.

OTHER APPROACHES

Lester Levinson, the founder of The Sedona Institute, has created another approach to ending the "approval game." He calls it "The Release Technique." According to Lester, approval is one of the most essential human frailties and one's willingness to deal with it is one of the most direct and powerful paths to personal freedom. He believes one of the most productive ways to deal with an addiction to approval is to be willing to be present and aware each time the need for approval arises.

Each time you recognize this need, ask yourself a simple question: "Are you willing to let go of wanting approval?" If your answer is "Yes," then ask yourself "When?" If you cannot answer yes, keep asking the original question until you can honestly feel the willingness to let go of wanting approval. Don't let yourself off the hook until you are able and willing to come up with an affirmative answer. Once you are genuinely able to answer the questions with "yes" and "now," feel the feeling of wanting approval. Feel it and then let it go. Let the feeling go as easily as you would a cloud passing overhead or a balloon that is attached to your hand by a string.

No matter what techniques you use or discover to deal with freeing yourself from the "approval game," however, the most valuable key is to practice giving yourself approval and acknowledgment—a lot of it. In fact, we recommend that the first thing you do in the morning is to splash a little water on your face, express your gratitude for the gift of the day and then stand right there looking at yourself in the mirror and start listing all the things that are pretty terrific about yourself. If you have trouble doing that, start by identifying some of the things you are grateful for. Start with your cat or dog or the tree outside your window. Start with whatever you can feel grateful for, but above all, start someplace. No matter how awkward it may feel, no matter how silly or unfulfilling it seems to you, keep giving yourself feedback and approval for the stage you are at and for the progress you are making, for the courage and commitment it takes to keep learning and moving closer to your authentic self. Give yourself approval often, abundantly and lovingly. It is one of the important steps on the path to creating greater meaning and purpose in your life.

TODAY'S REFLECTION

My need for approval from others can be a sign that I am out of touch with myself. Therefore I will stop looking outside of myself for the approval of others and start looking to myself for my own wisdom and recognition. By living authentically and practicing excellence and love today, I can maintain my own self worth. From this moment on, I agree to celebrate the wonder of my life and to give thanks for the incomparable person that I am.

PART TWO
Penetrating Those Thorny Myths that Limit Authenticity

◆

God Ain't No Lady or Gentleman!

The Sage does not hoard. Having bestowed all he has on others,
he has yet more. Having given all he has to others, he is richer still.

⊸[Lao Tzu]⊷

In *Memories, Dreams, Reflections,* Carl Jung tells a story about a rabbi who is asked by one of his students why there are so many instances of God appearing to Man in the Old Testament, whereas in the New Testament there are no sightings reported. According to Jung, the rabbi ponders the question for a while and then tells the student that he believes the reason is that modern man no longer has the ability to bend that low.

Clearly, from Jung's point of view, humility and surrender are necessary in order to glimpse the mystery that is God, and modern man does not exude either of these qualities. In fact, many of us today not only lack humility but also have lost both the willingness and the ability to surrender—to anyone or anything. In what could well be called the Age of Arrogance, surrender has become a pejorative term.

We do appear, however, to have a pretty tenacious grip on a number of other qualities—disharmony, imbalance, impatience, aggressiveness, anger and all of the tensions and pressures they produce. These qualities are not only a part of the legacy of our times, but the pushes and pulls they produce tend to separate us from each other, from ourselves and most especially from a way of life that has genuine meaning and purpose. So as we take our next steps on the road toward greater authenticity, it seems essential that our path lead through the subjects of humility and surrender and into that tricky territory called God.

From the early scratchings on the cave walls of Altimira to the latest scientific and theological writings and the mapping of DNA, there is a clear record that our search for meaning has always involved a quest to understand the mystery of God. Indeed, in each age, and ours is no exception, this subject has been as powerful as it has been controversial. It is one of the primary reasons many of us find ourselves at odds with members of our own families and with neighbors across the fence, across town, across the border and the ocean. God is such a personal, numinous, and vital experience that even the most cursory entrance into the subject triggers some of our deepest needs, longings and, above all, fears.

We know that the subject is fraught with challenge, and that we run the risk of offending you. That is truly not our intent. We have no desire to tread on your personal religious or spiritual beliefs or try to impose ours on you. Instead, we trust that through our exploration of various beliefs about God and other bedrock beliefs we will explore in the chapters that follow, we will encourage you to take some time to re-examine your own beliefs and discover if they limit or expand your ability to lead a life that is truly authentic.

To facilitate this part of our conversation, we will share some of our personal beliefs with you. Again, we recognize that you may not agree with us, in part or in whole. In fact, you may find that your beliefs are diametrically opposed to ours, but we ask you to stick with us anyway. And we do this not because we want to convince you of the rightness of our beliefs but because we think that one of the most important things any of us can do is test the relevance of the fundamental beliefs we hold against the life we are currently leading by comparing them to the life we were leading when we first learned these beliefs. It's vital to ask ourselves if we are still the same person with the same requirements we were when we were first introduced to our beliefs.

There are many life forms that require a particular kind of nurturing, protection and support when they are young but have quite a different set of needs when they are older. A seedling, for example, is often staked and supported when first planted, but later outgrows the stake and indeed the stake sometimes can become an inhibitor to full growth if left in place too long.

Baby elephants are trained to stay in place by having one of their back legs wrapped with a rope and staked to the ground. When the elephants are small, the rope and stake are more than sufficient to hold them. When they get older, the rope and stake alone are ridiculously insufficient, but the futility of the struggle during early training keeps them from even trying to pull free.

There are numerous examples in which early training and support systems are eventually outgrown or impede growth if left in place too long. The point here is to explore the essential premise that all life forms eventually outgrow their initial need for certain supports and boundaries. The only question is whether they move beyond them or instead choose to remain restricted and miss the experience of their own truth and authenticity.

ON THE SEARCH FOR GOD

In the early portion of our lives, we both spent a significant amount of time learning about and trying to come to terms with God by doing what people have always done—we copied the beliefs of those we trusted and learned to define God in human terms. It was our way of trying to make the infinite and incomprehensible more finite and comprehensible. And who can blame us? The mystery of God is beyond a child's capacity to express in words. Of course, this does not imply that as children we are not in more direct communion with God than most adults, but to gain acceptance in the world of adults, most of us struggle to adapt to adult language and images. As adults, especially for those of us who depend almost exclusively on our intellect to explain life, the challenge of living on the edge of the unknown is a lot more difficult. For both children and for adults, however, the quest to develop a direct connection with God is not for the faint of heart. This is bedrock stuff.

It's understandable that to get a handle on God, the two of us transposed what we were told and what we experienced in our childhoods onto the Heavenly Realms. And because both of us had a father and mother, when we heard God referred to as Father, we used our personal experience to help us understand the image of God. Perhaps you did something like this yourself.

Add to this image the religious and historical teachings and images we were exposed to in our early years, the books and films we watched and the religion classes we attended, and it's easy to understand why we grew up believing that there was "Someone" out there in "The Heavens" who looked kind of like a person—much more stately and imposing, more powerful and loving—but still a human-like figure who had extraordinary powers and who was in charge of it all. Just as there were people in our lives who we called "parents" and "preachers" and "teachers," there was this "Someone" out there in the farthest reaches of the universe who we called God and who was the Father/Mother of us all!

OUR ANTHROPOMORPHIC GOD

In our case, this anthropomorphic version of God no longer holds the same meaning it did when we were children. We both have worked hard to eliminate the belief that God is a kind of substitute "parent." Though comforting, this belief imposes a limited emotional concept on a mystery that is far more magnificent.

Freeing ourselves from this anthropomorphic image of God has not been easy. In fact, for a good part of our lives we clung tenaciously to this image and attempted to build our world on it. And in the interest of accuracy, there are probably a number of places in the still-to-be-examined folds of our consciousness where remnants of this belief still lurk. In her book *When Things Fall Apart*, Pema Chodron suggests that at some level our desire to anthropomorphize God issues from our desire to find what she calls "ground" and clearly "ground" includes the idea that God is a kind of alternate parent or babysitter. The only problem with this belief, as Chodron points out, is that just when we find a decent babysitter, they or we seem to move on.

As a result of holding onto this belief about a human-like God who is a substitute parent, when a circumstance arose in either of our lives when we did not feel supported, taken care of, or protected by God, we would feel disappointed, confused, betrayed, rejected, unworthy or just plain pissed off.

Just as we had transposed the physical image of our human father/mother onto God, we also had transposed the same emotional qualities we knew in these earthly relationships onto our relationship with God.

A HARD STORY TO VALIDATE

The fact that it was impossible to find anything that verified the existence of this human-like God did not deter us from believing that the romanticized images represented by statues and depicted in movies were true and that it was only our limitations that prevented us from experiencing it. We therefore continued believing that God existed in this form and that if we were good enough and did what we had been told in Sunday school, we would someday gain God's approval and eventually be granted entrance into a perfect place called Heaven.

We are exaggerating, of course, to make a point rather to make light of what is very sacred. We both are deeply spiritual and have our own personal experiences that enforce our faith. At the same time, we believe that if any of us are ever going to step beyond conformity and toward greater authenticity, we must explore the belief that God must look like us, walk like us, talk like us or think like us. This belief may actually keep many of us from what we most seek—a direct, full and joyful experience of God.

Why? We remind you of the parable about the man standing at the window waiting for the guest to arrive when the guest is already at the door. This parable has a lot of application in our lives. Our insistence that God show up in a form we imagine He/She should is one of the ways we may be missing the fact that God is already here and there and everywhere, now, always, waiting only for our recognition, for our surrender.

SOME IMPORTANT QUESTIONS

If you are willing to continue exploring what we know is a sensitive subject, ask yourself if your belief in God as a human-like figure and your expectation that your relationship with Him/Her should be pleasing, supportive and always loving, assists or retards your actual experience of the divine.

As a point of departure, consider the number of times in your life that you have had something to learn, and before or during the learning you have found yourself objecting to or troubled by the circumstance or form in which the learning was taking place. Also consider the number of times in which you have had something to learn and found yourself objecting to the teacher, to the place or conditions under which you were being asked to learn, to those with whom you were learning or to what was being asked of you in the process of that learning.

Can you hear your voice complaining? Can you feel a little of the heat or frustration rise inside you when you feeling that your complaint was falling on deaf ears? Sure you were willing to learn, you said. You were even ready to learn, but you were ready to learn in a different way, an easier or more convenient or a better way. You were willing to learn in your way. Sound familiar?

Let's look a little closer. What exactly did your expectation about how you were supposed to learn or the kind of teacher you were supposed to have, do for you? Did your expectation advance or retard your learning? Did you find that your insistence on the teacher having a particular look or style assisted you in the learning process? And if you insisted on learning in your way, how much did you really learn?

BEYOND THE KNOWN

Not much of a surprise, is it? After all, your expectation about the way things were supposed to happen or the look or style of whomever was supposed to teach you only went as far as your knowing allowed you to go. And since the word "learning" implies that a level of knowing exists beyond our current level of knowing, it should not surprise any of us that our expectations get in the way of our ability to learn. In short, our known gets in the way of the unknown.

This message reminds us of the message ancient cartographers used to communicate to travelers. Prior to times when the world as we know it had been fully explored, cartographers often depicted all of the land or water beyond their own territory as dangerous. In fact, they would draw frightening images around the borders of their maps and print the words "Here There Be Dragons." By comparison, contemporary author and healer Depak Chopra suggests that it is not the unknown we should fear but the known, for it is the known that imprisons us. It is the known that makes up the boundaries between what is familiar and unfamiliar. It is the known that provides the filters through which we view life and, in this case, God.

Fortunately, however, no matter what expectations any of us may have, no matter what form we think learning is supposed to take "our" way isn't necessarily "the" way learning happens. In fact, if we are really honest with ourselves, most of us will admit that a lot of things do not fit our preconceived images. Could it be possible that God is one of those things?

We believe that the essential, infinite power of life we call God, Spirit, Oneness, or any of one of the hundred sacred names is much too all-encompassing to ever fit our concept of a substitute parent. In fact, we believe that God may not be all that concerned about what we think He/She is supposed to think, do or be because God ain't no lady or gentleman.

Instead, we believe that God *is* and God does whatever needs doing. We believe we have this whole proposition reversed and that instead of God being a parental disciplinary force in an unforgiving universe, God is a neutral force, a central, organizing force that is part of us and everyone and thing around us. It is our job to be aligned with God and that it is not God's job to take some kind of paternal/maternal care of us.

How does this relate to authenticity? We believe that what we call pain and suffering happen when we fall out of alignment with God, when we turn away and lose our awareness of our connection with the divine organizing principle of the universe. We believe that all of the motion and struggle that goes on in our lives is natural and results either from the unavoidable mistakes we make along the way or from our stepping off our path and turning away from our search for meaning and purpose. As a result, it is not so much that God punishes us for our sins as that we keep turning up the heat in our own lives—experimenting, making mistakes, turning back to the path, and repeating this process over and over again until we "know." This process, at least in our experience, can sometimes get pretty uncomfortable and downright challenging.

TODAY'S REFLECTION

My image of God may be too small and limiting. It may, in fact, be the very thing preventing me from experiencing God every minute of every day. God is as specific as this Earth and this breath, and as infinite, unlimited and intangible as the mystery hinted at in the night sky, and yet, I am never separate from God. Wherever I am, God is and for this I can be very grateful each and every moment of my life!

What Do You (Really) Believe?

I do not seek, I find.
-·[Picasso]·-

No matter what form your God takes or the seriousness or casualness of your worship, it is our experience that when most of us are challenged on the strength of our belief in God a significant number of us react strongly, at times passionately, dramatically, and even on occasion, heatedly. In fact, sometimes the reaction is so strong and so dramatic that we are prompted to argue, fight, abuse, maim and even kill each other in the name of the God in whom we believe.

Much of our world's history is, in fact, is a record of these various expressions and reactions over our various beliefs in God. Eckhart Tolle, the author of *The Power of Now*, suggests that as a species we managed to kill well over a hundred million people during the last century and much of that killing was done in the name of one God or another and under the sanction of one religion or another. And it is precisely this history, this record of intense and uninterrupted violence that our species commits in the name of God that prompts us to wonder how it is we have been able to get away with this giant contradiction for so long. How is it possible that in defending our belief in God—or in anything for that matter—we can exhibit and justify behavior that contradicts almost every fundamental tenant on which these beliefs are founded?

As we take a few more steps along the road toward great authenticity, we invite you to examine this contradiction for yourself. We invite you to ask yourself if you believe that any of us can ever bring real meaning and purpose into our lives if we continue to live with this kind of hypocrisy.

Based on our own experience, we think it is safe to assume that many of us who believe in God also believe that our God is omnipotent and omniscient. And we also think it is safe to say that because many of our concepts of God include this all knowingness and all powerfulness, it must follow that anything we have ever done, do or are about to do, our God must know about and that anything we have ever done, do or are about to do, our God could do at least as well if not better than we are doing it or will do it.

And if we follow this line of reasoning another link or two in the chain and assume that God is also omnipresent, that He/She is everywhere and in all things, then it must follow that God not only knows all that we know and do, but God actually is the knower and doer of all of these things through us. In short, that we are the instruments of God.

TRUST IN GOD

Now here comes the real rub. If God is all knowing and all powerful and all present, and if we believe in God, why don't we trust Him/Her?

"I do!" you say. "I trust God!"

Well, if you trust God why do you worry about things? If you trust God why do you expend so much energy trying to control things? Why do you think that you need to make things happen? If you trust and believe in God and God is all-powerful and all knowing, why are you so intent on manipulating and forcing so many things to happen? Why do you believe in scarcity and lack? Why are you so intent on winning at any cost, on subjugating others or denying them the same rights and privileges that you have? Why, indeed, do you struggle so, complain, judge, condemn and doubt?

If you believe in God and your God is all-powerful, all-knowing and all-present, why are you so afraid and what are you so afraid of? Why are you so concerned about outcomes and risks? Why do you avoid being present in each moment? And when you are present, why do you sometimes exhibit such bias and prejudice against others who have different beliefs, different cultural practices, different colored skins?

Truly, if you believe in God, why do you let other human beings starve or go without basic necessities? Why do you hoard things? Why do you allow others to be maligned, mistreated and abused in the name of one belief system or national sets of values? And lest you think we are picking on you, please understand that we ask ourselves these questions each day and each day we find that we come up stumbling and fumbling in our own responses.

Indeed, if life is an expression of the God that so many of us say we believe in; if life is an expression of our God's power and knowing, why do so many of us have so much stress and anxiety? And if we really get down to basics and if we are really honest with each other, what would our lives really be like if we genuinely trusted and served the God we say we believe in?

TODAY'S REFLECTION

Today, I am willing to admit that my life will be different in this and every moment if I trust in the God I say I believe in. So from today on, I will demonstrate my belief and trust in every thought, word and action. Today I will serve every person, object and event I encounter. With each breath I take, I will be more and more authentic.

◆

To Thine Own Self Be True

When you lose your mind, you'll come to your senses.
⋅⊰ Fritz Perls ⊱⋅

Although we hate to admit it, neither of us popped into the world saying, "Okay, God, let me have it! I want all the learning I can get." Instead we grew up thinking that school and learning were necessary steps toward living the kind of life we wanted—a life we mistakenly believed would be different when we got to be adults. Of course, when we got to be adults and began our work life we did much the same thing. When we joined the army of the employed, we thought work was something we had to deal with in order to afford our time off. Work was something we would do until we retired.

Sounds a lot like the story we told ourselves about school, doesn't it? We are exaggerating, of course, but isn't it true that most of us separate school and work from "real life?" And once we get to this so-called "real life," we tend to resist going back into learning environments. Even when we are at work and our well-being depends on it, many of us resist learning some essential lessons until we find ourselves in one of those can't-avoid-it-any-longer moments.

As we discussed in the chapter titled "The Secret Is in the Basics," however, our failure to learn a number of these primary lessons results in our sometimes stumbling along in lives and careers that don't work as well as we'd like. These lessons, of course, include fundamentals about our career and are based on a number of primary academic disciplines, but perhaps of greater importance they also include: how to relate effectively to others; how to communicate constructively; how to cooperate and collaborate; how to differentiate between and honor different points of view; how to resolve conflict, how to create greater balance, harmony and peace. These are lessons about ordinary things that many of us did not learn during our school years and, as we discussed earlier, they have confounded and confused us ever since.

As a result of these unlearned lessons, we often find ourselves running over some things, and in turn, being run over by some others. We get hurt and we hurt others, disappoint and are disappointed, disillusion and are disillusioned. We mislead, confound, confuse and abuse; in turn, we are confounded, confused, and abused. We get angry, doubtful and upset and often miss the goals we have set for our lives and careers or equally important, miss the present moment and the process called "life" because we are struggling so hard to achieve our goals while believing that the end justifies the means and, of course, the pain. We do all of this and much more while living in this grown-up thing called "real life" that happens after our school years are over.

CYCLES OF PAIN

These unlearned lessons also cause us to make some of the same mistakes over and over. Multiple marriages or primary relationships that run aground on similar obstacles; friendships and other relationships that fail for the same reasons; career opportunities that flounder because of the same incapacities, the same limiting beliefs and the same un-mastered skills.

For many of us, these patterns continue undiminished until we die or, if we are lucky, until something happens that brings enough hurt or confusion, pain and sadness in our lives to require that we finally deal with them. We lose someone we love. We get fired or divorced or become ill. We have an accident or are the victim of a crime.

When life brings us up short, we generally fall to our knees and admit how exhausted and afraid we feel. We finally admit that all of our trying to keep this together, all of our pretending that we are okay, is more than we can handle. Even if we have always denied the existence of a Higher Power; even if we have never believed that this Higher Power would listen or, perhaps more telling, would actually respond to us, we call out into the great void, asking, hoping, praying for some kind of assistance.

We cry out, "I've had enough" or "I can't take the pain of this loss, this broken relationship or this failure at work one moment more. God, I do not want this job that sets me against my own conscience or values. I do not want another conversation in which I am misunderstood or cannot understand. God, why this tragedy, this disease, illness or divorce? Why this loss of my friend, my child, or my parent? God, why did this happen? Why is my life so hard? Why me?" No doubt you've known such moments. To be alive is to know them. In these moments we sometimes find ourselves asking our Higher Power to show us another way. "I'll do anything," we say. And of course, on this day we mean it.

A GIFT OF GRACE

We have had a number of days like this in our lives. We are also aware that not long after we ask for help from this deep aching place in our hearts, a remarkable thing happens. Help actually shows up. Of course, it may not and generally does not appear in exactly the form we expect. No, like the guest who is already standing at the door, help does always come in the form we can even recognize at first. This is one reason many of us miss its arrival. But come it does and when we finally recognize its arrival, we tend to take it as a sign that reaffirms our faith and allegiance to the Higher Power we may have forgotten or neglected, to the Higher Power we may think of as our "substitute parent."

Of course, as good for the soul as one of these periodic re-affirmations of our Higher Power may be, there is a danger. While we can't speak for you, in our case getting an answer to our request sometimes allows us to justify our inclination to lay both original blame and credit at God's doorstep. Why do we say this is a danger? Because in assigning blame and credit to God we miss one of the key points of the whole experience. When we delegate our personal accountability to God we fall back into that old habit of anthropomorphizing God. In short, we turn our Higher Power into our substitute "parent." And as we discovered in the last chapter, that is not only an illusion, but even more consequential, it is a dead end on the road to authenticity. Indeed, to have a direct experience of our Higher Power we must remember that we are responsible for aligning with the will of the divine even when it is not perceived that it is always in the highest and best interest of our egos.

THOSE OLD HABITS

Delegating our accountability to God is dangerous for another reason. It allows us to pretend we can avoid learning some of the lessons we still haven't learned because if we get into trouble at home or at work and cry out again our Higher Power will save us. We can go back to our old belief that learning is a necessary inconvenience we must endure and that work is something we have to do until we retire. We also go back to our old habits and our unconscious ways both at home and at work, and before long the hurt, confusion and challenge builds up again. The pain and the disillusionment increase. That's when we either start to dismiss God again or start to blame our woes on our Higher Power.

Oddly enough, when we start to sink back into this old habitual and unconscious pattern, God seems to let us do just that. That's right! Our Father/Mother Who Art In Heaven seems to let us flounder, moan and whimper, whine and gripe, cry, strike out and even withdraw because the truth, as we talked about in the chapter with that title, is that God ain't no lady or gentleman.

On the surface this image may not fit our anthropomorphized Higher Power, who is supposed to be loving, but it certainly seems to work. It gets our dander up and forces us to identify and examine some of our illusions about ourselves, about life and, eventually about God. It forces us to ask the "big questions." When we do, we are sometimes lucky enough to discover that some of our concepts of life and self and God are too small, that beneath our concepts of what is loving and caring lies a different reality—a loving greater and more profound than we have ever known before. We discover that underneath our former, limited definition of God is a level of generosity, wisdom, and joyfulness, greater than we imagined.

Does this awareness show up in a form we expect? Maybe, but generally not. In fact, sometimes it does not even seem like love or wisdom. Instead, this new experience of our Higher Power is so large, so all-encompassing, that inadequacy is forgiven while, at the same time, excellence is encouraged. And even though the experience sometimes prompts us to resist or deny this level of loving and return to the safety of our old unconsciousness, God stays with us. Not that old anthropomorphized version of our Higher Power, but a God that is so much more remarkable, a Higher Power that waits for us to remember that we are responsible, that we are capable, that we are, indeed, a critical and essential part of the divine, a God who is present for us in each and every moment of our lives.

A DIFFERENT KIND OF GOD

This is what we mean when we say that our Higher Power is not responsible for us. As we have discussed, we believe God does not punish us. Instead, we are responsible and accountable to ourselves for ourselves. It is we who do the punishing. It is not God's job to let anything as inconsequential or transient as manners or politeness or political correctness stand between us and true alignment with our souls. And for that we can be thankful, for if God followed the same rules and behaviors that our earthly fathers and mothers often do, our weaknesses and inadequacies might well be extended into eternity.

Instead, our Higher Power, in Its infinite willingness and knowingness, reaches out in grace and waits for us to remember that it is time to wake up, to grow, to learn so that we may come into higher levels of consciousness. If we are fortunate and wise enough, we listen, and on that day the next important stage of our life begins.

Therefore, our Higher Power may not be a substitute "parent" or the perfect lady or gentleman, but God is God. God is not limited by what our egos think, but instead God and that aspect of God we call our souls prompts us to follow our true longings and follow our destiny. God, in fact, provides the opportunity and then waits for us to remember that our first and final job is to be true to ourselves and for that we can be extraordinarily and eternally thankful.

TODAY'S REFLECTION

Today is as good a day as any to learn the lessons my life holds for me. Today and every day I will remind myself to give up my limited version of God and inherit a truer and deeper experience. Today I will be true to myself and open to the awareness that I am in God, that God is in me and that God and I are One.

◆

The "I" of the Beholder

If you always do what you have always done
you will always get what you have always gotten.
-⟨ Anonymous ⟩-

We have discussed the fact that lessons we have not yet learned, avoided learning or left incomplete account for a lot of the problems and pain in our lives. Now let's look at the relationship between some of these sources of pain and the things we tend to judge most often about others and about the world around us.

We call this phenomenon "the mirror complex," a practice that severely limits our search for greater meaning and purpose. It's the habit of getting so caught up in what we see in life that we forget that what we see is most often determined more by our beliefs and emotional state at the time of the seeing than it is by the image itself. We forget that whatever is going on "out there" has more to do with the "I of the beholder" than it does with what is beheld.

For example, neither of us is particularly patient—especially when we are engaged in conversations on subjects about which we have strong opinions. In fact, under these conditions we both have the tendency to interrupt others before they are finished speaking. As a result, neither of us qualifies for easy admittance into the Good Listeners Club. This habit of assuming we know where the speaker is going and formulating our reply and sometimes even responding before they finish is not very effective. Although neither of us is particularly fond of this habit, and on occasion even admit to having it, guess what habit we are both offended by or judge harshly when it shows up in others? When we look into the outer world and experience some interrupting or assuming they know what we are talking about before we finish talking, we criticize them.

Perhaps you have some qualities or habits you are not fond of in yourself and tend to judge in others. You also may have noticed another important aspect of the mirror complex: no one is quite as critical of a particular sin as someone who suffers from the same sin or as someone who has recently been delivered from that sin.

Have you ever found yourself getting indignant or righteous about a quality or habit that someone else is displaying that you have just mastered? Smoking is a good example. In our case, there was a time when we had recently quit smoking and found ourselves being particularly intolerant of folks who smoked. More intolerant, in fact, than some people we knew who had never smoked.

Have you also noticed that those of us who tend to be the harshest judges are often those with a limited exposure to the world? They tend to view a large part of the world and its practices as wrong or, at the very least, as strange or different. Without the benefit of enough experience with what is different or the kind of perspective that comes from exposure to new things, the lens through which we look at life tends to be very narrow and distorted. This tendency helps to explain why there is so much judgment and distrust between different cultural, ethnic, philosophical and religious groups.

A WORLD FULL OF JUDGMENT

This practice is called "projection" and although it is a natural ability that allows us to experience and learn things from a distance, it has a shadow side as well as a light side.

A quick glance at today's newspaper will give you a number of examples of the shadow side of projection. The minister or priest who talks about morality and preaches about family values is caught having an affair or molesting children. The politician who campaigns on the issue of political corruption is arrested for taking bribes or is investigated for having accepted illegal campaign contributions. The public service commission responsible for regulating public utilities violates our trust and contributes to a crisis of confidence in government. The hospital that promotes a message of community service turns a seriously ill patient away because the individual does not have insurance.

Our world is full of people talking about the sins of others, criticizing, condemning and moralizing as if these 'sins' and these 'others' were somehow separate from them. There are people who spend time and energy talking about, worrying over and crusading for the causes of justice and freedom. Still others who spend at least some portion of their lives bemoaning 'the system' or pointing to soft money in politics, poverty, poor health care, faulty education, the plight of the homeless or the abuses of drugs and alcohol as the primary cause for society's problems.

OUR OWN REFLECTION

We do not mean to imply that taking a public stand on critical issues is inappropriate. The point is that our opinions and efforts would be a lot more effective—not to mention inviting—if we acknowledged that sometimes what we are judging, criticizing and condemning out there is connected to our own personal issues or frailties. In fact, in many instances it is this inner connection that first brings the outside issue, person or event to our attention. Furthermore, our experience suggests that when we own this connection and deal first with our own vulnerability, frailty or fear, our efforts on behalf of various causes carry less emotional distortion and, in the end, are much more constructive.

THE BATHROOM MIRROR

Another interesting aspect of the mirror complex is that even though most of us get caught up in negative outside projections, few of us look in our own bathroom mirrors and blame the mirror for the image it reflects to us. Even if we don't like what we see. Even if we wish we were taller, shorter, thinner, younger, more handsome or beautiful, graceful or expressive, joyful or interesting, we know that the image is indeed an image of ourselves.

But when we look in the Mirror of Life, we blame life and the world around us for the inconsistencies, imperfections, differences and unknowns that we see. Even though we realize that no amount of judging and criticizing of our bathroom mirror will change the reflection, we assume that condemning what we see in The Mirror of Life will somehow create a change. Why?

The answer is simple. We are afraid. We are afraid of what is different, afraid of what we do not understand and perhaps, of greatest consequence, afraid that what we perceive as being "out there" may actually have something to do with tendencies we have or suppress.

We are also afraid that what is happening out there may have some connection to what we have experienced or know in our own hearts that we are capable of experiencing or expressing. We are afraid that the pain, confusion, frustration and dysfunction we view out there and in others might have something to do with the amount of pain, confusion, frustration and dysfunction we are holding or avoiding inside ourselves.

In fact, more and more moments these days we are both forced to admit that the amount of judgment and criticism we level at the world or at each other is actually a direct indicator of the amount of sadness, pain and despair we are holding inside ourselves.

We also are beginning to know—often by virtue of the moments of grit or grace and forgiveness that life offers us—that the images we see in the Mirror of Life show us that if we were better at demonstrating our own moral responsibility, our own brand of justice and freedom, our own loving kindness, then perhaps the world would begin to reflect a better, more positive or at least, more empathetic and authentic image. We both count these moments as gifts.

Here's another example of how this works. While visiting a client company for a strategic planning session, we overheard a manager criticizing a subordinate for a report that was "shoddy and unacceptable."Although we only heard the end of a much longer exchange, we could tell by the manager's voice and the body language and downcast look on the subordinate's face that it had not been pleasant. It was also clear that the manager had violated a number of rules of effective communication and leadership.

Under normal circumstances, we probably would have communicated to one of the company's senior executives about ways his managers could deal with their people more effectively. In this instance, however, the manager, who we will call John, was part of a team of managers with whom we were working, and so we had some additional insight on him and some of his issues.

Yes, you guessed it. One of the qualities John had identified in our evaluation process that he wanted to work on was his habit of being overly critical and confrontational with people who did not perform to his liking. In fact, John had been candid with us, admitting his performance in this area had always been a problem for him. He also knew this tendency stood in the way of his rising higher in the leadership chain.

When we had previously explored this subject with John, he said he had grown up with a father, a retired Marine major, who often had been critical of him, sometimes in ways that were rather dramatic and punitive. He also told us that his first boss used a similar style and that whenever this boss criticized him, he tended to shut down.

To further complicate matters, John reported that when people tried to point out this weakness in his communications style, he would try to justify his behavior with statements like: "What do you mean? Look at the sloppy or inconsiderate job they did. Didn't you see the way they responded?" His defense of his actions was filled with more judgments directed at that someone or something out there that had offended him.

Although it was not possible to meet with John at that time, during a coaching session the following week, we shared our experience with him and noticed that his initial reaction was to turn that gun of criticism toward us.

Because this was not exactly the best use of his energies and since we were not at all intimidated by his manner, John eventually admitted that his reaction had as much to do with how he was feeling about an event that had occurred earlier in the day as it did with what his subordinate had done. He also admitted that he had assigned a meaning to his subordinate's actions—mainly, that his subordinate did not respect his authority. In short, John took the subordinate's actions as a personal affront, instead of understanding that the incomplete work could have been the result of any number of factors that had more to do with the subordinate or the conditions in his department than with John. To his credit, John also acknowledged that instead of owning that some of his irritation was the result of the earlier event and that the quality of his subordinate's report was just the trigger, he had turned the full weight of his frustration on the young man.

In many ways, this coaching session proved to be an important point in John's development. During our next session he said he had begun to see the connection between things he was judging harshly in his subordinates and his own traits, qualities or moods. He also was able to see that the more compassion he had for himself when he made mistakes, the more compassion he could feel for others. Eventually, these understandings were translated into different behaviors. His subordinates and superiors reported that he was far more effective in his communication and that he was beginning to turn some of those negative moments into ones of real connection and assistance for others.

BEYOND THE SMOKE SCREEN OF PROJECTION

We experience this process in our personal lives. Depending on how busy, pre-occupied or stressed we are, we forget we are looking in a mirror and instead get lost in the smoke screen of projection. When we remember that the judgments about fairness, morality or justice we make about "out there" are reflecting things to us, we have the opportunity to actually learn something. The more we accept the fact that our reality is shaped by—or at least colored by—our projections and that these projections are primarily about us and not about the world, the more quickly we grow. In fact, this awareness also helps us to avoid judging our families, friends, colleagues, ourselves, strangers, the world or God because of what we do not know and what we fear. Judging and criticizing are, in the end, only ways of trying to shield ourselves from our own fears.

When we remember that we are looking into a mirror, life ceases to be about moralizing or condemning, about pouting or playing the victim, about judging and criticizing, or about being a passive observer. Instead, life becomes an engaging, proactive journey of getting to be better at being who we really are and what we have come here to do.

POINTING THE FINGER AT THE MOON

So when you project your sins and frailties onto the outside world, remember that judgments are the first sure signs that you are projecting. Judgments also are specific ways to remind yourself that the feelings of outrage, blame, judgment, criticism, and helplessness do not suit a being as powerful as you. They are indications that you are coming from a place of hurt and separation and that you have some work to do.

Just as in the parable of the man who kept looking at the end of his finger rather than at the moon toward which it was pointing, this awareness can remind you that you may be gazing at the reflected image of your own unfairness, immorality or injustice instead of recognizing the moon of new greater possibility, purpose and meaning.

Of course, in making this admission you may also have to admit that one of the reasons you spend so much time judging what you see in the Mirror of Life is that you are afraid you do not know how to change those aspects in yourself. Our experience has shown both of us that when we have been willing to look at ourselves, we have found that the way through the fear is "doing" whatever we have to do to learn or unlearn, to feel or stop feeling, whatever is causing us pain and distress in our lives. It always comes back to us.

So the next time that sense of moral outrage, criticism or judgment of others or of the world around you comes up, remember it is your cue that some personal work needs to be done. And instead of getting lost in the outer image, go to that place inside where the pain, judgment or fear resides, feel your anger and pain, your fear and self-judgment and begin to shine the light of your awareness and acceptance on it. Awareness and acceptance are two of your best allies.

Another thing that helps us is to take a few long, slow deep breaths. Breathe in the feeling we are trying to avoid—anger, frustration, impatience. Then breathe out compassion and caring. We do this for a while and then, when we feel a little more grounded, we begin a dialogue with this feeling that we have been avoiding by projecting it out onto the world. In Buddhist circles, this practice of breathing in what we are afraid of and breathing out spaciousness and greater ease is called "tonglen."

Because this practice is so effective, we invite you to experiment with identifying and befriending your feelings. We suggest you listen to what your feelings are trying to tell you. Remember, to be successful, you must acknowledge whatever you feel and actually feel it. It may be fear. It may be panic, confusion, sadness or something else. Whatever it is, however, simply invite it in and feel it. Allow the feeling to disclose its message to you, breathe into the feeling and accept it without censoring or softening its meaning. When you are ready, one action, one instance at a time, let the pain or the fear or the judgment become your teacher. One step, one thought, one breath at a time let that feeling instruct you on how to bring greater caring, courage, patience, hope and understanding to what you are judging most in others, in yourself or in the world around you.

We had the privilege of spending a week recently in the presence of someone who is a master of this process. Thich Nhat Hanh is a Buddhist monk and a Nobel Peace Prize nominee. One of the many valuable lessons we learned from him is the practice of mindfulness—the process of being present with each breath, each action, each thought, each feeling. To be in Thich Nhat Hanh's presence is to witness mindfulness. He walks with such care and speaks and listens with such presence and directness. He demonstrates the enormous power of being in the present moment. And when he suggests a way of dealing with emotions, it makes such sense. He cautions us not to fight against them. Instead he says, "Hello, my little anger" and welcomes the emotion into his life so that it can teach him.

If working with your emotions in this way sometimes does not bring you greater clarity or emotional balance, you can always go to other people, other resources, friends, colleagues, acquaintances, or counselors and ask for assistance. Above all, go to the most incredible place of all—go within yourself to that wisdom that flows through you, go to that which you call God.

OBSERVATION IS A KEY TO TRANSFORMATION

Accept the many views you get in the Mirror of Life. Allow the lessons to disclose themselves to you and, above all, commit to learning the lessons and to taking the next step and then the next. Keep moving until one day you find that you are able to look in the Mirror and see an image diversity, beauty, strength and wonder, a world that reflects remarkable achievement, clarity and authenticity. One day your mirror will reflect a celebration of possibility and learning, an exclamation of the infinite variety of you and your life.

We know this is not easy, but we also know that it is well worth the effort. If you are willing to see what is reflected in the Mirror, you will be greatly rewarded. And the truth is, you've already tried most of the hard stuff—avoidance, denial and attempts to blame everyone else—and look where that has gotten you.

In those moments when you find the going a little difficult remember this quote by British author W. Somerset Maugham. "If you only expect the best, that's what you will get."

TODAY'S REFLECTION

The Mirror of Life reflects my own image back to me. I can pretend that this is not so and get caught up in the illusion. Or I can accept that what I see in the Mirror is actually in the "I" of the beholder. In this way, the Mirror of Life can become my guide and teach me how to be more authentic.

◆

Love By Any Other Name Is Not Love

Give love.

·≡[Mother Teresa]≡·

The quote by Mother Teresa that opens this chapter has a story attached. Apparently, Mother Teresa was visiting Boston and at the end of a Sunday mass, she and the pastor retired to his rectory for a light lunch. During lunch the doorbell rang and the priest excused himself, tended to whoever was at the door and then returned.

A few minutes later, the bell rang again. The priest excused himself. This process was repeated a few more times until, on one of the priest's returns to the table, Mother Teresa asked him if everything was okay.

"Yes," the priest said, "It's just that on Sundays I always make extra food for the homeless and so they come by after mass."

"I understand," said Mother Teresa. "And what do you give them?"

"A sandwich generally."

"Is that all you give them?" she asked.

"Well, sometimes I give them something to drink."

"Anything more?" she asked.

By this time the priest, thinking that Mother Teresa thought his gifts of food were not large enough, went on to explain that he had a modest budget and was giving all he could afford.

Mother Teresa was not deterred, however, by this explanation. She asked again, "Is there nothing more you can give?"

Finally the priest smiled. Remembering a talk Mother Teresa

had given several years prior, he said, "Yes, Mother. I could give love."

Love is another of the essential topics on our path toward authenticity. To be alive is to be inextricably drawn to or repelled by this remarkable, troubling, seductive, and extraordinarily confounding emotion called Love. Empires have been won and lost because of it. Armies launched. Crowns gained or denied. Rich or poor, it does not matter; we all are subject to its charms. Families have been torn apart, kingdoms crafted, religious schisms birthed and careers made and lost all in its name. Some of us, in fact, spend our entire lives in its service, while others, badgered and damaged by early encounters within its complex realm, do all we can do to avoid it. In the end, we are all under its spell. Love is that mysterious territory where the sacred and the profane meet. Love is both ethereal and tangible.

Love is a word that is not often used in the corridors of government, in the bastions of corporate privilege and on the playing fields and courts of competitive sports—except of course in speeches, memorial services or in those unguarded moments called victory celebrations. For those of us who spend a lot of time in these territories, public expressions of this emotion feel awkward and seem much better suited for churches, homes and, of course, our bedrooms.

Under Love's spell one can breathe all that is fine and noble, all that is pure and innocent, elevated and Divine, and yet, in the blink of an eye, one can also taste the deepest despair and unnamable agony. Turn toward yet another of its faces and we can immerse ourselves in its fruit, get dizzy from its earthy scent and overwhelmed by its powerful, beating pulse. Love is the gossamer dream we chase and in the chasing suffer some of our deepest wounds and achieve some of our greatest breakthroughs.

IN SEARCH OF LOVE

On your road toward greater authenticity and purpose, examine the role love plays in your life. Try to determine if the beliefs you hold about love limit or propel you to your next level of consciousness.

Is love fact or fantasy? Real or illusory? Is love the thing mystics and poets describe, or is it the tawdry bangles and cheap beads of cynical society? Is love found only in traditional churches and formal prayer, or can we find it in primitive chants and even in the wedding chapels of Las Vegas? Is it love that is depicted on soap operas and promised in Victoria's Secret catalogues? Is it love that drives us wild with jealousy and passion? Is love that tender, extraordinary emotion we feel when we stand in the doorway of our children's room at night and watch them sleeping? Is love what we see in the eyes of a faithful dog who waits for his morning walk or sleeps beside our bed when we do not feel well?

Is it what motivates the choices made in government chambers and corporate boardrooms? Is it that which prompts some among us to lash out, to disown, and to disenfranchise? Is love at the root of the desire to control, to own, or to limit? Is it love that wets the sheets with sweat and juice of passion? Is it love that causes us to go on quests and accomplish the impossible?

Love is all of these things and more. In the final analysis, only you can judge what love is for you. Only you can answer from the depths of your heart. But one thing is clear—from Eve's first seduction to Britney Spears shaking her schoolgirl charms, from Atlas lifting his awesome burden to Brad Pitt flashing his boyish smile, we are all captured in its mystery. Yes, even though one of out every two marriages ends in divorce, we still walk down the aisle with astounding frequency, enormous courage and remarkably little thought.

"Money can't buy you love," the Beatles tell us, but in the world we live in, a large number of us certainly seem to do our best to refute this song's message. Indeed, it appears that many of us believe that money does buy love or at least a version of it we are willing to settle for. And by this we are not just talking about prostitution. We are talking about all the other forms of exchange; those in which so many of us so-called ordinary, decent men and women stand on one side or another of the auction line, putting in our bids to either purchase the affections and companionship of those of lesser means and greater need or to exchange our affections for the price of security and safety.

Why this apparent cynicism? Are we down on love? No, if anything the longer we live and the more encounters with the strange and wonderful experience we have, the more we both know that to arrive at true authenticity, to explore and eventually experience a life of true meaning and purpose, to get from this place of confusion and longing to a place of real honesty and originality, we must be willing to put this most precious commodity under the microscope of truth and discover if the beliefs we hold lead to or away from love. And perhaps of even greater consequence, we believe that each us who walks this path to greater self-knowledge and legitimacy must determine what we will do about the answers we arrive at when we ask, "What is this thing called love?" "How do I love?"

DEFINING YOUR LOVE

Before we leave you to answer these questions for yourself, let's look a little deeper at love. Let's answer a few more questions. Is love really unconditional as many claim? The love of a mother and father for a child is said to be unconditional. Are severely disciplined and controlled children loved unconditionally? Are children who are made to live a life in their parent's image loved unconditionally? Are abandoned children loved unconditionally? Abused and neglected children? Doesn't seem so, does it? And unless our figures are wrong, there are an awful lot of controlled, severely disciplined, abandoned, abused and neglected children in our world today.

What about the love between children and their parents, especially aging parents, parents who brought them into the world, nurtured and protected them, and sacrificed for them? What about the time when these same children have the opportunity to bring their parents in from the world to nurture and protect them and to sacrifice for them and then chose to turn away? What about this kind of love? Is it unconditional?

And then, of course, there is the love we hold for our husbands and wives. Unconditional? In addition to the divorce rate, there is the murder rate and the suicide rate. There is the domestic abuse rate and the rape rate. Love? Perhaps these and so many other aspects of what passes as loving are part of the Dharma of life, the duality of love. For as we have said before in regard to happiness, hope and other subjects, one cannot have the light side of a quality without also experiencing the dark side.

What about other kinds of love? The love between brothers or between sisters? If these forms of love are unconditional, why is there so much disharmony within families? And on a more global scale, why are there so many instances in the Family of Man where brother kills brother and sisters betray their faith with each other?

And what about the love we have for humanity? Is that what motivates the international policies of most governments? Is that what underlies the strategic plans of most multi-nationals? Is that what motivates most of us to produce and deliver the products and services with which we make our livelihood?

And what about love for ourselves? Do we truly love ourselves? In a world that often asks us to barter away or sacrifice some of the things, people and values that are most dear and sacred to us in order to be hip or to belong, do we love ourselves? When we put ourselves in harmful, negative situations and eat foods that poison us and drink water that makes us ill, is this unconditional love? When we abuse other life forms, is that love? In short, do we love ourselves enough to take care of our hearts, our minds, our bodies and our souls?

And what about lust and greed? Do these common experiences fall under the wings of unconditional love? And what about attachment, obsession and, on the other side, sacrifice, dedication, and trust? Quite a conundrum, isn't it?

So there are a few more questions we invite you to ask yourself. Am I capable of loving? Am I willing, in my search for greater authenticity, to look truth in the eye and discover what love is? And above all, how I can express and practice love more often, more deeply and more genuinely in my life today?

TODAY'S REFLECTION

My heart knows where I am faithful to love and where I am not. Starting today, I make a commitment to myself to bring greater honesty, compassion, willingness, courage and trust in my relationships. Where I find that I have limits on my willingness to live with an open heart, I will seek honestly to remove them. Where I find that I am using love as a form of barter or manipulation, I will stop. Where I find that I am not present, not available for love, I will come into the present and surrender to love.

In the Name of Loving

*Enlightenment consists not merely in the seeing of luminous shapes
and visions, but in making the darkness visible.*

⋅∉ C. G. Jung ∋⋅

In our quest to bring greater meaning and purpose into our lives, we have found ourselves having to look at what we and other members of our species have done in the name of loving that have not been very loving at all.

In the name of loving we have proclaimed our commitment to high ideals and lofty values and then proceeded to criticize, judge, condemn, punish and avoid those who do not practice our values according to our standards. In the name of loving we have pursued and wooed and then, in turn, turned away and betrayed. We have pledged our undying commitment and then gone back on own word, demanded more than our share, damned, disavowed and turned our backs on the needs of others.

In the name of loving we have been less-than-supportive parents, unfaithful partners, unwilling lovers, less-than-honorable friends, insensitive neighbors, and unconscious and irresponsible members of our global family. Not exactly a pretty picture and not exactly a path that leads us to real meaning and purpose in our lives. In the name of loving we have been biased and prejudiced. We have abused the environment and allowed others to abuse it. We have let fellow human beings go without basic necessities and, in some instances, die of starvation. Yes, we have done all of this and more.

Perhaps you have also done some of these things in the name of loving. Perhaps you have you promised to love a person and then loved them only as long as they have done what you wanted them to do or been who you wanted them to be. Perhaps you have loved another person but only as long as they have exhibited or pretended to exhibit behavior you found acceptable or appropriate or responsive.

Yes, in the name of loving we all do small, petty, selfish and hurtful things. Of course, we also do large, ugly, cruel and terrible things in love's name. In fact, as the Dalai Lama says, "Deluded by empty concepts such as racism or nationalism, people who are not criminal on the face of it, commit acts of extreme violence and cruelty." We go to war in the name of love. We maim and kill in the name of love. We even abandon entire races and ethnic groups, and conquer, divide and subjugate other nations, all in the name of loving.

SUCH A CONTRADICTORY DEFINITION OF LOVE

Seems strange, doesn't it, that we should spend so much time in pursuit and apparent worship at the altar of love and yet act in so many ways that contradict the very essence of loving? We speak the word often but spend so much time doing things that do not look, feel, touch, taste or smell anything like love.

What do you think accounts for this seeming contradiction? Is it just the natural consequence of living in the physical world, the world of supply and demand, the world of seeming scarcity and lack? This is, after all, the land of illusion where "the stuff of ego" is more familiar than the state of loving. This is the planet where our bondage to limited ideas and negative thought forms—to all the 'isms'—is sometimes more comfortable than the responsibilities that go along with true "freedom." This is, in fact, the planet where a lot of us spend indifference, confusion, violence, and manipulation as if they were acceptable coins of the realm.

"No," you say. "Not true. I don't do that." Well let's explore this a little. Do the people in your world use the currency of openness, tenderness and vulnerability more than they use coin of avoidance, anger or indifference? Is your world free of prejudice and built on acceptance? Do the people around you really care what happens to their brothers and sisters of different colors, nationalities and religious beliefs—those who live next-door and those who live on the other side of the world?

And what about you? How aware are you at this moment about what is going on in the room upstairs or the house across the street? How aware are you of what is going on in this very moment in some other part of the world that either lifts people or pushes them down? And if you are aware, what do you feel, think and do about it?

When we ask ourselves these questions, we often come up more than a little short. So we are not asking these questions of you to be accusatory or superior in any way. We ask you because if any of us are ever going to bring true meaning and purpose into our lives, we will have to be a lot more willing to look our frailties and avoidances right in the eye.

So if you believe there is not as much love expressed each day in this world as there could be, if you find that there are not enough of us who equate love with acceptance and compassion and understanding and that too many of us settle for cheap substitutes, then perhaps it is time to do something.

Sure, most of us know the right things to say and the right gestures to make. We have seen a lot of the same films and read some of the same books. We have listened to many of the same pious words from the same high pulpits and from the front of classrooms. But knowing the words and the music is not enough. Eventually we are going to have to start really singing and dancing the Song of Love. In short, if we believe in love, we are eventually going to have to do something about a world that is so full of divisiveness, violence, hatred and hurt.

A LOT OF WHYS

There are thousands of reasons why, of course, but we are coming to believe that one reason for this dichotomy is particularly relevant—

love is scary. To express love we need to open up to life and opening to life means opening to vulnerability, to pain as well as to pleasure, to confusion as well as clarity, to loss as well as to gain, to betrayal as well as to trust, to death as well as to life.

Opening up puts us directly in touch with our sensitivity, our frailty and, our old friend, fear. Opening up puts us on the edge and requires something of us. It wakes us up. It reminds us that we are responsible and demands that we become more conscious. Above all, opening up reminds us of our inconstancy and impermanence. You know—death and all that.

For those of us who do not want to be reminded of these things or to feel the reality and pulse of life, this is a real problem. For those of us who have been closed down to loving—and that includes all of us at least some of the time—opening up can be painful. Isn't that why we closed down in the first place? We want to avoid feeling?

At the same time, even the most closed among us occasionally has one of those moments of grace and awakening when someone or something comes along and touches our hearts. And in these moments we glimpse again what it is like to feel love. Of course, when that happens some of us run for the hills or the nearest bar, vacation, drug, sexual partner or other diversion.

Both of us have claimed that we want to live more fully, more openly and joyfully. In fact, when someone asks us if we want more love, abundance, and joy, we answer with an enthusiastic "Yes." But sometimes when we have to take the risk, to put ourselves on the line, open up and really feel vulnerable again, there is often another voice, one that says, "Not so fast, please."

In his inaugural address in 1994, Nelson Mandela said, "Our deepest fear is not that we are inadequate. Our deepest fear is that we are powerful beyond measure. It is our light, not our darkness that frightens us the most."

Yes, it is our light that frightens us, the light of our loving, so even when we say we want to love fully, even when we say we want to live fully, when the choice comes a lot of us turn down the volume and hold back because the condition of holding on or holding back is more comfortable and familiar. Sad, but true. It is often more comfortable to be shut down than to be open. And sometimes it is also a lot more acceptable, especially to those around us who are shut down as well.

So we tell ourselves a lie. We tell ourselves we are learning to be loving. We tell ourselves it takes time to love. But of course that's another lie. It doesn't take time to love. It doesn't even take practice, though practice can't hurt. Love isn't something we have to learn. It is something we have to be willing to express. Love takes courage. Love was there before the pain. It was there before we started hiding. Love was there before the judgments and the imperfections, the divisions and the hatreds. Love is, was and ever will be.

LOVE WAS THERE IN THE BEGINNING

Yes, love was there first. Long before the feelings of the fear, doubt and the rest of the stuff that makes living on this physical level so damn challenging and painful. Love was there before all of the artificial and synthetic stuff.

Do you spend at least some of your life trying to be safe rather than opening up to love? Do you sometimes do more of what dulls you, wears you out and keeps you in that familiar comatose state than what it takes to let love in?

We are painting a somewhat negative picture, but our purpose is not negative. We want to point out the giant contradiction that so many of us talk about love at the top of our voices, but express love in our lives at with such hesitation. And the irony is that it takes very little of the real thing called "loving" to produce all of the feeling and all of the experience we desire. An explosion, a magnificence, a Fourth of July of Consciousness is always present in the smallest expression of honesty, in the littlest gesture of genuine concern, of commitment and tenderness. And this awakening to love is so real, exciting and extraordinary that it can carry us—as lovers and as beloveds—beyond the limits of numbness. In the simplest, tiniest expression of the best and most natural that is present in our hearts there is richness beyond compare.

But to get to this tiny, simple moment we need to be willing to give up our frayed blankets and our old, bedraggled stuffed animals. We need to be willing to practice feeling and then expressing what is actually going on in our hearts. We need to be willing to live in the real magnificence of life, the tingling, vulnerable, ever-nowness that happens when we move beyond the familiar and the safe. We need, in fact, to risk.

Yes, in the name of love we do many things. Wouldn't it be nice if one of these things could be to live life authentically, to live the love that we are.

TODAY'S REFLECTION

Today I commit to stop talking about loving and start living it. I will let love guide me even in the face of fear. I will remember that before there was pain and hurt, before there was separation and division, there was love. And to rediscover my loving, all I have to do is to stop doing whatever I am doing that is unloving and open my heart to the gift of the present.

Original Sin

This is the true joy in life, the being used for a purpose recognized by yourself as a mighty one; the being a force of nature instead of a selfish little clod of ailments and grievances complaining that the world will not devote itself to making you happy.

⊸[George Bernard Shaw]⊷

A lot of people seem to believe that life is supposed to be different from the way it is in any given moment. As a result, a lot of us feel frustrated, impatient, ineffective, sometimes inadequate and, of course, hurt. This hurt, in turn, prompts us to be defensive or to withdraw and build a shell or wall that we hope will protect us from our disappointment with life, with others, ourselves, and of course, with God.

Building shells is a pretty common practice among the members of our species. For some of us the level of disappointment is not great, and therefore our shells are relatively thin, while for others the disappointment is much greater and therefore our shells are very thick and end up isolating us from the world. Whether thick or thin, most of us build shells and use them as a defense against hurt.

Of course, each of us seems to have a different strategy when it comes to building shells. Some of us make it a full-time occupation and we let the world know it. Some of us take great pains to camouflage our shell building and even pretend we do not have one. Others paint their shells outrageous colors to draw attention to them. Some of us wear our shells like badges of courage, while others go into a process called therapy and spend long periods trying to remember and understand all the reasons we built the shell in the first place.

No matter what strategy you employ, however, you probably spend a significant portion of your life and a reasonable amount of your money either reinforcing your shell or in pursuit of something that will relieve the hurt that caused you to build the shell in the first place. If you are in this latter group, you may believe that if you could finally arrive at an understanding of the basic cause of your hurt you would be able to come out from behind your shell.

THE ROOT CAUSE

Whether you avoid or analyze the causes of your disappointment and hurt, you might catch a glimpse of what you think is a root cause and, like an amateur detective, begin to pursue this clue with fervor. The hurt began, you think, when your father hit you, or maybe it was when your mother did not give you what you asked for or what you thought you needed. Maybe it was when your father left home or your mother passed away or when a teacher criticized you or a coach shamed you or the kids at school laughed at you or taunted you.

Whatever "it" is, there "it" is. The root cause, the source and beginning of hurt! But the euphoria doesn't generally last, does it? In fact, life has the habit of challenging our new-found understandings. Indeed, very soon after celebrating our liberation from the root cause, we are tested on the strength of our discovery. And while we cannot speak for you, we can say that in our own experience we often come up short in a lot of these tests. We discover that rather than being free, we are still captives of hurt. This realization, at times, leads us to deeper analysis and others into greater avoidance.

If this is true for you, we have an off-the-wall suggestion. Accept that "hurt" is always going to be hanging around. Consider the possibility that hurt is one of the best things that could ever happen to you. Instead of leading to either deeper analysis or greater avoidance, hurt can lead us to heightened awareness and greater authenticity.

We also suggest that hurt was there in the beginning, but not because of some childhood wound and certainly not because someone talked someone else into eating an apple. Instead we believe that hurt is natural, necessary and unavoidable. It is also a blessing. As author and teacher Ram Das says, hurt is "grist for the mill."

So if hurt did not originate as the result of some event in our childhood or when Eve seduced Adam, where did it come from? We believe it comes into being the moment we separate from God and make our way into this thing called life. In short, hurt is what we feel as a result of leaving home—a kind of ultimate homesickness—and therefore, in our opinion, hurt is the true "original sin."

ORIGINAL SIN

Yes, we know, the story goes that "original sin" began when Eve talked Adam into eating of the fruit of the Tree of Knowledge. In that moment, they both became aware of their nakedness and the existence of good and evil. We are taught that this is the "fall from grace" that the rest of us have to spend our lives trying to atone for. We must, by extension, live in an unhappy state and work very hard to regain the favor of a dissatisfied God so that eventually we can return to that time before Adam's bite and get back into this place called Heaven.

We've all heard the story many times, but have you really paid close attention to it? Have you ever wondered why thousands of years of history should rest on the shoulders of this one guy who got a little daffy over the charms of his girlfriend and ate an apple? Really? An apple? Apples are the things we are encouraged to eat each day "to keep the doctor away."

Where we would be if Eve hadn't talked Adam into taking that bite? Would we exist? Would the earth exist? If what traditional religions call "original sin" had not occurred, would God's experiment called the Earth ever have happened?

To explore a different story line, what if Adam's bite was perfect and essential? What if it was not a "fall from grace," but the first and most necessary step on the path to a new kind of grace—conscious grace, whole grace, loving, aware, extraordinary grace? What if that is what being human is all about? What if the "original sin" that produced "original hurt" was and is absolutely critical as a means of encouraging us to leave home and set out on this journey into life and into this experience called awareness? What if "hurt" is an ache, a longing, a kind homesickness that keeps us awake? What if it's God's way of reminding us that when we take on human form our job is to make mistakes? What if mistakes are an essential part of being in God's garden? What if "hurt" is God's way of encouraging us to continue our journey to return to ourselves, not as an unconscious, unaware soul, but as a vibrant, experienced, alive, wondrous, powerful, co-creator, as a contributor who brings our strength and our limitations, our mistakes and our victories back home to add to the whole story of creation?

If you are willing to consider this possibility, perhaps you will recognize the rather ironic, unmitigated cosmic humor of the whole process. Perhaps you will remember that, in any present moment, you are and always have been on a journey home. In fact, you have never been on any other path or on any other journey. You are the payoff, and all paths lead you back to you.

The only difference between the various paths we select is the speed and directness with which different paths allow us to proceed to our destination and the range of experiences we choose to have along the way. Perhaps you will remember that hurt, both the original hurt of separation and the continual hurt of life, is there to help us remember our vulnerability and own our intimacy and gentleness. And the sooner and faster we remember all of this, the sooner and deeper we accept this condition of life, the faster and more wondrous our progress will be. Perhaps that is what Thich Nhat Hanh means when he encourages those he works with to use a simple mantra to practice mindfulness: "I have arrived. I am home."

WAY BEYOND CLOSURE

Of course, there are times when our shell serves a purpose. There may be moments in the growing and learning process when something organic is happening or a need for privacy exists. In these moments, our shells can serve a useful purpose. But beyond these natural moments, we are not intended to live our lives in shells. They are like cottages or inns along the path where we can take shelter and rest for a little while.

So if you are living in isolation and separation, discomfort and defensiveness, consider the possibility that "hurt" is your ally and companion, pointing the way toward greater expansion, toward surrender and openness. Hurt may exist not as a justification for closure but as an aid to expansion, an aid to greater caring and communication, innocence, tenderness and joy.

Do not spend your life trying to avoid hurt or endlessly reviewing it or analyzing it. Be thankful for your "hurt" and let it do its job. Don't resist your hurt. When it shows up, embrace it. In fact, breathe into it and allow it to pass into and through you. Resistance will only cause it to hang around longer.

Hurt is part of the unavoidable wonder of who you are. It's a signal alerting you to something important. Also remember that it's okay to have a shell and that you are in charge of opening and closing it. Above all, remember there is a pearl of great price within you and this pearl is your authenticity. All you have to do to live it more fully is to consciously accept your hurt. Let it become your teacher and allow it to assist you to remember the presence and wonder of God.

TODAY'S REFLECTION

When I feel hurt I have a choice. I can defend against it or embrace it and allow it to teach me what I am here to learn. Hurt is a guide helping me on my way home. Today, I will make peace with my hurt.

◆

Death, Granddaddy of All Beliefs

Let go of the mind and die into The Heart.
⊸[Stephen & Ondrea Levine]⊶

D eath, annihilation, termination, the end of the line, passing over, giving up the ghost, kicking the bucket, crossing over, the other side, the doorway into the beyond. We have heard it called by many names. We have sensed its impact on the lives of others, felt its tentacles reach into our lives and perhaps even had it touch our bodies directly. Some among us have had a direct experience of leaving our physical bodies at the moment of an accident or trauma or a brush with an alternate reality. Some of us have passed into what is called the "tunnel of light" and returned to tell others about our remarkable experiences. Some of us have experienced death in dreams, while others among us have entered altered states of consciousness with the aid of drugs or rare foods or breathing or other forms of stimulation.

Most of us have wept at its arrival in our families, pulled back in trepidation and fear from it and tried, in ways far too numerous to mention, to avoid even the slightest recognition of its existence. The perennial search for the Fountain of Youth is motivated by it, played out each day with varying degrees of obsession over exercise, cosmetic surgery, wonder drugs and healing waters. And yet no matter what we do, no matter how much we avoid or deny it, death is with us constantly.

Even if we could push death aside for a little while, the media certainly will not let us forget it. Death is the media's bread and butter. In fact, the first numbers we hear in any news report are the death statistics—the casualties in wars, accidents, epidemics, natural catastrophes, and of course, on holiday travel fatalities. These are the lead stories. The detailed and highly specific accounts of grizzly crimes always dwell on the number of deaths as if a sufficiently large number makes one death somehow less significant. Then, of course, there is the national obsession with obituaries. Some of us, in fact, have trouble starting the day without them. It's a cup of coffee and the news of who is no longer with us.

Yes, the death toll seems to have become a way of keeping score. It almost seems that the media considers life to be a kind of sporting event and death is the opposing player.

Of course, the media is feeding us these sensational stories to peddle more newspapers or raise their ratings so they can sell more cereal or cars, beer or feminine hygiene products. But lest we lay too much burden on the media, remember whose voracious appetite for sensationalism is being fed. Also remember that one of the interesting things about this subject, as Stephen and Ondrea Levine point out in their book *Who Dies?*, is that the really sensational number never gets reported. Over 250,000 people die each day. Yes, approximately a quarter of a million people leave the earth each day and that translates into approximately 75,000,000 human beings each year.

We are we exploring what many consider a depressing topic because as long as men and women have recorded their stories, death has always haunted our consciousness—The Grim Reaper, The Dark Specter, The Unwanted Guest, The Shadow Behind Us. And therefore we know that unless and until we learn to deal with it, we will never learn how to live.

If we are ever going to lead empowered and authentic lives, if we are ever going to uncover real meaning and purpose in our lives, we must learn to look death in the eye and relax our fear. That is the purpose of this chapter. We invite you to step back from all the things you have to do right now and explore some of your beliefs and fears about death. If you do this now, in the next moment and the one after that you can be more awake, more aware, and more committed to living your life fully. Let's face it: deep in our hearts we know that of all of the crimes we can commit, the one we fear most is to die without having truly done what we have come to the earth to do.

DEATH OVER OUR SHOULDER

The Yaqui Indian known as Don Juan once told Carlos Castaneda to "always keep death over your left shoulder." When Castaneda asked his teacher to explain, Don Juan told him that consulting with Death each day will enrich his life and remind him of its value.

Keep this lesson in mind as you take these next steps on the road toward greater authenticity. In fact, find your own way to keep death constantly in your awareness—not as a depressing image or as a reason to be afraid but as a consultant and ally who can teach you how to live your life more fully.

Imagine for example, that today is the last day of your life. What will you do? With whom will you spend it? What will you say? How will you want the legacy of this day to reflect the legacy of your life? Will you put certain affairs in order? Will you have conversations with people in your world that you have wanted to have for a long time? Will you experience regrets over things you wanted to do and have not yet done? Will you regret things you want to contribute and have not yet contributed? Will you take new paths and explore new options? Will you pray more or play more or spend more time in quiet intimacy with yourself or others?

This "keeping death over your left shoulder" can make a significant difference in how authentic, original, and natural you are in each moment. Indeed, death can be feared and dreaded, held at bay temporarily with distractions, but in the end it gains our full attention.

AN ALTERNATE VIEW OF DEATH

If you stopped long enough to imagine that this is the last day of your life, and if you answered some of the questions about what you would do, you probably have some new awareness or perhaps have re-considered some things you have thought about before and put back on the shelf. No matter what you learned in answering these questions, including perhaps that you did not want to answer them, if you are truly interested in bringing real meaning and purpose to your life we strongly suggest you do this exercise often or, at the very least, periodically.

We also suggest that today you start doing some of the things you would do if this was the last day of your life. And if you need a little more motivation, we suggest you take a few moments and write one of those obituaries that some of us are so fond of reading with our morning coffee. Write your own obituary and ask yourself what Tom and Mary Smith sitting in their kitchen in St. Louis or Boston or Dallas might say about your life. Would they find it interesting or meaningful or valuable? Would your obituary instruct them, motivate them, and touch their hearts or would they skim right over it?

CONVERSATIONS WITH DEATH

As we have said, death can be a wonderful and wise companion with whom you can take this journey toward greater authenticity. Death also can inform you in a number of ways. For example, you can have one-on-one conversations with death. We use this technique a lot in our work. It is a powerful way of gaining insight and greater connection with ourselves, exploring our beliefs and learning how to identify some of the things that limit us and others that promote greater consciousness. The process we use has a number of different roots. The one we tend to favor comes from Carl Jung and one of his earliest disciples, Maria Louise Von Franz, who developed a process called "active imagination."

Let us give you an example of how these conversations work. George was having one of those days in which everything he tried seemed to end up in either confusion or delay. It was one of those days in which he wondered what was going on and if and how he had gotten out of alignment with God and his own wisdom. You probably have days like this as well.

Lately when days like this arise, George turns to his journal and has conversations with some of these frailties and confusions. We will have more to say about this in the next chapter. For now, you may find it instructive to listen in on a conversation George had with Death.

George: Death, can we talk?

Death: I will save you some breath. There is nothing but Death. I occur in each second, each moment, each event, word or action. I am simply the passing beyond of this moment so the next moment can arrive. I am the way of transition, the avenue by which change happens. So all of this fear and dread of me is a waste of time.

This fear and dread are part of the misconceptions and illusions that the mind and the ego make up in an effort to cling to life. But I am not anything to be afraid of. I actually occur thousands of times each day in each life. Yes, the reality is, every time anyone turns their attention from one thing, one word, one action to the next I am there—like an eraser—cleaning the board so that the next thing, word or action can be written.

You see, this illusion keeps the appearance of continuity. It is like a theatrical conceit that allows the story to be told. At the same time, it is only a conceit and without it you would remember that you are simply experiencing good theater. You would also acknowledge me—not as a specter or dreaded and unwelcome guest—but as a valuable part of life. You would not build me into something large and dreadful, but instead see me as a friend.

George: Some friend!

Death: Yes, and a good one. I am suggesting that you not feel badly when this or that project isn't working or this or that person doesn't understand or want what you want. It is all just temporary. All just passing by. Of course your project or your relationship dies. How could they do anything else? They die every time you turn your attention away from them or walk into or out of a room. Projects and tasks die every time you turn your focus to the next project or task and relationships die as soon as you turn your attention to the next person. Conversely, your relationship or your project is reborn each time you walk back into the room or turn toward it again.

You see, continuity and permanence are some of those conceits created by your overworked and exhausted mind; they are like emotional/mental sleights of hand that allow you to maintain the illusion that all of these separate moments and actions and words and thoughts are part of a continuous, never-ending story.

It is your mind collaborating with what Eckhart Tolle calls your "emotional body" or "pain body" that keeps the story alive. If these partners did not cooperate, the story, the never-ending continuous story that you call your life would be seen for what it really is, a series of separate thoughts, words and actions. And what a gift that would be. A gift of freedom. This moment you are free to have, do and be whatever you require or desire. This moment, unencumbered by the last. What a gift!

This morning, for example, just before you began this conversation with me you were thinking about yesterday. But yesterday ceased to exist when today started. That did not, however, prevent you using your mind and your emotions to allow some of the pain and confusion that occurred yesterday to color and infect today.

Meanwhile, the truth is, there is no pain present today. At least, not yet. None of the events that occurred yesterday are occurring right now. If you are experiencing remnants of previous yesterdays, it is only because your mind is struggling to keep them alive in this moment.

I sometimes think that is why you and so many others are afraid of me. I interrupt this game of illusion, this game of hide and seek and call you to a different, a more responsible and higher game. To befriend and accept me is to accept that you are free and that, of course, places this extraordinary challenge on you. It requires that you live this moment with reasons, justifications and explanations. It requires that you loosen you grip on the past and live.

George: As I listen to you I'm aware that I am still afraid that if I let things go, if I let things end, you are all I am going to ever feel—you and sadness and regret and despair and depression.

Death: Perhaps that will be true, but it's equally possible that you will experience and relief and joy and freedom and a lot more. In the end, of course, it does not matter. No matter what you experience, eventually you will realize that it is only a projection, only part of the theater of life, and as you know, every projection, every evening at the theater—no matter how good or bad the play—ends. How long you hold on to it is largely your choice. In short, you can celebrate or suffer for as long or as little as you choose. Some primitive tribes go very deep into suffering. They, in fact, are extreme in their actions for a very short period of time, but then they move on quickly to what is next. That is the true rhythm of the natural world. In short, they let whatever the story is go.

So in your case, you can hold onto the pain you experienced yesterday. You can, in fact, hold on to it for the rest of your life. Some members of your species do that. One of their relationships ends and then for the rest of their lives they are sad or angry or blaming or miserable.

But the truth is that relationship died hundreds of thousands of times during the time it was being held as continuous and constant. The same is true of thousands of other experiences and opportunities in the workplace and at home. These are born and die thousands of times each day. Each has its own cycle of birth and death and rebirth and re-death. And it is up to each person as to if and how they live each of these moments.

George: You are giving me a lot to think about, but, of course, the challenge is to put your guidance into practice.

Death: Yes, or you can let my advice just die. You see, there is nothing to worry about. If you trust the process of life, whatever you need will be there at just the time you need it. That's what this remarkable and interdependent mystery called life is all about. So you don't need to struggle with it or with me. You don't have to try to remember what's important. All you have to do is to live and if you get in trouble, all you have to do is to "look over your left shoulder." I'll be there.

Have your own conversation with Death. Yes, we know you may feel awkward or foolish at first. You may find yourself hoping no one you know comes in and asks what you're doing. But remember, if this was the last day of your life would you really care what someone else thought or would you be doing whatever it takes to complete your life in an authentic way?

TODAY'S REFLECTION

I have a choice today. I can try to pretend that death does not exist. I can pretend that I am not afraid of dying and treat death as an unwelcome guest or I can welcome it. Death can be my ally. Death can be one of my best teachers about life.

PART THREE
Turning Deliberately Toward Greater Meaning & Purpose

Learning to Dialogue with Yourself

My words are very easy to understand and very easy to put into practice,
yet few in the world can understand them or put them into practice.

-◦[Lao Tzu]◦-

To be alive in the twenty-first century is to be at least a little media mad. In fact, most of us have been trained to live in a world of ten-second visual cuts and a continuous, multi-track dialogue, the kind of dialogue that Robin Williams performs to make us laugh but that drive us crazy when they occur in our own heads.

It is probably more accurate to describe this dialogue as a chorus of voices, often more contentious than polite, a group discussion or committee meeting gone whacko with each of the many voices vying for attention, arguing, and offering conflicting points of view. This inner argument masquerading as a conversation often distracts us from being present and prevents us from accomplishing our goals. This inner discord is not only limiting and troubling, it also precludes us from living authentically. The noise distracts us from getting to the truth.

An old Sufi story speaks to this situation. A disciple asked his teacher, "What is truth?" The teacher replied, "Something I have never, at any time, spoken, nor shall I."

Lao Tzu, in the *Tao Te Ching*, examines the result of this outer-directed focus:

The way that can be told
Is not the constant way;

The name that can be named
Is not the constant name;
The nameless was the beginning
Of heaven and earth;

And William Faulkner, borrowing from Shakespeare, described aspects of contemporary life as being, "full of sound and fury signifying nothing."

If your interior committee is at all like ours, there are probably plenty of times when you would do almost anything to silence the racket. But finding the off button is the trick, isn't it? Do you also find that there is at least one voice among the many that is stronger and more disruptive than the others? It's not always louder than the rest, but this voice is identifiable by the power of its negativity. This voice can be so negative, in fact, you may try to hide it, to lock it up inside as though it were an "insane child" you want to keep out of sight of friends and neighbors.

No matter what you do to hide this particularly discordant voice from others, however, you hear it, don't you? You cover it up, camouflage, deny, defend against and perhaps even try to rationalize the things this voice says. Yet the more you try to keep this voice hidden the more rebellious it gets. The more you attempt to deny and avoid it, the more this whacko dialogue seems to heat up.

How do we know this? We do the same thing. Most people do. So in case you thought you were alone, please know that we are all in it together. While the thought may not be very comforting, it's a form of mass psychosis and there are some powerful techniques you can apply to deal with it.

Sedena describes one of her run-ins with her committee in this way.

Sedena: "Sometimes when I wake up in the morning the committee is already in session. One voice is nagging about all the things I forgot to do yesterday. Another voice is anxious about what I have to do today. A third voice is complaining about something George did and a fourth is angry at me for not saying what I should have said in an interaction with a coaching client. This is only the start of my morning conversation and I haven't even gotten out of bed yet."

A MORE CONSTRUCTIVE APPROACH TO THIS DIALOGUE

Instead of trying to avoid or deny or distract yourself from one or more of your particularly negative voices, listen to what it being said. Instead of trying to drown it or them out with additional noise and activity, allow it to have its full say and participate in your inner dialogue as an equal and respected member of the committee.

You might resist this approach, because you know how this scenario plays out at work when that loud and disruptive member of your team takes the floor or when a child at home goes off in a vocal rampage. But give it a try. Allow your disruptive voices to speak as you would invite that disruptive team member into the project or that unruly child into the game rather than insisting he or she stay on the sidelines. Disruptive voices actually have something to say and by allowing them to speak, you'll find they eventually start to express themselves in ways that are more understandable and sometimes— and here's the kicker—very valuable.

We have found that the more we allow the disruptive voices— within ourselves, in our client companies and in the complex relationships with individual coaching candidates—to express themselves as equal and recognized participants, the less troublesome they become. In fact, the very voices we resist sometimes become the doorways through which some of our most substantial learning opportunities come.

Just as some of us find that some of our most important lessons and breakthrough discoveries come through relationships with a friend or a child who is physically or mentally challenged, we have discovered that some of our greatest lessons come from listening to the odd and strange voices within us. The seemingly disruptive voices we have been denying for years can become bridges to another level of loving and understanding.

Of course, there are instances when some of our original fears are justified, times when these awkward voices react with smallness, narrowness or with fear. But these instances are more than offset by moments of extraordinary new learning and opportunity.

So we invite you to begin a different kind of dialogue with yourself. Explore your inner dialogue and discover if some of the voices you have been avoiding might not have some things of tremendous value to say. Remember that the more you allow these inharmonious and inappropriate voices to speak out the more you will discover that what they have to say is a bridge to your greater meaning and purpose in life.

THE RISK IS ITS OWN REWARD

We know our suggestion may sound silly or dangerous or troubling. You may have been told that your true nature is sinful and that you should defend yourself against it. But what if your true nature is not sinful but good? What if your inner voices—even the most cantankerous of them—are trying to lead you to a higher, better, more expansive way of life? What if your inner committee contains voices that have some very important messages for you?

Having kept some of these voices locked away for years, you may feel foolish letting them speak. But if you trust the process, we know that the risk will be worth your effort.

You can test this hypothesis by considering the most recent experience you have had dealing with a friend or colleague or family member who is out of sorts. Have you noticed that more often than not the primary cause of the person's mood is the desire for attention or because the opportunity to participate in something has been denied? And even though it takes patience and time to re-establish trust and open the channel, with the investment of a little attention the individual generally comes back into balance, don't they?

It is this kind of attention and love, simple and direct, that the voices inside you want. They want to contribute. They want to do their job, which is to share what they know. Sometimes, in fact, these voices are the keepers of your unexpressed desires, fears, doubts, longings and dreams, and once you listen to them, you start to remember, you start to re-inherit the energy and pathways to greater authenticity in your life.

YOUR CHALLENGE

Tune into the wisdom of these voices, allow them to be powerful agents for your transformation rather than unwanted disruptors. Conduct this experiment with yourself for five minutes each morning and each evening. Just sit down, close your eyes and literally talk to yourself. And "talk" includes that other essential component called "listening." In short, give voice to the voices within you. It will be like a five-minute party at which everyone gets to talk and to listen. No matter how obnoxious or distasteful, no matter how silly or disruptive, no matter how critical or contrary any of the voices may be, give each of them your attention. Be the patient listener who sits at the conference table and acknowledges the contribution. Listen to their grievances, hurts, angers and, above all, listen to what is between and beneath the words.

Of course, like a garden hose that's been lying unused in the sun for a while, there is a chance that sediment will come out first. So what? It's time. In fact, it has probably been a long time since you felt the cool clear water of your own refreshing and authentic wisdom. You don't have to do anything. Just listen, and resist defending or justifying. Listen to that wild, wacky and wonderfully original series of voices that comprise your inner committee.

Twice a day, five minutes of your time, that's all you need to invest. Have the kind of conversation we shared with you in the chapter on death. One day, in one of those conversations, you will realize you are no longer listening to discontent but to something else. You will realize that the harangue has stopped and something wonderfully intimate and interesting has begun. You will discover that these dialogues within yourself can prove to be as interesting, informative and engaging as your best conversations with others. You may just discover how truly extraordinary a conversationalist you are.

TODAY'S REFLECTION

Some of my disharmony is the result of my not listening to all of the voices within me. Today I will stop resisting and start listening. Today I will start listening and stop criticizing the voices on my committee. Today I will begin a true dialogue with myself, listening to that "still small voice" that is guiding me home.

◆

Turning Toward What Scares You

Fear is a natural reaction to moving closer to the truth.
⊸[Pema Chodron]⊶

After more pain and confusion than either of us cares to remember and certainly more than we ever want to relive, we have finally discovered that in dealing with a number of the challenges that come up in our lives, we have been making a fundamental mistake. We have been turning away rather than toward the things—both inside and outside ourselves—that frighten, trouble, confound, confuse and scare us.

You might think this doesn't sound like such a big deal, but we are here to report that it *is* a big deal. We are also here to say that if you are willing to take even the next few days of your life to test a new strategy, we guarantee that your life will never be the same again! Guarantee? You bet! This is a one hundred percent sure thing that will absolutely bring greater meaning and purpose into your life.

Think about it. How many times each day does something come up that troubles, pains, scares, confuses or disturbs you, and how many times do you turn away from it? Maybe you don't always turn physically away. Maybe you turn up the sound a little on the television or your CD player. Maybe you keep your eyes directed toward the person you think is the cause of your confusion or pain, but you turn your mind toward other things. Maybe it's just a slight adjustment you make in the temperature in the room, in the direction the conversation is taking, or maybe you shift what you are doing in some other way. You run a little harder, take another exercise class or, on the other side of the coin, eat another doughnut or cookie. Maybe your turning away literally involves a redirection of your eyes away from a person who is old, physically or mentally impaired, homeless, threatening or clearly disturbed. After all, you would not want to embarrass someone by staring, would you?

Do you know what we are talking about when we say that we have been facing in the wrong direction, turning away rather than toward what the things that trouble us? Do you also do this sometimes to avoid parts of your life that you find disagreeable, disturbing or challenging? Do you sometimes use little or big avoidance strategies, time-filling, mind-numbing strategies to prevent yourself from dealing with your own truth and discovering greater authenticity in your life?

And please, remember the caution we have offered previously. Our questions are not meant as accusations, nor are they designed to be used by you against yourself in the form of guilt. They are not intended to imply that either of us has this stuff down pat. In fact, for us this reversal of our habitual pattern, this turning toward rather than away from the things that scare us, often requires every ounce of courage, stamina and honesty we can muster. Indeed, this is not a minor course correction. Because so many of the currents of contemporary life flow away rather than toward our challenges, this decision to move toward the things that scare, confuse and cause us pain, sends some pretty serious shudders through the Ship of Self.

From our experience with a number of corporate leaders and folks on the international stage, we know that these shudders are equally great even for those who appear to have great courage. For example, Lech Walesa's name is obviously associated with the cause of labor unions. In a Communist country at the height of paranoia about workers' rights, he organized the shipyard workers. Did he have an easy road? No. Was he afraid? Yes, at times he feared for his life, for the well-being of family and associates and for the future of the Polish state. At times, he was even afraid of leaving his country, afraid that if he ever crossed the border, he would never be allowed to return. Even with a very large number of people from the international communi-ty working on his behalf and even with the support of the U.S. gov-ernment, George could not get him out of Poland for an internation-al event. Despite these fears and obstacles, Lech Walesa turned toward his fears and as a result, the labor union movement was given new life in Poland.

LIVING IN A ONE-MINUTE WORLD

Whether you are working to change the face of workers' rights in a non-Democratic country or struggling to deal with more personal challenges, the truth is that you did not get turned in the wrong direc-tion easily or overnight. It took a whole army of well-meaning but equally misdirected folks to teach basically innocent children to move away from troubling challenges. It took thousands of hours of secular school, hundreds of hours of Sunday school, millions of moments of at-home and out-in-the-world instruction, movies, books, television commercials and the lyrics of thousands of popular songs to train us to look for immediate relief from pain and to avoid anything that resembles trouble.

No one has time anymore for anything but work and the corre-sponding reflex reaction of pain avoidance. No time to cook food at natural temperatures or to take whole courses on subjects of interest. Instead it's a world of microwaves and condensed book clubs. No time for balance, for just being, or for allowing things to develop. We are too busy getting ahead or to the top or on to the next thing or to whatever we think will make us famous and thin, rich and happy, acceptable and safe. We are members of the abbreviated culture prac-ticing an abridged version of life in a time-crazed world.

Radio, television, movies, CD's, DVD's, drugs, alcohol, food, exercise, sex, sleep, you name it, and we have personally used it to avoid, soften, defer and dull the things that make us fearful and doubtful. These things force us away from the center and to the edge of the world where authenticity happens and meaning and purpose can be found. In some ways we are like those ancient cartographers we mentioned earlier. We have spent far too much of our lives in the territory of the comfortable and the familiar, telling ourselves scare stories of what lies beyond the border. "Here There Be Dragons!"

THINGS THAT SCARE US

As long as our minds are free to roam in the past and the future, we will always be afraid. When we are afraid we tend to avoid the tough places, the mysterious places, the edgy places. In this over-medicated, therapy-mad, entertainment-focused culture of ours we have learned to avoid our feelings, to suppress or sublimate them or to interpret and analyze them.

On the surface, the purpose of all of these actions is to feel better and the mantras of our age certainly remind us to feel more. But feel what? Feel good, feel young, feel motivated! When we feel sadness, grief, or loss, we medicate or analyze to death. We do our best to fit these feelings into carefully outlined lists of symptoms and pathologies. We call these feelings dysfunctions and have a whole set of practices and processes designed to eliminate, reduce and cure them.

The only trouble with all of this "conditioning" is that it has trained us to avoid facing or telling the truth. Not since Buddha was brave enough to tell it like it is—that suffering, pain, confusion, despair, and loss are part of life, part of what he called the Dharma, the duality—has the truth really been told. And yet, sometime after he (and Jesus and Mohammed and others) told us that our addiction to pleasure is inextricably linked to finding pain, that our quest to find clarity is attached to confusion, that seeking gain and possession are sure paths to loss, we turned onto this self-defeating path. You know the story, already. Up leads to down. In leads to out. Love to hate. Opposite sides of the coin, and we can't spend one side of the coin without spending the other.

So are we advising you to give up all the painkillers and live life cold turkey? Yes, for the most part, that is precisely what we're saying. We agree with author James Thurber, who said, "All men should strive to learn before they die, what they are running from and to and why." Although we know how challenging this path is, we have found no other choice that actually works. No matter how much instant gratification we seek, no matter how many new jobs, geographies, lovers, or diet programs we try, no matter how many new teachers, healers or therapists we work with, in the end it comes down to one simple, totally and absolutely unavoidable truth. If we want to lead lives that are authentic and full of meaning and purpose, if we want a direct connection with God rather than settling for an intermediary, we must go directly to the source. We are going to have to face the music and dance the dance that only we can dance. In short, we are going to have to start turning toward rather than away from the things that scare us. We are going to have to do what poet David Whyte calls, "going into the ashes of the world to feel the fiercer edges of experience."

We are not suggesting that therapy, guidance and education are inauthentic or bad. There can be very helpful. There are also times when a piece of cake, a sexual fantasy or a great movie is just what we need. What we are saying, however, is that if you are using any of these activities or experiences as substitutes for investing your full and undivided attention in the search for your own truth, if you are holding on to beliefs that any of these things is enough or that if you can only get through the day, the week or the month you'll be fine, you are kidding yourself.

TURNING TOWARD

Troubling as this thought may be, in the end it is nowhere near as troubling as the life you will end up leading if you continue to suppress, deny and avoid the things that scare you. So please, consider our recommendation. Give yourself the gift of greater self-discovery. Follow Thurber's advice and give yourself the gift of knowing how courageous, remarkable, and wise you are.

You don't have to start with the big stuff. Begin with some of the smaller things that scare you. Start with things that are reasonably small inconveniences or disturbances that may be limiting you at work, at home or in the world around you.

For example, you may have some confusions or misunderstandings that show up in your relationship with someone at work or at home. You may have some concern about a minor ache that has shown up in your body. You might have a glimmer now and then that you are not living in a place or under conditions that serve your deeper dreams for the life you want to live. You may be just about to start a new job or begin a course of study and some small concern keeps coming up. Or perhaps these first hints of dissatisfaction or confusion, these tiny harbingers of future pain or loss, have something to do with a new group you have joined, a new religious or spiritual practice you are beginning, or a new place you are planning to settle.

No matter what the source, name it and then feel the feelings associated with it. If you are willing to feel what you feel and to turn toward rather than away from this feeling, you will be taking one of the most courageous and valuable steps you have ever taken. But you have to actually feel the feeling. That is the key. It may begin as a physical discomfort. You are too hot, too cold, too itchy, too close, too restless, too something. It might come up in other ways, emotional ways that are attached to the physical sensations. You may feel a little nervous, anxious, sad, or angry. Perhaps there are thoughts that hint at deeper feelings such as doubt, despair, confusion, indecision or boredom.

No matter what you feel, acknowledge the feelings, feel them and then turn toward and not away from them. Invite the feelings in. Welcome them. No matter how uncomfortable they may be, do not cover them up with some distraction or diversion. Just welcome them. Ask for their assistance. Observe them. Talk to them. And then—and this is the real secret—listen to them.

If you use the dialogue technique we discussed in the chapter on death, writing an actual conversation with whatever scares you (death, anxiety, confusion, pain, hate, anger, and so on), you will be amazed. In fact, having a conversation with whatever you are afraid of, addicted to or troubled by can be one of the most liberating experiences of your life. Let what scares you disclose a little more about its purpose for being in your life. Find out what you can do to make peace with it. Is it a first warning or alert or a lifetime companion? Is there something you can do so that it does not morph into a physical, emotional or spiritual disease?

There are many other "hows"—spending time in silent meditation, quiet reflection, artistic expression, yoga, honest conversation with other people in your life, genuine, committed forms of therapy that allow for the mystery and do not analyze life to death, constructive forms of play, intimacy with those you love. There are also techniques that Thich Nhat Hanh recommends and the remarkable life-affirming strategies that Eckhart Tolle has introduced.

The list is as limitless as your imagination, courage and commitment to your own freedom allow. Frankly, in the end, the "how" does not matter. What matters is your moving beyond believing toward knowing. What matters is not being perfect or doing it right, but your willingness to explore the true mystery and wonder of your life. What matters is not that you find God, but that you are willing to surrender to God. Yes, what matters is your willingness to turn toward and not away from life.

STAYING DOWN LONG ENOUGH CAN MAKE A REAL DIFFERENCE

When you are passing through one of those really challenging times that happen when you lose someone you love, when you have a serious health problem, lose your job or your way in your career or make some other major life transition, please avoid the tendency to come up from the depths too soon. We know the natural tendency is to move out of the darkness toward the light, to move away from the sadness or pain toward relief, but we also know that staying with your feelings until they have given you all of their gifts is a very important key to real authenticity.

TODAY'S REFLECTION

I will make a major adjustment in the course of my life today. I will trust in my ability to turn toward the things that scare me rather than away. Today I will acknowledge that none of the "aspirins of life" that I have ever taken have given me true relief. Today I will take my next real steps toward greater meaning and purpose in my life and inherit more of my authentic self.

———————————————————— ◆ ————————————————————

If You're Not Here Now, You're Nowhere

As a thing the way is shadowy, indistinct.
Indistinct and shadowy yet within it is an image:
Shadowy and indistinct yet within it is substance.
The essence is quite genuine and within
it is something that can be tested.

⋯∎ Lao Tzu ∎⋯

We have been talking about the value of learning to have a different kind of dialogue with ourselves, about learning to listen to our own wisdom, and to make peace with some of those disruptive voices that are part of our inner committee. We have also been talking about having the courage to follow the prompts our inner voices offer in our quest for greater authenticity and meaning. And we've been talking about changing our strategies and turning toward rather than way from the things that scare and trouble us.

Let's turn our attention to how our inner dialogue and some of these inner prompts can lead us to live more fully in the "now" where everything we require and everything we desire can be found. Let's talk about some of the obvious things we may be overlooking that can make a real difference in the quality and content of our lives.

There is a story from the Sufi tradition about a merchant who for years traveled the same trading route that took him through a narrow mountain pass to markets across the border in a neighboring country.

Each time the merchant arrived at the border crossing the guard in charge would stop him, insist he take every pack off of every one of his donkeys and then thoroughly search each pack for contraband. This practice continued for many years. In fact, it continued until the border guard finally retired.

One day as the merchant was making his way through his own village, he heard his name called and turned to see the retired border guard waving to him from a nearby café.

They sat for a while and made small talk. Eventually, the retired guard said, "I am retired now and can no longer do you any harm, so I wonder if you would mind answering my question."

With a wave of his hand the merchant indicated that he would.

"So tell me, am I right? Were you smuggling?"

The merchant nodded.

"But I don't understand. I went through each of your packs so carefully. I can't for the life of me believe I missed the contraband. What were you smuggling?"

"Donkeys," replied the merchant.

The point of the story parallels a discovery we have made in our own lives. In our efforts to find the hidden contraband or so-called treasure we often overlook the obvious. For this reason, take your next steps on the journey to greater authenticity by looking at some of obvious things you may be overlooking.

There is a Zen expression that encourages us to, "eat when eating, sit when sitting, stand when standing." When we first came across this expression a number of years ago we thought it was a worthwhile but rather obvious and simplistic concept. After all, what else could one do with eating, sitting or standing? Clearly not all that difficult to accomplish and certainly nothing revolutionary in nature.

We could not have been more mistaken.

All of these years later, we are both just beginning to glimpse how challenging living in the "present moment" can be. Of course, in some ways our first impression was correct. That Zen statement does point to the obvious but also to our error. The error lies in the assumption that the answer can be found anywhere else. Indeed, although the wisdom imparted to us by many wise and noble beings who have come before us discloses that only in the "now" is life to be found, we have gone on our not-too-merry way seeking it everywhere but where we are. Only in the "now" does life disclose its secrets to us. Only in the "now" can we uncover what is ours to learn, to live, to experience, and to enjoy.

MORE COMMON SENSE

Another Zen expression issues from the same deep well of common sense. It is that old cliché about busy hands keeping us out of trouble. In this instance, too, the longer we both live and the more we experience, especially our failures, the more obvious and relevant this expression becomes. For when our hands are deeply involved in doing something, a practical something, a physical something, it is not possible for us to go away from what our hands are doing. In fact, it is quite the opposite. We need to stay present in order to do that particular something and when we do stay present, remarkable things occur.

First and most important, we actually get the doing done and generally with a lot more proficiency and excellence. Second, when we are really involved in the doing we also experience a sense of fullness and satisfaction. Third, we remember how valuable it is to do something for the value of the doing instead of as a means to an end. When we are present we are also able to identify our resources, both those we have and those we need. We also remember that whatever we need is either already available or the present moment becomes the doorway through which we can obtain whatever we need.

IN THE NOW EVEN PAIN DISSOLVES

Another remarkable thing about staying present is that by living in each "here and now" we greatly reduce the amount of pain we experience in our lives and, as a consequence, in the lives of those around us.

Reflect for a moment on how much of the pain that you experience is "physical" pain and how much is "emotional" or "mental" pain. Unless you have been particularly challenged with a significant physical limitation or a debilitating illness, you can probably report that most of the pain you have experienced in your life has not been physical, but instead has been "emotional" or "mental."

Most of your pain is the result of an emotion, feeling or thought you have held on to from a previous moment. Most of these emotions, feelings and thoughts issue directly from your belief that you or an event, circumstance or relationship is not the way it is or was supposed to be.

This thwarted desire to be, do, have or experience something different triggers a thought and the thought stimulates a feeling and the feeling in turn rubs against and reinforces a limiting belief, such as "I'm not good enough," or "Things never go my way," or "I'm not loved." In this way a continuous cycle is kicked off. This cycle produces what we call "emotional" or "mental" pain.

Sadness, a sense of loss, loneliness, unworthiness, hopelessness, abandonment, anger, frustration, confusion and thousands of other emotional pains issue from this cycle. If you slow feelings down, however, if you observe the sequence carefully, you will discover that the seeming source of your emotional pain is generally not present in a current moment but is part of a past moment, a kind of ghost from the past.

There is a well-known Zen story that speaks to this situation. Two monks were walking along a quiet country road one day and as they rounded a bend they saw a river ahead and a young woman standing on the bank. As they approached they could see that the young woman was pacing back and forth and weeping.

The younger of the two monks, known for holding a very rigid sense of the rules of his order, turned away. In his view, his order prohibited him from speaking to women or having any interaction with women and that rule had to be followed. The other monk, however, turned to the woman and asked what was troubling her.

"The river is so swollen by the rains," she said, "and I am afraid that if I try to cross I will drown."

Understanding the depth of the woman's fear, the monk offered to carry her across, and when she agreed did precisely that. Then he and his companion proceeded on their way.

About a half hour later, the younger monk, clearly disturbed, turned to him and said, "You violated the rules of our order. Not only did you talk to that woman, but you picked her up and carried her across the river."

"Yes," said the second monk, "but I find it interesting that I put her down almost an hour ago and you are still carrying her."

We all are often like the younger monk. In our personal and professional lives, we sometimes carry things in our minds much longer than we do in actual time. Our emotions and thoughts are our constant companions, and when we look closely at these emotions, we realize that to keep carrying them we have to do something quite unnatural. We have to go away from the present moment to think, project, worry, obsess, fantasize, consider, and replay.

We are not saying that the cause of your sadness, anger or confusion, rejection or betrayal is purely mental. We are not saying the cause of one of your emotions is not something real or threatening or damaging and that it did not actually occur in one specific present moment. The conditions and experiences that promote our emotions are often all too real, an undeniable part of the fabric and challenge of our lives. We are saying that these events, conditions and experiences occur in one "now" and then that "now" passes and is replaced by another "now" in which there are other experiences, other sources, causes and opportunities for new pains and new pleasures. Laughter, wonder, excitement, loss, befuddlement, joy or a thousand other experiences that you define as good or bad, positive or negative occur in each of these new "nows."

THERE'S NO FUTURE IN THE PAST

Meaning and purpose are contained in present moments, and far too many of us miss our present moments because we are captured by emotions that result from previous moments. Literally and actually, the majority of new moments do not contain the old experiences or events or conditions except by virtue of the mental and emotional energy we expend to hold on to them. And this is true even when the same people continue to be present.

To continue to experience emotional or mental pain from a past moment, we have to step out of the flow of time and try to stop Time

Present to try to hold on to Time Past. In doing so, we become time's prisoner. And this is precisely how our emotional and mental pain arises. When we step out of time—or into what Eckhart Tolle calls "psychological time"—when we turn way from the present, we become a prisoner of the past or a captive of the illusion of a future. When we are not here, we are nowhere.

Since this is an unnatural act, however, some part of us must go on with the present while another aspect of our consciousness, energy and attention remains a prisoner of the past. This creates a chasm or gap between where we are and where we place our attention and as a result of this gap emotional and mental pain becomes a continuous rather than a momentary or passing experience.

WHERE DOES FUTURE FOCUS COME IN?

When we talk about staying in the present, a lot of our clients and the folks who attend our public programs ask us what to do about planning and focusing on the future. They want to know if we are suggesting that they stop doing strategic planning, envisioning or goal setting.

Our answer is simple. If you use strategic planning, envisioning or goal setting to avoid the present—like Hesse did originally with his summer house—then these practices are not constructive. If, however, you elect to utilize a present moment to participate in a creative experience that provides you with the ability to simulate a more positive, constructive and powerful set of alternative futures, then strategic planning, envisioning and goal setting are not violating time's boundaries.

The key is to bring the future state into a present moment and experience it consciously, not to use a present moment to project a goal into some future moment. While this may seem like double talk, if you take the time to explore the difference, you will understand that trying to go ahead in time is not possible. In fact, projecting goals into the future always keep them slightly ahead and removed from realization because the future does not yet exist. Only the "now" exists.

The only way to achieve a positive, constructive and powerful outcome from envisioning, strategic planning and goal setting is to use these tools in a present moment to experience alternative outcomes.

AN ALTERNATIVE TO PAIN

We believe there is a very viable, achievable and available alternative to a life of pain. And this alternative is as obvious and simple as the Zen expression we quoted earlier: "Eat when eating. Stand when standing. Sit when sitting." When we learn to live as many moments as we can in the here and now, we significantly reduce the amount of emotional and mental pain in our lives. When we pay attention to whatever is going on right now and then when this moment passes, we let whatever has been a part of this moment pass with it. In this way, we can discover the possibility of unlimited choices. Discover curiosity. Discover new opportunity. Discover wonder. Discover surprise. Explore the promise and the challenge that each new, present moment offers. In this way become a part of the flow of life, the oneness. In short, let the past go and "be here now" as Ram Das has told us for years.

In order to get to greater authenticity and meaning, we have to do our best to live each moment with as much truth and awareness as we can. Above all, our experience reminds us daily that we are human and imperfect and that life requires great courage and even greater compassion.

TODAY'S REFLECTION

Eat when eating! Sit when sitting! Stand when standing! Everything I need is here and now. All that I am is here and now. This moment and then the next moment. Each distinct and different. Each contains its own wealth, its own mystery. If there is pain in this moment, I will experience it and then let it go, just as I let the actual physical moment go. Today I will remember that life is a series of moments, each of which has its own experiences and presents me with the opportunity to be free of pain, whole and authentic.

Moving Beyond Pain

*Our doubts are traitors and make us lose
the good we oft might win, by fearing to attempt.*
-◦[Shakespeare]◦-

In the previous chapter we talked about physical pain and the fact that it either exists in a given moment or it does not. Physical pain is the specific result of something we have done or failed to do to, something that is done to us, a specific physical disability we develop or are born with or, if you believe in it, the result of karma. Accident or trauma causes physical pain that is measurable and, in a lot of instances, pain can be reduced or treated through the process of natural healing, the taking of herbs or drugs, or by an allopathic medical intervention or procedure.

There is, however, the other kind of pain that we have discussed at greater length, "emotional pain." Unlike physical pain, emotional pain is not as tangible or measurable and it is not located specifically in any one area of the physical body. Although medical research now strongly supports the premise that emotional pain can and often does eventually manifest as a physical disease and dysfunction, emotional pain is not as easily traceable to any one physical event, threat, accident, or body condition as physical pain. Instead, emotional pain most often results from perceived consequences we believe will come about as a result of something that has occurred in the past or that we are concerned will happen again in the future.

Emotional pain also comes from the thoughts and beliefs we hold about what we want and do not have, what we think we should be and are not, and what we believe we ought to do and have not yet done.

It also issues from thoughts and beliefs we hold about who we believe we are versus who we want to be, what we can do versus what we want to do and what we have done and cannot undo. As we get older, it often arises from what we once were able to do and can no longer do.

In short, emotional pain does not necessarily come from specific and current physical events, actions or experiences, but instead from our assumptions, hopes, concerns, doubts, wishes, and projections that compare past or possible future events, actions and experiences with our present.

A LIFE-ALTERING DISTINCTION

What has all this got to do with authenticity? We find that understanding and learning to work with the distinction between physical and emotional pain can be one of the most powerful and immediate tools any of us can employ to reduce and, in many instances, eliminate much if not all of the emotional pain we experience in our lives. And this is no small thing, especially when one considers that the amount and frequency of our emotional pain far exceeds the amount and frequency of our physical pain. Of particular consequence here is the fact that in reducing the amount of our emotional pain, we not only substantially improve the quality of our lives, but we also have more energy, passion and clarity to devote to bringing greater meaning and purpose into our personal lives and our careers. So let's look more specifically at the process by which we create and amplify what we call emotional pain.

"Do first things first," Stephen Covey, The 12-Step Program and others remind us. So what is the origin or first thing to consider when exploring emotional pain? Our thinking mind! We know, of course, that this conclusion may trouble those of us who are very devoted to our minds. And yet like it or not, this is just the truth of it and eventually even the most mindful among us will have to admit that our ability to think, while a great gift, can be and most often is a serious challenge and a significant deterrent to our ability to live lives of true meaning and purpose.

Thinking can enliven, awaken, uncover and add to almost any subject or experience. Thinking is one of the tools that helps us to understand, analyze, evaluate, consider, discern, reflect and comprehend. And these clearly are just some of the positives that our thinking minds do on our behalf.

There is, however, another side of thinking, the shadow or negative side. Overused or abused, thinking becomes compulsive, obsessive, dominating, closed, and much more. When we abuse thinking it becomes the primary residence of doubt, judgment, criticism, deception and more. When given free rein, thinking becomes our tormentor, the abductor of our energy, the dissembler of our joy, and the detractor of what we perceive as possible. Thinking also distorts our feelings, raises obstacles, denies real experience, expression and love and acts as the consummate means by which we avoid the present moment.

While thinking can sometimes enhance our vision, at other times it blinds us. Thinking is one of the means by which we make new discoveries but also the means by which we deceive ourselves. Thinking assists us in living more fully, but it also can betray us and lead to the most severe delusions. Thinking can open us to understanding and awareness, and it also can be the primary way we split our focus and deny ourselves the ability to live authentic lives.

Strange, isn't it? This one tool can be such an extraordinary gift and such a source of danger at the same time. Used effectively it provides us with the opportunity to live a life that is almost free of emotional, and in many instances even physical, pain and yet it is most often is the primary source of most of our pain.

BEYOND OUR PREOCCUPATION WITH THE PAST

How is this possible? As we've discussed, most of us believe we live in a highly evolved society and one of the justifications we use for this belief is that we are so complex. We point with pride to how complex our lives are and to the number of things we can do at the same time.

We call it "multi-tasking" and multi-tasking is one of the most sought after qualities in today's business and personal environments. In fact, to many leaders and managers and to those of us who find ourselves frantically struggling up the ladder of success, the ability to juggle a lot of tasks at the same time is worth its weight in gold. We sit in meetings and write memos at the same time. We drive and talk. We listen to the radio, look at the scenery and participate in long-distance phone conferences. We have phone conversations while reading our email or walking along city streets. We apply make-up while driving and talk to friends miles away while we are shopping, walking through airports and doing a thousand other ordinary things. We watch television, read and converse all at the same time. We work on two or three or twenty different projects during the same day.

We pride ourselves on our ability. The truth, however, is that all of this thinking is hurting us. Thinking reinforces the illusion that our rational mind is the center of the universe and the sole or primary source of our intelligence. Thinking also hurts us because our rational thinking mind not only creates and measures time, it maintains the illusion that time is divisible into subcategories called past, present and future.

This arbitrary and very dangerous preoccupation with time—this artificial juggling and dividing of it into past, present and future—provides the thinking mind with the opportunity to create and sustain pain. Take away this illusion, deny the thinking mind the opportunity to divide time into past, present and future, and suddenly the source of most of the emotional and some of the physical pain we experience disappears.

How can this be? One clue lies in a consideration of all of that multi-tasking we are so proud of. In many ways, even though we think we are doing a number of things at the same time, we are actually doing a series of individual things consecutively. Why do we make this distinction? Because this awareness that we do things consecutively rather than simultaneously provides us with the understanding of how subtle and dangerous the shadow side of the rational thinking mind can be. It also gives us the opportunity to observe and witness how out of control our mind has become.

The fact is most of us can no longer tell the difference between thinking and doing. And because we also obscure the difference between simultaneous and consecutive "doings," we also miss the fact that there is space between the actions. And while this space is sometimes only a fraction of a second, it contains a great secret about life.

If we can learn to recognize this space or gap, if we become a witness and observer within this gap, we can learn how our thinking extends, exaggerates and, in some cases, creates our pain. We can become aware that each moment contains or does not contain pain, either physical or emotional. We can also become aware that each moment is separate and that one moment gives way to the next.

This may seem painfully obvious, but let's go deeper. When each moment passes and another moment arrives, if the thinking mind was doing its assigned job, it would shift its attention from the moment that is passing to the moment that is arriving. But it doesn't. Instead, the thinking mind, which is the home of the ego, pretends that gap between this moment and the next does not exist. It pretends that the arriving moment is connected to and a continuation of the previous moment.

The thinking mind artificially tries to make these two moments one by continuing to focus attention on whatever has occurred in the passing moment. Of course, if there is loss, anguish, disturbance, confusion or any of the other thousands of causes of emotional pain in one moment, these emotions are extended into the next moment. This is why we have so much emotional pain.

AS SIMPLE AS THAT

Is it really as simple as that? Yes, in many ways we believe it is. Clouds pass. Rain, thunder, sun, night, day, fire, flood, wind, breath, the physical body, even land masses come and go. We are aware of the spaces and the gaps between these things. We recognize where one begins and another ends. We know the difference between the land and the sea and would not think of trying to deny the existence of either. When we look up at the sky we do not allow our minds to pretend that there are not spaces between the clouds. We do not try to hold onto the wind or make the rain a continuous condition. Even in our own bodies we acknowledge that there is an in breath and an out breath and even a slight pause in between.

So if all of this is true, why do we allow our minds to deny and obviate the difference between one present moment and the next? Why do we pretend that time is a continuum and that what is past is still present?

TODAY'S REFLECTIONS

If I allow my life to unfold, moment by moment, I will experience only that which is mine to experience in this present moment. Where there is real pain I will experience it and where there is real pleasure and joy I will experience that as well. My commitment today is to give myself permission to experience each and every moment and then to let go of each moment as it passes and all that it contains, pain as well as pleasure. In this way I will greatly reduce the amount of pain in my life and discover more of my true meaning and purpose!

◆

Crossing the Zone of Risk

Security is mostly superstition. It does not exist in nature,
nor do the children of men as a whole experience it.
Avoiding danger is not safer in the long run than outright exposure.
Life is either a daring adventure or nothing.

◦[Helen Keller]◦

The history of our world comprises stories about men and women who have faced various challenges, incredible odds and seemingly insurmountable obstacles. These people either achieved their goals and broke through to new levels of accomplishment and consciousness or failed in the effort. From the legends and myths about the gods to the true exploits of some of us ordinary mortals, the underlying messages and morals instruct, uplift, sadden and motivate us. These stories break our hearts, trigger our outrage or bring tears of wonder to our eyes and cheers to our voices.

Many of these stories form the basis of the hero's journey— Arthur pulling the sword from the stone, Joan raising an army to free France, da Vinci leading esoteric societies and changing the face of art and Einstein riding beams of light through the universe. These stories ennoble our lives and remind us about both the frailty and extraordinary strength of our fellow travelers.

During our careers we have been particularly blessed to have met a number of men and women whose stories have encouraged us on our journeys toward greater authenticity. In our professional lives we have spent a great deal of time with the men and women who have made the exploration of space a reality. These people include not just those gifted men and women astronauts who actually go into space, but the thousands who spend their lives on the ground solving the incredibly complex technological, scientific, electrical and mechanical problems that make manned space exploration possible. Although there are some today who question their competence, criticize their efforts and fault their commitment, we can say from thousands of hours of first-hand experience, that the men and women in the space industry are among the most devoted, committed, talented and courageous human beings we have ever met.

Our lives also have crossed with many people who are not so high profile, but who instead make thousands of other well-known companies and government organizations work. Many of these men and women have remarkable stories to tell. Their stories may not be as glamorous or seemingly heroic, but when we look beyond the obvious we find people who overcome odds to invent new systems, develop and deliver new products and services, and sometimes bring their organizations back from the edge of bankruptcy. We see people who go way beyond the call of duty to serve their employees and their customers. They do this with pride and excellence while obtaining a second degree at night to advance their careers and sometimes to support children they raise as single parents. We see people who manage, with physical disabilities, not only to hold jobs but also to lead entire companies to new levels of effectiveness. We encounter people who, in their spare time, contribute to the lives of others and to their communities in astounding ways, mentoring young people who are at risk, creating outstanding art forms, volunteering in thousands of organizations and discovering and sharing new life strategies. Yes, our world comprises people who make us proud to be human beings.

So, as we set out on this next part of our journey toward greater authenticity, let's look at one of the essential qualities these men and women have in common—their willingness to risk. This willingness is a critical and essential ingredient in discovering lives and careers of true meaning and purpose. It is both the gateway to success and also the place at which those of us with less courage sometimes falter.

THE R FACTOR

Risk is an essential component of action, a prerequisite for participation, for moving outside the boundary of the usual, the predictable and the comfortable. Risk is also an essential for adventure, new discovery and the exploration of opportunity. Risk embodies the quality of willingness from which all things are possible.

Risk is a state of mind, an expression of proactive energy and, above all, a zone through which each of us must pass to get from possibility and opportunity to actuality, from conception to manifested or materialized reality.

Call to mind the image of one of your life's current possibilities or desires: a relationship you would like to have, a place you want to live, a career or business opportunity you are seeking, a new talent you would like to develop, a personal goal you want to achieve. This image is like the view of a lush garden you can see from an open window. As you look out from your current perspective toward this garden filled with flowers, plants, and trees heavily laden with fruit, you notice there are wonderfully inviting pathways and shaded arbors that seem to lead from the spot you are standing in to the garden itself. For the sake of our example, let's call the window where you are standing "the present moment" and the garden "your future state or desired goal."

As you gaze out from the "present" toward this "future," you may be aware of feeling a degree of discomfort—discomfort that may range from slight to extreme. Why discomfort? Because you know that to get from the place where you are standing to that inviting garden you will have to leave the comfort and familiarity of your current position and make your way out into the unknown territory of the pathway to the garden. The moment this realization occurs you have arrived at the edge of what we call "The Zone of Risk."

This Zone of Risk separates possibility from actuality, hope from fulfillment. It represents the territory many of us have heard so much about and sometimes gone to great lengths to avoid. Even though most of us like gazing off toward the garden and enjoy fantasizing about all of the new opportunities and possibilities it represents, we tend to cling tenaciously to what we believe is, at the least, our comfortable place at the window.

Even when present conditions in our personal lives or at work are nothing to write home about, even when we moan about our pains and our challenges, even when we acknowledge (and loudly) that our present lot is much less satisfying than we want it to be, some of us remain at the window.

Why? Our old friend fear, of course. Fear and the comfort of the familiar and the habitual. Then there are the horror stories others tell us about their one great and harrowing excursion in the winter of '25 or '99 or even last week into the Zone of Risk. They tell us how painful it was, how disappointed they were to discover all the forces that were arrayed against them and all the people who failed them. They don't often tell us about their own missteps or short steps or timid steps. They don't often tell us they only made a partial effort, a kind of peak-a-boo venture into the territory. Nor do they often admit that if they had applied the same strategy and made the same number of attempts when learning to walk or speak or ride a bicycle they would still be sitting on their behinds silently looking out at the world. They would never have felt the thrill of riding and walking and talking.

But this is not a criticism. We both have been many times to the edge of the Zone of Risk and pulled back, deciding it was far better to stay in the familiar than to venture into the unknown. What's that old saying about a bird in the hand?

Still, our admission that we have been timid in the past and may be in the future does not give us any special dispensation from truth. And so we offer this encouragement to you as well as to ourselves to move forward toward more genuine alignment with and inheritance of our destiny. The fact that we surely will encounter this hesitation, this drawing back, at other times in our lives when the Zone of Risk presents itself, does not give us reason to deny our right, our privilege, and our need to keep moving forward toward greater authenticity.

Of all of the reasons we hesitate—and they are as numerous and as varied as the imaginations and fantasies of those of us who stand at the edge of the Zone—one reason stands out above the rest. Most of us have ventured into the Zone at some earlier time in our lives and found that discomfort showed up.

We also have found that once we stepped into the Zone, the route from the window to the garden itself was often harder to find, the distance farther than we expected and the path more arduous than we imagined. When we could no longer see the window from which we departed or the garden to which we were heading, we felt lost, alone and afraid and so turned back.

Many of us have some version of this story to tell. It might be a moment of youthful enthusiasm and passionate longing in which we decided to roll the dice with Fate. Or perhaps it was a moment later in life when we took a shot at something new: a new career, a new business we wanted to start, a new love we felt ready to explore. Perhaps our new something involved taking a chance at developing a skill or talent or starting some community project. Whatever goal prompted us to leave the window and go in search of the garden, we set out in pursuit of it and met disappointment.

THE GARDEN OF POSSIBILITY AND REALIZED DREAMS

Have you ever wondered what would have happened if you hadn't turned back? Perhaps you have asked yourself this question before or maybe you have avoided it completely. Perhaps there have been times, times when your life has been particularly painful, when you have thought about that earlier aborted adventure and considered taking another shot at your dream.

We both have our own moments of this kind of wondering. Sedena is an actress and each time she speaks of her craft there is a special light and fire in her eyes. For years she pursued her craft, taking classes, studying with various teachers, going to auditions, doing all of the things that actresses do on their way to greater skill and recognition. She was willing to be an extra in a number of movies, act as a spokesperson in industrial films, and act in commercials so that she could make her way up the ladder and into television and motion pictures. She also produced pieces for the theater and television. While her skills are adeptly and wonderfully used in the healing and motivating work she does today with people all across the country, there are moments when that special place lights up in her eyes and I know she is wondering if she is finished with her acting journey and if she went far enough into the Zone.

In George's case, his largest questions come up around his sculpting. Discovering that he had talent for it in his early thirties, he took the plunge and rushed headlong into the Zone in pursuit of his dream. But somewhere between the window and the garden, he encountered fear. He started looking around at a lot of the artists he knew who had been struggling for years with little recognition and even less financial return and he pulled back. He did not know if he wanted to pay the price, and so he retreated to the ground of the familiar. Whenever he is working on a new piece of sculpture or when someone comes into our home and is touched by the unique beauty of his work, he also wonders what his life would be like today if he had not turned back toward the safe and the familiar. He wonders if he ever will be finished with that particular crossing of the Zone.

A SHORT EXCURSION

With these examples in mind, let's pretend for a moment that we are experiencing one of those moments of fear together. Let's examine what it might require for us to get through the Zone of Risk and take up residence in our garden of realized dreams.

The first stage of the Zone is the place, of course, where our concerns become the strongest. Here we are often joined by some of Discomfort's traveling companions, Doubt and two of its most faithful friends, Fear and Confusion. We can be certain these characters will show up when we step into the Zone of Risk.

"Where are we going today?" they ask, often with a leer and that high-pitched laugh.

Doubt and Fear are two of our constant companions in the Zone of Risk. At face value they are a troublesome duo and, if we take their stories seriously, we'll find ourselves turning back and running for safety.

But if we look closer and listen more intently to their stories, we may find that, like so many other companions we meet from time to time, they are not what they at first appear to be. Doubt, in its most common disguise, promotes things like restriction, resistance, confusion and procrastination. When doubt wears this face it fits the acronym **D**riving **O**urselves **U**nconscious **B**y **T**hinking.

However, we have found that Doubt can also be an ally, and as an ally it can prompt us to pause, consider and evaluate our circumstance, take stock of the challenges we face, the resources we require and the opportunities that are present. In short, Doubt can assist us to be better prepared to make a more successful crossing of the Zone of Risk. Doubt can remind us of the supplies and resources we need, the reserves we may want to have in place and even some of the other allies and companions we might like to invite along on our passage.

Fear also has different faces. Like physical pain, physical fear is an ally. It is part of the fight-or-flight mechanism. It prompts us to defend ourselves by alerting us to danger and getting us out of harm's way. One of fear's other faces, however, is its emotional side. In this disguise fear gets in our way, causes us to hesitate and to freeze in place. In this disguise it calls up in us the feelings associated with all of the horror stories that are filled with terrible consequences.

While physical fear can be catalyzing, emotional fear is often traumatizing. While physical fear produces clarity, emotional fear often causes paralysis by analysis. In its negative guise fear is an acronym for **F**alse **E**vidence **A**ppearing **R**eal. We think a thought, a negative thought, a thought about risk. This thought triggers a feeling, a negative feeling based upon a perceived negative outcome or consequence (False Evidence Appearing Real) and then we react as if the feeling we feel is real. Not only real, but independent of the thought. In other words we act as if our feeling constitutes "reality." This is how we create illusion in the physical world.

A HOUSE OF CARDS

If all this sounds a little like "The House That Jack Built," it should, because in some ways this is a fairy tale. The only problem is that for far too many of us the fairy tale quickly becomes a horror story, one that sends us scurrying out of the Zone of Risk back to the familiar and the habitual; back to the ordinary and away from the original and the authentic.

What's wrong with that, you ask? Plenty and nothing, depending on your desired outcome. If not living your dream is acceptable to you then retreating from the Zone of Risk is not such a bad thing. If living your life in the familiar, the known and the habitual is all you require or desire, then turning your back on the garden is no big deal. We won't overdo the use of acronyms by giving one to Confusion or Complaint or Resistance. Suffice it to say they are close companions of Doubt and Fear and most of us are familiar with these characters too. We encounter them daily in some form or other: whining, bitching and moaning, anger, cynicism and frustration are a few clues that one or another of these odd folks is around. They show up often and at rather predictable moments when there is something we want to do or be or have and we are afraid to pass through the Zone of Risk to do or be or have it. This same phenomenon occurs when someone else invites us to cross the moat into our next great adventure.

From this moment on, however, you are forewarned and to be forewarned, as the old saying goes, is to be armed. Now when any of these companions of Doubt show up you can't pretend you do not have a choice. Choice One: you can take them at face value and fall under their spell. They will love it. It's part of the grand game of life. Yes, you can take them at face value, throw in the towel and abandon your quest for the garden.

Choice Two: you can recognize their presence as a sure sign you are in the Zone of Risk and your resolve is being tested. You can turn toward them, look past their theatrical disguises and have a real dialogue with them. Find out what they want you to know. Ask how you can be better prepared. Inquire as to how they can assist you in becoming more authentic in your journey.

THERE IS ONLY ONE AUTHENTIC CHOICE

Although there appear to be two choices, there is only one. For after any of us has seen the garden, it is not really possible to return to the window, is it? Oh sure, we can pretend for a while. We can tell our friends that the adventure was not all that important anyway. We can tell them how good it is to be home. But we know the garden is out there. Still waiting. And we know that one of these days the pain of trying to maintain stasis will build up again. We will begin to tire of our restrictive walls and we will begin to wonder if it is time and if we have what it takes to cross the Zone of Risk.

Even if we manage to get back to the comfort and familiarity of the window in the physical sense, the "we" who arrives there is different from the "we" who departed. That's what T.S. Eliot meant when he said, "Fare forward, fellow travelers, he who arrives at the terminus is not the same as he who departs."

Right here and now, in this space of quiet intimacy between us, let's be ruthlessly honest with each other. Let's give each other the respect that fellow travelers show to those who walk the same path. Let's admit there is no real going back. Let's acknowledge that life and God sometimes allow us to rent some space near the "window of the familiar" for a while, but there are no low-cost, long-term rental agreements, no condominium ownerships available in the comfortable and the limiting.

We could pretend that fear and doubt, confusion and frustration are justifiable deterrents for a while. But eventually we will all be called by the undeniable flow of life to redouble our efforts and make that passage through the Zone of Risk to the realization and fulfillment of our destiny.

THERE IS NO SUBSTITUTE FOR THE OBVIOUS

How do you redouble your efforts? You simply pick a path and then put one foot in front of the other. You take the next breath and then the next. You remember that home is where you already are and that all paths lead back to you.

In addition, you look for the next specific physical action and you do it. It may be the next word that needs writing or saying, the next note that needs playing, the next step that need dancing, mathematical equation that needs solving, the conjugation or vocal intonation that needs investigating or expressing. Whatever it is, however, the next effort is always simple, almost immediate and always available in each present moment.

The next step involves a specific and very physical doing. You can make it a lot more complicated, or you can recognize life for what it is— a remarkable and yet very practical series of opportunities to practice and to demonstrate, to express and explore your innate and God-given ability to pass through the Zone of Risk to your next level of mastery.

If the next physical action doesn't present itself right away, perhaps it's time to rest or play or wait or pray. Life does not have to be complicated when we are cooperating with its rhythm. Life just presents something or someone in one moment and then lets it go in the next. No good. No bad. Just life. So we can take life's lead and remember it is not just about working or doing more. It is not just about sitting back and doing nothing. Life is comprised of cycles and these cycles are available for observation each moment all around us. All we have to do is to open our eyes and take them in. Trees bud and leaves grow to give us more oxygen and shade and then they turn wonderful colors and eventually fall so that new buds can form. Life is a process. We have been told this so many times. As the saying goes, "life is a journey not a destination."

The next time you find yourself standing at that window and some vision tempts you—you might as well pack your bag and whistle a happy tune as you begin your incredible journey through the Zone of Risk toward the realization of your destiny. And if along the way some traveling companions called Doubt, Fear or Confusion show up, remember that motivation wears many disguises. Give them a smile or a laugh or a thank you. And then allow them to assist you to renew your dedication to freedom and self-mastery. If you find yourself stumbling, losing your sense of direction, then sit down for a little while and breathe, breathe and wait for the next sign.

About waiting, author Joyce Sequichie Hilfer, says, "constant motion seems more important than waiting, but waiting is the time to prepare, to build up the spirit and be rested and ready."

So practice a little waiting. Ask your inner wisdom for the next clue and then allow the next breeze of courage to blow. Your inner wisdom will take you far past the place where Doubt and Fear leave off. It really is as simple as that!

TODAY'S REFLECTION

Risk is not something to avoid, but something to embrace. Risk means I am alive, that I have things left to know and experience and accomplish. As to doubt and fear, they are the signs that I am on the verge of something new. So today and every time I find myself standing at the window of the present gazing off at the garden of the future, I will call upon and trust my inner wisdom and step courageously and passionately into the Zone of Risk. One step at a time I will open to life, to new possibilities, remarkable lessons and the expression of my authenticity.

What Needs to Be Done Is (Only) the Doing

*If you expect to see the final result of your work,
you have not asked a big enough question.*

-◦[I.F. Stone]◦-

One of the interesting things we have noticed in our work with organizations, the people who lead them and with those who come to our public programs, is that many of us spend a great deal more time thinking about things than actually doing them. In fact, when we reflect on our own process and observe the workings of others, we find that our most challenging problems and obstacles are often the very things about which we are doing little, and sometimes, almost nothing.

We may be thinking a lot about these things. We may be studying them, reflecting on them, and evaluating and analyzing them. We may be fretting, complaining and worrying about them. And while all of this attention and busy-ness gives us the sense and others the appearance that we are really working on these challenges, when we dig down a layer or two we discover that "thinking and talking about" are not the same as "doing."

If you take time to reflect on your own process, you probably will find that the degree of worrying, complaining and thinking about things is often in direct proportion to the amount of "not doing." Thinking about something often serves as a stalling technique, a substitute for doing. In other words, thinking is a substitute for being.

THE DIFFERENCE BETWEEN REAL AND IMAGINED ACTION

Of course this "substitute doing" does not provide us with satisfaction for long, does it? Somewhere in our consciousness we are aware that this "thinking about" is keeping us—like a child who wants to swim but hesitates—on the edge of the pool. We look longingly at the water and imagine what it is like to swim, but swimming remains a vicarious experience. Living vicariously, as many of us know, rarely satisfies our true longing.

As a result, a lot of us tend to redouble our "substitute measures." We think harder. We analyze more. We worry longer. We raise our voices louder in complaint. Sometimes we also add our negative judgment of the challenge or the obstacle or the person who presents the obstacle. Sometimes we go so far as to deny our original desire. And we do all of this and more while still on the edge of the pool. We do it rather than face our fear of jumping into the actual water of life.

Of course while this drama is going on some part of us is not fooled, nor are the other swimmers. "Jumping in" is the only answer. Only through a direct and specific action can we get beyond our fear, doubt, procrastination or worry. As for others in the pool, if we are in reasonably kind company, they just go about the process of enjoying and celebrating the water and leave us alone. You know what happens when others are not so kind.

THE LITMUS TEST

Test this premise against your own experience. Think back to a time when you were particularly unhappy or dissatisfied with some aspect of your life or your performance at work. It may have been years ago or perhaps only weeks or moments ago. Ask yourself if it was a time when you were actually doing a lot to deal with or overcome the challenge you faced, or if it was one of those times when you were thinking about, evaluating, wishing, hoping, and considering doing something.

If you are like most of us, chances are you were spending more time in your head than in your life. And this is not to imply that all thinking and evaluating are limited or negative. They can be valuable and important steps are precursors to doing, but they are not substitutes for it.

Look again at that specific period or event you just called to mind. What was the reason for your concern or fear or dissatisfaction? Can you identify it? Were you feeling overwhelmed by the size or scope of the project or undertaking? Did you think you lacked certain skills or information you needed? Were you troubled by the fact that you seemed to be doing it alone or with or for someone who was not responsive or appreciative?

No matter what the conditions, how would you compare the amount of time you spent actually doing that something to the amount of time you spent thinking or worrying about it? If you were doing specific things, were you present in the doing of them or were you distracted by your thoughts about the possible outcome or consequences of what you were doing? Were you concerned or preoccupied by your thoughts about possible failure?

If you are like us, you were probably doing some, if not all, of these things. When you were not distracting yourself in this way, you were thinking about something or someone else while doing what you were doing. Perhaps that someone was not there with you. Perhaps it was someone you wanted to have there or someone with whom you had unfinished business. Perhaps that someone or something else you were thinking about was someone or something thing you loved or hated. No matter what the cause of your distraction, however, if you slow down the memory, you will discover that some of the fear, concern or discomfort you experienced was directly proportional to the amount of time spent thinking about that someone or something else.

As a result, you were not present. Now here comes the rub. Your fear, concern or dissatisfaction would have disappeared to the exact degree you turned up your involvement in the doing.

As a way of discovering if this premise contributes to bringing greater meaning and purpose into your life at home and at work, make a list of the things that need to be done at this time. They can be things at work or at home or both. They can range from short correspondence and verbal communications that are incomplete, to major projects and both long- and short-term goals. They can involve life-long ambitions or minor things that need to be fixed or replaced, serviced, cleaned or discarded. Do this exercise now before reading any further.

BEYOND THE OBVIOUS

You may notice that the things on your list tend to fall into one of three basic categories: "Practical Doings" that can be done in your immediate environment that will bring about a visible change, such as washing the dishes, organizing your desk or fixing something that is broken, etc; "Doings With/For Others" that could involve taking a trip, assisting someone with a project or being of service to someone; "Doings With/For Oneself," such as exercise, study, rest, meditation, learning, art and so on.

After you have created your list, select an item from one of the three categories, and do whatever next physical action you can that will lead to completing that item on your list of incompletes. It might be something as simple as washing the car, writing an email or letter, calling your friend, or opening the dictionary to check on the spelling of a word. Whatever it is, there is a simple and obvious next physical action. Turn on the hose. Pick up a pen. Open a blank document on your desktop. Create a list of objectives for your proposal. Pick up the telephone.

Next physical actions are always obvious, simple, practical and doable actions. Do this simple exercise and we guarantee you will discover a significant difference immediately. Using this strategy every time the "thinking monster" shows up will produce a transformation of noticeable proportions. We might even go so far as to suggest that this transformation will be revolutionary in scope. You will find that one of the reasons your life sometimes feels so bogged down is that what needs to be done is (only) the doing!

TODAY'S REFLECTION

A great deal of the dissatisfaction and confusion I face in my life is the result of thinking too much and doing too little. So from today on I will make this agreement with myself: I will utilize thinking as part of my planning process, but I will stop using thinking, worrying, procrastinating and complaining as a way of avoiding doing! Today, I will do the next physical actions. Today I will invite greater authenticity and originality in my life.

◆

Where Is it Written?

Living itself is a task of such immediacy, variety, beauty and excitement that one is powerless to resist its wild embrace.

⋅≺[E.B. White]≻⋅

Energy follows thought and manifestation follows energy. Thoughts persisted in produce states of consciousness, and states of consciousness persisted in produce physical manifestations.

If these statements are true—and our organizational and individual change work clearly suggests that they are—then it must follow that what we are currently doing to create the content of our lives is creating the limitations as well as the opportunities, the boundaries as well as the possibilities. It must follow that, as Henry Ford is reputed to have said, "Whether we believe we can or we can't, we are right!"

There are times when we do not like to be reminded of this power we have over the shape and content of our careers and our personal lives. At least, we don't like the part suggesting that we create the bad as well as the good. While most of us are more than willing to take credit for our victories and accomplishments, even if they are not entirely ours, we are not as anxious to take credit for failures and losses even if we only contribute in some small way to them.

Though some people take credit for the failures and problems but not the successes, the vast majority of us are quick to point out our achievements, while selectively underplaying our mistakes, errors and limitations. But whether we like it or not, admit it or not;

whether we are inclined to claim only our victories or primarily our failures, the truth is that we have a great deal to do with creating both our losses and our wins. Indeed, where else could our failures, mistakes and limitations come from, if not from the same source that creates our successes?

FOLLOWING THE TRAIL OF OUR THOUGHTS

If energy follows thought and manifestation follows energy, it must follow that some of the thoughts and beliefs we currently hold are the source of our limitations and failures. For example, there are some in government and in the private business sector who believe they are not responsible for the damage they inflict on others through inferior or flawed products or services or through damaging policies and practices. Nothing could be further from the truth. These beliefs, policies and actions are not only enormously damaging to large numbers of people, but in the end they are self-defeating as well. For how can anyone find true meaning and purpose in life by denying truth, meaning and purpose?

On the opposite side of the coin, many of us believe that in some very large ledger, controlled no doubt by the gods, it is written that we can't have what we want or that we are not entitled to live the kind of life we want. Some of us also believe that written in the same book are beliefs like: "I am not worthy"; "Life needs to be hard"; "Nothing is achieved without a lot of struggle"; "Only the tough or the brilliant succeed"; "Money is the root of all evil"; "I am not one of the gifted or lucky ones"; or "I can't win without slaughtering my competition or dominating others."

It's strange that beings capable of creating extraordinary wealth and performing remarkable feats should go through our lives holding onto and expressing such limiting beliefs. Isn't it strange that such bold and highly evolved life forms should use thoughts to create stories in which we lose rather than win, get less rather than more, experience pain and loss rather than gain, take from others for our own success or destroy and limit others rather than elevate them?

So what's the alternative? Awareness first. Followed closely by understanding, acceptance, and commitment in rapid order.

Commitment to what? To live a much more authentic, connected and aligned life. To live according to a rather simple formula, guaranteed to produce more joy, contentment, grace, openness, meaning and purpose. This formula has six steps with three guidelines, and they apply to organizations, groups and families as well as to individuals.

SIX STEPS TO GREATER AUTHENTICITY

These steps are not foolproof, but they work effectively if you work at them. They require consciousness, effort and, above all, a deep commitment to living a more aligned and harmonious life. Here they are:

1. Above all else be grateful for what you have—the good and whatever you define as the bad.
2. Ask for guidance and then have the humility, patience and wit to listen.
3. Identify and define what you want, and then break these goals into specific action steps that will help you achieve them.
4. Pay attention to your thoughts and notice the underlying beliefs that cast doubt on your ability or right to have what you want. Then replace these with positive, supporting and expansive thoughts and beliefs.
5. Complete all of the action steps with genuine respect, attention to detail and love. Make each word, thought and action an act of love.
6. Be sure all that you manifest is for you own and others' best and highest good and then trust in the outcome.

THREE SIMPLE GUIDELINES

As you implement the six steps, measure your alignment against these three guidelines.

1. Pay attention to what works and do more of it.
2. Pay attention to what does not work and do less of it.
3. Experiment with new things.

Is it really this easy? We believe it is. Our experience suggests that each of us, as an individual and as a member of various organizations, has the power to move beyond limiting thoughts, words, actions and beliefs.

Our own lives and the lives of many of the people we work with continue to demonstrate this truth. We do not mean to imply that these steps will end all suffering, remove all obstacles or make you or your company rich and famous. In fact, if we follow the guidance of some of the extraordinary souls who have come before us, suffering and obstacles appear to be part of life and only by accepting them and accepting ourselves as we are in each moment can we ever truly take steps toward greater authenticity.

Still, acceptance of what Buddha called the Dharma of life does not mean we cannot explore the limits we have placed on our destinies. In fact, if we are prepared to live more on the edge and less in the middle, to turn toward rather than away from our discomfort and fear, to step out of the habitual and the familiar and into risk, then we will have the opportunity to achieve what is right and appropriate for us. At the least, we will know we have been to the edge and gone after our dream.

THE FUTURE IS ALREADY HERE

It is not only a choice but also our responsibility to step forward and claim what is truly ours, what is already ours. Everything we are capable of conceptualizing and everything we require and desire is already ours. Everything we are struggling to achieve is already achieved and all we have to be willing and courageous enough to do is to step out of the ordinary and the habitual to claim it.

Of course, it doesn't always feel this easy, does it? On some days the process of accepting and claiming the wonder and magnificence of who we are feels almost impossible. Some days, in fact, when we look in the mirror at ourselves or out into the mirror of the world at our companies and organizations, it can feel like we are paddling upstream against the wind towing a very heavy barge. On these days we need a little more compassion, courage and patience and sometimes a lot more acceptance and love. On these days we have to reduce our expectation about the progress we, our families or our fellow employees, are making and focus a lot more consciously on the things for which we're grateful.

Sometimes we have to be satisfied with taking smaller steps and achieving fewer gains. When the process seems too much, we even can put up our feet for a little while and find something to laugh about, or we can roll up our sleeves and work a little smarter and harder. We also can listen to music, talk to a friend, take a walk, say a prayer or give someone a little acknowledgment before we can go on. There are times when remembering to breathe and to stay in touch with your heart before the next ascent is essential.

There are also times when exercising patience and waiting is a terrific way to build up your staying power. Trust yourself. You will know the difference between turning away and turning toward. On other occasions, when the tide is with us, we can build momentum, celebrate our gains and above all, give away a little more than feels comfortable to those in need.

THE CHALLENGE IS NOT IN GETTING WHAT YOU WANT

Consider the possibility that the real challenge in life is not in getting what we want but in preventing it. We expend a lot energy keeping what we want away, and the only thing we have to do to get what we want is to acknowledge it and to stop the worry, the doubt and the disbelief that may be standing between us and the legacy we want to live.

Nelson Mandela said, "You were born to make manifest the Glory of God that is within you. And as we let our own light shine, we unconsciously give people permission to do the same. As we are liberated from our own fear, our presence automatically liberates others."

If this truth applies to each of us, imagine what startling and revolutionary results can be achieved if whole companies or government agencies or associations do it. Imagine what could happen if our entire nation did it. Imagine a whole world doing it.

Yes, imagine that! It may be that all you have to do to inherit the world you desire is to pay attention to your thinking, get in touch with your heart, with your essential wisdom and being and then use the gifts you already have to materialize and experience what you already possess. Imagine that you can do all of this without experiencing most of the frustration, pain and struggle you are now experiencing.

Like all of the premises we discuss in these pages, we invite you to test this one. Explore if, when and under what conditions you may be limiting your life at home and at work. Ask yourself where you, your family or your organization may be resisting risks, new challenges, change, opportunities to learn, new relationships, new interests or skills.

Where is it written that you or those you love and work with cannot do any or all of these things? Where is it written that limitations are real or that you or your organization must keep them forever? Imagine what your life will be like without whatever you define as limitations. Imagine what will happen every day if you are not afraid to do all the things that issue from your heart to your mind as prompts. Imagine what will happen if the things you admire and envy in others are actually traits and abilities you possess and that all you have to do to experience them is to open to them and live them. Imagine what today can be like if you accept the fact that you and every person in your family, your company, your community, your nation and your world are the authors of your own stories and that the next page is blank and waiting for you to write or draw anything you want on it. Imagine what today can be if you live it full of real meaning and purpose.

TODAY'S REFLECTION

I am responsible for my life whether it is abundant or limited, closed or full of opportunity. I am the author of the good as well as the bad, the sadness and frustration as well as the joy. Not because I am guilty of a crime but because I am alive and am responsible for my attitude. As the author of my life, I am grateful for this day, for my life, for my destiny. Today, I claim my authenticity. I welcome greater meaning and purpose into my life.

◆

Who Cares Why...How Is the Answer!

If you don't get what you want, you suffer;
if you get what you don't want, you suffer;
even if you get exactly what you want,
you still suffer because you can't hold onto it forever.
Your mind is your predicament. It wants to be free of change,
free of pain, free of the obligations of life and death.
But change is a law and no amount of pretending
will alter that reality.

-ɛ[Dan Millman]ɜ-

here was a carpenter whose reputation as a master craftsman had spread so far he was one of the principal reasons the construction company he worked was so successful. Each detail in the homes he built was executed with the finest material and with the most exacting attention. After many years of service, however, he decided to retire, and so he told the firm's president of his intention.

Having sensed that this day was coming, the president was not surprised, but he was saddened and told the carpenter his feelings. The two men had spent much of careers working together, and they sat for a while reflecting on the past. When the carpenter finally got up to leave, the president asked him to wait a moment longer and then explained that there was one last project he wanted the carpenter to complete.

The carpenter was about to object. After all, he had made his decision and he felt the president should understand. The president did not know the carpenter had finally agreed to take his wife on a trip, and this final project might interfere with those plans. When it became apparent, however, that the president would not take no for an answer, the carpenter reluctantly agreed.

And so over the next few months, he worked on this last project. There was a difference, however, in his work. Because of his decision to leave and his concern about his promise to his wife, he found himself rushing certain aspects of the job. Not a lot at first, but as is the way with construction projects, one delay here led to another there and before long the project was behind schedule. This led him to rush a little more, to cut corners here and there, substitute material that was on hand for that which had been special ordered but not yet arrived. And while he regretted some of these choices, he excused them by reminding himself that he was ready to move on to the rest of his life. Finally, the day came when the project was finished and he went again to say goodbye. The president thanked him for his outstanding service and said he would be greatly missed. Then as the carpenter turned to leave, the president once again asked him if he would wait just a moment longer and then moving out from behind his desk approached the carpenter with an envelope in his hand.

"This is for you," the president said. "A little token of our appreciation."

Surprised and touched by the gesture, the carpenter took the envelope. Being a shy man, he was not going to open it until later, but seeing the president's expectant look, he did. At first he did not quite understand what he was looking at, but then the contents of the envelope became clear. What lay in his hand was the deed to the new house he had just built.

One can only wonder what the carpenter thought as he looked at the deed in his hands. One can only wonder how many times in the days and years ahead as he walked around his new home he replayed the choices he had made during his final months of work.

Is it possible you sometimes have similar thoughts going on in your mind as you go about the business of your business in the world each day? Are you still passionate about what you do? Still committed to the same level of excellence you brought to your work at the outset of your career? Do you remember that early enthusiasm, that desire to do a great job? Are you still working each day to make a contribution to your colleagues and your customers or are you simply working for the money you make? What meaning and purpose do you find in and bring to what you do in your work in the world each day?

THE ANSWER IS NOT IN THE WHY

Keeping the story about the carpenter and these questions in mind, let's turn to the subject of this chapter. In previous chapters we have talked about the fact that "energy follows thought and manifestation follows energy." We have explored our belief that as co-creators of our lives, who we are and what we do and have are things we have created, promoted or allowed. We have also agreed that it is essential to pay attention to what we think, because our fears and doubts as well as our desires do indeed come upon us. Finally, we have determined that one of the keys to a more engaged and authentic existence is our ability to shift beyond our thinking mind to the state of being present and that in such a state a truer form of wisdom and a deeper commitment to real meaning and purpose becomes available to us.

Napoleon Hill, a protégé of Andrew Carnegie, said it this way: "Whatever the mind can conceive of and believe in, it can achieve." We realize, of course, that depending on the quality of your life at this moment, these premises may be either palatable or indigestible. We also know that some people abuse these concepts. Instead of accepting them as tools to find their direction when they are lost or to motivate and inspire when they are stuck or tired, they use them as reasons to beat up themselves or others.

Be aware of the significant impact these negative practices have on the course of your life. Also, put away any resistance and doubt you may be feeling, at least for now, and allow the possibility that whatever is occurring "out there" that may be obstructing or tyrannizing you may be the result of a belief or perception.

THE OUTSIDE MIRROR

On some levels, of course, it is difficult to believe that we would choose to tyrannize or limit ourselves, but sadly enough, our experience shows that this is the case. As we have discussed before, a significant number of us appear to believe we are limited beings and that long before we were born two other beings existed who violated one of God's laws and that as a result we must spend our lives seeking release and forgiveness from their offense.

While we have already explored this belief in the chapter on Original Sin, we think it is worth repeating that our continued adherence to this and other limiting beliefs reinforces the concept that we are earth-bound, limited beings and not powerful co-creators.

LEARNING FROM THE OUTSIDE IN

When this awareness is coupled with the knowledge that a lot of us delegate our sovereignty to an external source, it is easy to understand why so many of us accept mimicry as a form of learning and view collaboration as a form of cheating. It is also easy to understand why so many of us are not self-validating and self-directed.

Are the beliefs that prompt this delegation of sovereignty malicious? No, but they certainly are restricting and limiting and, what is particularly relevant is that in the end they are false. In our opinion, our God, the God who is the source of this mystery called life, would not have designed a system that defeats itself. Perhaps some of those who wanted to build a base of earthly power and serve as intermediaries might have found value in such an awkward system, but clearly no one committed to living a life that is joyful, open, loving and fulfilling would.

With the burden of institutions trying to build their own edifices to power, it is really not much of a surprise that so many of us find it difficult to discover a life of greater authenticity. This world teaches us we are born with a stain of sin and that if we work very hard, are very obedient and delegate our sovereignty, perhaps someday we will be forgiven.

No wonder so many of us spend our lives feeling dissatisfied and unworthy. No wonder so many of us keep looking out there for someone or something to make us feel whole, complete and, of course, more acceptable. No wonder so many of us get captured by the illusion that our primary job in life is to turn ourselves from this "unworthy and sinful" being into someone who is cleansed of someone else's sins.

Do these beliefs serve authenticity? Do they promote empowerment and invite you into your rightful place as a co-creator? Are there other beliefs—old beliefs that may have served you earlier in your life—that may be limiting you?

BEYOND THE WHY TO HOW

Let's go back to the story about the carpenter. After accepting his final assignment he probably spent a lot of time asking himself why he had agreed to build that last house and why he had done all he could do to make the project go faster so he could get on with his life. In doing this, he let go of something he had used his whole career. He had let go of the "how" and focused instead on the "why."

"Why" is like a paddle toy with a ball attached by an elastic cord. The trick is to hit the ball so that it snaps back to the paddle and you can hit it again. The harder and more frequently you hit the ball the harder and more frequently it snaps back. "Why" attaches our experience to us and keeps returning it to us. In fact, asking "why" is like hitting the ball of experience into the air so that the universe can give it back to us.

When most of us have an experience, especially a negative one, we ask "why." And because God is always listening and willing to oblige, God appears to answer our request by sending more of that same kind of experience back to us.

UNDERSTANDING MAY NOT BE THE KEY

Have you lived a good bit of your life trying to "understand" things? Big things like 'original sin' and an unforgiving God and, by comparison, smaller things like why you don't have what you want, why a particular relationship failed or why you have trouble accomplishing this or that career or business goal. We certainly have. Like you, we have thought that understanding was valuable, essential and necessary to our success. In fact, for more years than we care to admit, we have been like greyhounds in mad pursuit of the rabbit called "understanding" that runs ahead of us on the rail called life. Always ahead, always just out of reach.

If our analogy about the paddle game holds true for you, if "why" is like that elastic that attaches the ball of experience to the paddle that is each of us, then ask yourself how long you are going to keep spending precious time in this game that continually brings limiting, hurtful and debilitating experiences back to you in repetitive cycles and patterns.

It is comforting to spend time analyzing what we did and when and with whom and, above all, "WHY" we did it! This is a familiar and well-regarded practice and a lot of us sincerely believe it is important to understand "why" we did what we did. But is it? Is "why" really the question we should be asking? Why? Why indeed!

Let's explore this question from a different angle. Has answering a "why" ever really assisted you getting the next project done? In smiling or laughing or being joyful? In your experience, has the search for "why" ever helped you to digest your food, write that report, clean your dish, have that conversation or wash your clothing? Has it ever assisted you in completing a task, expressing your love or feeling at peace with life? Has your search for "why" ever brought you one step closer to demonstrating self-mastery? Has it ever made the sun rise or set or allowed you to experience God?

If we seem to be pushing this issue, do you wonder "WHY?"

TODAY'S REFLECTION

"How" leads to knowledge, "why" to belief. "How" leads to doing, "why" leads to thinking and too often to procrastination. Today I commit to learning "how" to live my life more fully and to being responsible for how I live my life. Today, I commit to creating greater passion, joy and authenticity at home and at work.

PART FOUR
Practicing a Few Simple Strategies that Can Change Your Life

◆

Say "Yes"

The real voyage of discovery consists not in seeking new landscapes,
but in having new eyes.

◦[Marcel Proust]◦

If you have read our book *Say Yes to Change*, you know how strong-ly we believe in the power of this three-letter word. One of the rea-sons we champion its use is that most of us hear an overwhelming number of "No's," especially early in our lives—some 40,000 "No's" before we are seven years of age, some 900 "No's" to every "Yes." Most of them come from people who love us or who are charged with the responsibility for our well-being—parents, teachers, babysitters, min-isters, older brothers and sisters, coaches and friends.

These folks say "No" so often to keep us out of trouble and away from harm, to give us boundaries, and protect and control us. They also say "No" because that is the way they learned to live life. They say "No" to things they have never experienced, to things that intimidate them, things that they do not understand and, above all, to things that scare them.

We, in turn, learn to say "No" not only to things that can harm us, but to new experiences, new opportunities, new circumstances, new people and to the unknown. The implications of this situation are as startling as they are predictable. We say "No" to new career and job opportunities, to new life experiences, to new friendships and rela-tionships and to everything else outside our boundaries. Some of us continue saying "No" all our lives.

We also say "No" to a risk because someone else may have had a bad experience with it. We say "No" to certain activities and experiences because one of our caregivers or mentors may not have had the time or patience to allow us to do whatever our curiosity or energy or imagination prompted us to do. We say "No" because someone else believed that something we wanted to do was sinful or dangerous.

THE HABIT OF NO

After a while, this habit of saying "No" becomes so strong we say it even before we allow ourselves to consider the possibility of saying "Yes." We say "No" rather than risk disapproval or punishment. We say "No" to keep peace, avoid conflict or avoid disturbing the status quo. We say "No" even though a voice within us wants us to joust windmills, dream bigger visions, hope larger hopes, want wilder wishes, and live life more authentically.

We say "No" even though a voice within us wants to say "Yes" and to say it enthusiastically. We say "No" even when we know that being vital, alive, valuable, generous, kind, gracious, wise, tender, loving, bold, audacious, unafraid and full of wonder is on the opposite side of the line in the Land of Yes. We say it loud. We say it often. We say it even our sleep. "No!" "No!" "No!"

THE OTHER SIDE OF LIFE'S COIN

"Yes" on the other hand involves recognizing what already is. It is form of surrender to love and life, a vote of confidence in the mysterious, the infinite and the marvelous. "Yes" is a declaration of our openness to possibility, risk, and to the magic and spontaneity of life. Yes is the statement that each of us must ultimately make to find our way into wholeness, harmony and alignment with life.

When we say "Yes" we declare our belief in ourselves, our confidence in our ability to act. We step forward and allow the universe to support us and, in turn, we support and serve life. We declare our trust that God will provide us with all we require. "Yes" is an affirmation of God's benevolence, a declaration of our confidence that nothing will be given to us that we cannot handle or cannot use. "Yes" is a statement of our willingness to learn, change, grow and experience the unknown. "Yes" is a confirmation of our innocence and gratitude. "Yes" is simplicity.

But don't take our word for it. Lean back in your chair and close your eyes for a moment and sound out the two alternatives. Call to mind images from your life and your career—people, activities, possibilities. As you bring each of these images to mind say "No" to each. "NO...NO...NO!" Now exaggerate the "No." Yell it out! Snarl when you say it! Grimace and frown when you say it. Say it louder! Say it deeper. How do you feel?

Now review some of those same images and this time say "Yes" to those people, activities and possibilities. Say it joyfully! Say it enthusiastically! Say "YES."

How does your heart feel, and which of these words allows you to feel more of who your really are? When you say "Yes" do you feel more in touch with life, more energized? Do you feel the power? If you do, how can you ever want to say "No" again?

If "No" is sometimes a contradiction, a denial and limitation of life and "Yes" is an acceptance and an invitation to celebrate life, if "Yes" is a wonderment that leads you deeper and ever more confidently into life, why say anything else? Practice saying "Yes." Go into your world today and start saying it. Say it to all of the opportunities today presents. See what happens. After all, you are already quite familiar with the results of saying "No." So become someone who says "Yes" to greater meaning and purpose into your life. Become like those men and women who have come before you and whose courage and imagination has helped make the Earth more remarkable. Say "Yes" to your own greater meaning and to inheriting your true destiny.

TODAY'S REFLECTION

Today, I say "Yes" to my life, to its abundance, to its possibilities and to its wonder. I say "Yes" to the invitation to learn, to love and to reconnect with my passion and purpose!

◆

Divide and Be Conquered

If your mind is unclouded by unnecessary things,
this is the best season of your life.

--◦[Wu Mein]◦--

On the field of battle, as well as in our obsessive struggles to conquer life and to manage time, many of us often apply the strategy of divide and conquer. For centuries this famous war dictum has been touted as an excellent and useful life strategy. In fact, in today's corporate and government sectors various applications of this and other "war" strategies abound.

In our personal experience, however, when we apply these strategies in the primary areas of our personal and professional lives, when we divide our attention and split our energy and focus, we end up turning our lives into a battlefield on which instead of conquering some so-called "enemy" we end up defeating ourselves, our core values and many of our primary goals.

Rather an odd assertion to be coming from two people who consult and coach with some of the country's leading companies, government agencies, national associations and the people who run them. After all, two of the mantras that dominate today's corporate and government realms are "win at any cost" and "do more for less with fewer people and faster."

A lot of folks in our world also believe that the Gods of Productivity and Performance are insatiable and that to be successful we must propitiate them by making constant offerings of our own and our people's physical and mental health, family stability, and of course, sometimes our personal honor, dignity and values. Of course, in both the public and private sectors and especially among some of our colleagues in traditional consulting firms, our beliefs on this subject are considered sacrilegious. Fortunately for us, however, and unfortunately for them, more and more individuals and organizations are discovering that over the long run strategies based on the concept of divide and conquer are faulty.

The truly successful companies and organizations know that when they ask their people to divide their attention, overbook time, fragment their energy and focus their efforts on too many goals, their people do not function well, and when their people do not function well neither do their products, services, customers and balance sheets.

So, as we take these next steps on this path toward greater authenticity, consider if you are applying this old battlefield strategy in your personal and professional life. If so, what happens when you divide your concern, your caring, your patience, your focus and your love into multiple parts? Does this strategy elevate your consciousness and increase your level of commitment to excellence? Over the long run, does this strategy assist you in being more or less effective, more or less satisfied and authentic?

OUT OF THE LIVES OF BABES

Although it might seem like a strange next step, call to mind the image of a small child at play. Pay close attention to the quality of that child's focus. When children play they often become so engrossed that all else falls away. They are, as we often say, in their own world.

When we ask adults to describe these states of consciousness we generally get descriptors like "childlike and simple," and these descriptions are often accompanied by looks of nostalgia, as if this state of being is idyllic and forever lost. By comparison, when we ask adults about their own lives many describe them as complex and challenged and, by implication, important. They talk about the demands they face at work and at home and about a life that requires a great deal of multi-tasking. Indeed, they give the impression that as adults they are responsible and grown-up and that they no longer have time for the "simple" life they once knew.

NOT WHAT WE DO BUT WHO WE ARE

For many of us trying to make our way in this topsy-turvy world, this is the song we sing. And yet if some of the things we have discussed in earlier chapters are true, that our happiness and success depend more on how we do what we do rather than on how much we do, then it must follow that there may be something else lurking behind our seeming obsession to be more productive and efficient. Perhaps our compulsion to do more, to be grown-up and complex may be hiding something essential and fundamental, something that we fear—like the call to find greater meaning and purpose.

Perhaps we would be better served if we stopped asking ourselves how we can do more and start asking ourselves how we can learn to enjoy what we are doing. Perhaps it is time to look more closely at this practice of trying to divide and conquer and discover if we are pleased with beliefs and strategies that turn lives into battlefields and tasks and activities into enemies that must be conquered.

Neither of us believes that dividing our attention gives us the ability to be present in whatever we are doing. When we divide our attention and energy we tend to lose touch with our awareness. And when we try to apply this divide and conquer strategy to relationships, we often lose our sense of connection, our awareness of our feelings and our willingness to engage honestly with others. In short, when we divide our attention and try to conquer someone or something, we generally miss the true satisfaction, fulfillment and involvement that a more singular and committed focus brings.

Of course, in a world in which we are trained to have ten-second attention spans, to watch two or three channels of television at the same time and do three or four things at once, doing one thing at a time may, at first, seem to be an outmoded practice and certainly not a strong enough strategy to keep pace with the "competition." And yet, as we make our way through organizations that are struggling to stay afloat and into the lives of those who have lost their meaning and purpose, we wonder why doing one thing well is not enough.

Perhaps you wonder about this too. Perhaps you sometimes look up from whatever you are doing and see your child or grandchild across the room and wonder how you can get back to that state of singular focus and contentment.

These are important questions, particularly important for those of us who seek to live authentic lives and to engage in meaningful forms of work. It is vital to discover what we can do to make whatever we are doing more enjoyable. It is time to question this practice of dividing our attention and energy in order to multi-task and to start asking ourselves what we can alter or shift in this very moment to make our lives at work and at home more fulfilling and satisfying.

BACK TO THE PRESENT

Through this type of question we all have the opportunity to create more meaning in our lives and purpose in our work. Through honest inquiry with ourselves we can return our awareness to the present and here—and only here—have the possibility of finding truth, wholeness and authenticity. Through this kind of examination of life we can begin at last to make the choices that keep our attention whole and undivided and our meaning in sight. Indeed, in this way we can discover that our salvation lies not in complexity but in simplicity. To help you find simplicity in this tempestuous, noise-saturated, outwardly focused world, here are a few strategies that work.

Participate fully in whatever you are doing rather than give it your partial focus. If you are distracted by something, either deal with it at once or set it aside for later. Pay attention to your thoughts. Literally learn to witness them. Focus directly and physically on what you are doing rather than thinking about doing or thinking about something else. Pay attention to detail and to expressing each thought, word and action with excellence. Invest genuine concern and loving in each thing you do and for each person you encounter in the doing.

Instead of dividing and trying to conquer, bring your attention, full and whole, into your physical body in the "here and now" and you will discover a whole new level of enjoyment, energy and commitment re-emerging in your life.

Ignore any thoughts that include the words "but" and "can't" or "if only." They are divisive and do not contribute to greater awareness or harmony. All of this mind chatter ensures that you will continue to divide your attention and fragment your energy.

A DIVIDED HOUSE

If you really want greater meaning and purpose in your personal and professional life, your challenge is to come back into connection and communion with yourself. And your first step is to observe and witness the fact that the divided life you are leading is contributing to your discomfort, to the sense of ambiguity about your process and to the feeling of incompleteness that sometimes haunts you and raises your level of anxiety. Through paying attention you will recognize that anxiety prompts you to split yourself into so many pieces.

And who can blame you? It is not easy to make peace with our imperfections and our incompleteness, especially in a world that has become so results-obsessed and time-compulsive. However, overcoming these compulsions and distractions is the very thing we have come here to this school called the Earth to do.

If you do not agree with us and want to continue on your time-focused and results-oriented path, ask yourself how else you can discover what is incomplete and imperfect if you are not in the "here and now."

You can decide that life is not just about time and results, or you can continue to seek more results. In both cases, being directed and aligned, keeping your house undivided, will allow you to make your incompleteness more complete and your imperfection more perfect. Better still, when you live in the present you will even discover that incomplete and imperfect have more to do with our beliefs and perceptions than with reality.

So let's go back for a moment to that Zen saying we mentioned earlier. Consider the possibility that if we could learn to eat when eating, sit when sitting and stand when standing, we might actually rediscover the key to the joy we seek. We might remember that being present in every "here and now" is the only gift we can give to ourselves and others.

In this way each moment can become a source of its own joy or, at the very least, it becomes an opportunity to discover what is not joyful. With our forces undivided we can explore, examine and discover if there is something we can do, some new way of acting, some shift in awareness or belief that will make the moment more joyful.

If not, then we will be free to choose to go on to the next moment, and to the next. As for those instances when we believe there are no choices, by keeping our attention and focus united in the present we will have the courage to hold on until a next choice or a next lesson becomes clear.

TODAY'S REFLECTION

Now is all that I have. If I divide and try to conquer, I turn my life into a battlefield. If I unify my focus, energies and awareness I can experience the victory of wholeness and joy. I can discover my original, authentic self.

♦

Trust in Your Goodness!

Join the company of those who make the barren places of the earth fruitful with kindness. Carry a vision of heaven in your souls and you shall make your home, your college, your place of work and your world correspond to that vision.

--ᴥ[Helen Keller]ᴥ--

With all of the scientific, technological and social changes taking place in our world today, it is no surprise that many of us feel overwhelmed by pressures and demands. As we've discussed, these pressures affect every area of our lives and leave many of us feeling caught between that proverbial rock and a hard place, struggling on one hand to do what we believe are the right and responsible things to do, and on the other to do what we are sometimes led by our internal compass to do. We are caught between the demands that arise in our relationships with others and those that arise in our relationships with ourselves. Often these conflicts come up between the many demands our jobs place on us and the calls that issue from personal dreams.

For many of us this list of conflicts is long, and the results of the struggle are debilitating and exhausting. In fact, with levels of stress and burnout reaching unprecedented proportions, it is clear that unless we find a way to deal with these conflicts between inner and outer demands, our physical and mental health—and of equal consequence, our emotional and spiritual well-being—will continue to suffer.

When we talk in depth with many of the folks we work with we also learn that these struggles often involve a tug of war between forces they have been taught to believe are "good" and others that they have been told are "bad." They often equate "good" with selflessness, service to others (including propitiation to both the corporate and government gods), doing our duty, fulfilling the wants and requirements of others, and meeting the expectations of society as a whole.

"Bad," on the other hand, is often equated with being selfish, irresponsible, insensitive, uncaring, and sometimes cruel and hurtful. "Bad" implies we have little or no self-control, are immature and fall easy victim to our wants and what the world calls "temptation."

To be alive and engaged in contemporary society is to be familiar with this struggle. In point of fact, we have met few people who are immune to it. It is surprising, however, that many of us are not conscious of its long-term costs.

THE BOGUS STRUGGLE BETWEEN GOOD AND BAD

This struggle between what religions and societies often define as the forces of good (selflessness) and bad (selfishness) inflicts serious casualties upon us. Loss of energy and enthusiasm for life, feelings of guilt and shame, loss of passion, depression, resentment, physical and mental disease are only a few of these casualties. These costs are rarely talked about outside of counseling and therapy sessions. Their roots and causes are not explored by our media. Indeed, while the media appears to be interested in expending huge amounts of air time and print columns on their effects (crime, disease, war, and so on) it turns a blind eye to causes.

Solutions, of course, are complex and require not only effort, but significant shifts in belief, values, actions and lifestyles. In a world that operates on sound-bite consciousness and measures every change against only one barometer—its short-term impact on the economy rather than its long-term good—this is no surprise.

Still, whether our world is ready to make the changes or not, it is certainly ready to continue expending an enormous amount of time and energy posturing and preaching about good and bad. And yet, with the exception of a few basic acts, most acts we define as good and bad are not really different actions, but only different shades of the same actions that lie along a continuum. In fact, the line that separates good from bad is sometimes very thin, almost always subjective and sometimes hard to decipher. What one being, ethnic, religious or culture group elects to call good or bad is sometimes practiced in its opposite form by another person, group, religion or culture.

Furthermore, beneath all thoughts, words and actions, under all of the apparent differences and definitions, there is one common and unalterable motive: goodness. Every impulse, thought, intention, word or action that any human being has ever expressed or committed since the beginning of recorded time started out as goodness and love.

Even heinous acts do not refute this point. Instead, they speak to the imperfections and impediments in the instruments that play the music and not to the quality, elevation and purity of the music itself. Goodness and love are the primary notes in the Cosmic Symphony. Always have been. Always will be. The difference between harmony (good) and cacophony (bad) does not issue from the Composer (God) and is not inherent in the music itself (life), but it is the result of some of the imperfections in us as instruments.

Indeed, while many of our actions do inflict great harm, tragedy and loss on others and on ourselves, our actions do not make the music or even us as instruments bad. It only means we have taken some of the remarkable, neutral, harmonious and grace-filled music of God and, in the process of learning to play—which you may remember is why we have come to the Earth in the first place—we end up converting or translating the music from harmony to cacophony.

What has all of this got to do with authenticity? Well, we believe that in the end it doesn't really matter if we choose to laugh or cry, dance or stand still, go to work or not work, have sex or refrain, live alone or in society, go to church or not, wear clothes or run naked in the woods, share or hoard, see the positive or the negative, eat meat or to live as a breatharian, celebrate our Higher Power on Saturday or Sunday, at dawn or at dusk or not at all. We believe that each of these decisions results in learning and a different kind of quality of life. Choose to satisfy a personal desire over giving attention to others and there is learning. Reverse the choice and there is a different kind of lesson. Does it matter which you choose? On some levels, yes, if the choice you make injures or harms others or yourself, it matters. But that still does not mean that there are opposing forces of good and bad.

In fact, in the cosmic scheme of things, we don't think it matters all that much what choices we make. Eventually, all of us will make a lot of the same choices. We are all like actors who expand our craft by expanding the range of roles we play. One day we play the villain, the next the hero, one day the supplicant, the next the queen or king. In the end, we all have to dance the steps in the Dance of Life. The only difference between each of us is that we sometimes do these steps in a different order for different reasons and at different times.

In a world that already contains so much crime and is so overly permissive, this concept may sound dangerous. It may even appear to contradict a number of traditional beliefs that suggest that without the rules of morality and ethics, of right and wrong, our world would collapse. But if you dig around in these rules and are really honest with yourself, you'll have to admit that even with all of these rules, even with all of the preachers and teachers who talk about good and bad, our world has not yet become a Garden of Eden.

FOR THE GUIDANCE OF WISE MEN

Except for a few rules that are so obvious and common that most cultures and faiths have independently agreed on them (such as thou shalt not kill), most rules we live by are set by someone or some group at sometime and for some defined reason. They are not written in stone (unless a man has carved them) nor are they, contrary to what some would have us believe, written by God. They are Man's Rules!

And just as a rule or boundary that applied to us when we were children no longer applies when we are teenagers or adults, just as a rule established for us as students no longer applies when we graduate, it is so with all of the rules made by man when we move to different circumstances and different levels of consciousness. In short, rules are not permanent or inviolate. They must be constantly reviewed and explored. How else can we ever discover the natural laws and primary truths? How else can we allow ourselves to lead lives that are truly authentic?

Imagine, for example, how limited the world of contemporary art would be if Piccaso had followed the rules of classical art and never gone further than his Pink or Blue period. Imagine what physics would be without chaos theory or earth exploration without people like Christopher Columbus and Sir Edmund Hillary. Imagine what your life would be like if you still rode a bicycle with training wheels or if Moore's Law on the exponential growth of computers had never been articulated.

So the next time you find yourself in one of those struggles between what you think of as good and bad, the next time you are torn between doing something you believe you have to do and something you want to do, know that somewhere beneath all of that conflict there is only love and goodness. Also know that you will find this "underneath source" most easily if you follow your heart and learn to listen to your inner wisdom. And most often, of course, that will mean doing things against some of "man's" rules. Sometimes you will find great meaning and purpose doing things you normally avoid, the things someone else says are selfish and bad. When this conflict arises, remember that every impulse you have began in the heart of God as loving and to find it is to be deeply and extraordinarily, authentically present.

GOODNESS AND ONLY GOODNESS

By being present you will find only goodness, because you are goodness. Resident in each of your cells, in each of your breaths, there is goodness. Just now, here in this instant, allow yourself to glimpse your goodness. Close your eyes and feel it. Know it! You are a human being and you are good. You make mistakes. You are not perfect. You get lost sometimes, but you are human and human beings are here on this earth to live, to learn, to make mistakes and to experiment with life. Take a moment now and reflect on some of your struggles and then look beneath the surface. Feel the doubt, the fear, the not knowing, but don't do anything. Just observe your feelings. Feel how the desire for goodness resides beneath these feelings. Right there, feel the desire to be held, to be nurtured, to give and receive, to share, to listen and be understood, to support and be supported, and, above all, to discover your reason for being alive.

Follow the thread of your desire deeper and feel the level of loving that it discloses. No matter what desire you have, understand that it is driven by your need to understand, to connect, and to learn. Also remember, it would not be there unless you were meant to hear it.

Breathe in that knowledge. Feel the power of this knowing, this unending and extraordinary wellspring of goodness. Feel the resident virtues of your heart, compassion, harmony and love. Remember that all desires come from the same source, God. Also remember that there are no wrong choices, just alternative selections on the road of life and learning.

TODAY'S REFLECTION

There is no need to struggle between good and bad. There are no mistakes, only opportunities to learn and grow. It is what I do with my choice that creates positive or negative consequences. So I will choose freely and wisely and remember that as long as my choices do not intentionally harm anyone or myself, they are choices I am entitled to make as a human being.

◆

Listen for Your Meaning in the Silence

We shall not cease from exploration and the end of all
of our exploring will be to arrive where we started
and know the place for the first time.

-◦[T.S. Eliot]◦-

In a world filled with so much noise, it is hard sometimes to listen to ourselves and to separate what we know and feel from what the world tells us we are supposed to know and feel. And yet even though we know this, a lot of us continue to avoid going to the one place where we can truly find our meaning and purpose—the silence. Instead of choosing to be quiet, a lot of us seem committed to adding as much noise as possible to the cacophony that occurs both around and within us all the time. Sound, sound and more sound. Sound designed, it seems, to fill something that we have decided needs filling.

It is also clear that we have become so accustomed to living in this noise that many of us feel uncomfortable and awkward when it stops. In Sedena's case, there was a time in her life when noise was hard to escape—the noise in the world around her and the noise that was echoing inside her head. As a result she decided to spend a year living by herself on a quiet and beautiful piece of property her family owned in Northern California.

Though the adventure began as a way to get away from the glut and noise of her life, to spend time with her horses and to read some of her favorite writers—Emerson, Thoreau, Dickinson and

Whitman—after a while nature and the silence became much more than she expected. They offered a way of moving closer to the edge, to explore and uncover, to turn toward some challenges. It was a time to listen, to give space to what was trying to be born and could not be born in the noise. It was a time when the past needed to be put into perspective so that the future could be born.

George can also remember a time a number of years ago when he was living in New York and trying to establish himself as a sculptor. He had given up a lucrative career in advertising and was studying drawing and sculpting at the Art Student's League on West 57th Street and working on a set of stone sculptures he planned to enter in a juried competition for a one-year scholarship in Italy.

To make ends meet he was scrambling to fit in a number of part-time jobs—weekend bartender, freelance writer, evening administrator for a local technical school and occasional guest lecturer. It was a challenging time financially and in many other ways as well. As a result, he did not leave the island of Manhattan for a little over fourteen months. While this may not seem like a long time to some, anyone who has ever been to New York knows that although it is a remarkable city, life there generates a lot of tumult and noise. From the constant sound of traffic, fire and police sirens to the screech of subways, the squeal of buses, the sound of car alarms, the grinding of garbage trucks and dumpsters, the yelling on the streets and, of course, just the unavoidable and undeniable noise generated by twelve or thirteen million people going about the process of trying to live or come to work on a very small land mass can sometimes be assaulting and challenging. No wonder Ram Das calls living in New York the ultimate warrior training.

He finally had to take a break, however, and went to New England to visit his parents. At the time they still lived in the small town where he had grown up. On the first morning he took a walk in a wooded area adjacent to the house. It was just after sunrise. It was winter. As he walked he could hear the sound of his feet crunching on the surface of the frozen snow and suddenly he heard something else as well.

He was aware that he had a thought that seemed to rise up into the space around him and then return amplified and a little more comprehensible. In short, in the silence of that New England winter morning he actually could hear himself think. In that moment he could feel how deep-down exhausted he was from those fourteen months of uninterrupted noise.

No doubt, you have had similar experiences. Perhaps your awareness of the effect noise has on you happens when the kids suddenly go off to school or when you put them down for a nap. Perhaps it happens when you stay late or come in early to the office and remember how quiet and private and terrific the space feels. Early in the morning, late at night, out in the woods or down in your workshop or family room, it does not matter. What matters is the awareness that as a society we have become addicted to noise. In fact, many of us have become so accustomed to the noise that when we are alone we get uncomfortable.

Noise also gives us the impression we are doing something. And of course, as long as we are doing "something" we do not have to deal with our fear that we are less significant and more fragile than we often pretend. And most especially, because of all of the noise we never have to get to the "not doing" or the doing of "no-thing," which is called "being."

So stop for a moment and feel a little of this restlessness and discomfort, this undeniable urge to fill up and preoccupy yourself with noise. Feel this powerful urge to get away from yourself. Close your door, turn off the TV or stereo or the computer. Sit back in your chair, close your eyes and give yourself over to five minutes of silence. Five minutes is not such a long time. Just relax and follow your breath in and out.

If you took your five minute break, what did you feel? Did you have a little trouble just sitting there? Did you find your mind wandering or maybe wondering what you were supposed to do? Of course, you don't have to do anything and that takes a little practice. It takes awhile to get past the discomfort, discover why we have created a world in which there is so much noise and so little chance for silence.

We all have been trained to live in the noise. There is some form of media coming at us constantly when we are out in public. Billboards, flashing signs, music from loudspeakers, overflow noise from people talking on cell phones, visual displays, kiosk televisions. It's everywhere. In addition, most of us live in noisy landscapes. Listen to the sounds around you at this moment. No matter where you are, it's hard to find silence.

THE INNER NOISE

In addition to the noise that is happening outside and around us, if we stop for even a few moments we begin to hear the noise we create every moment inside of us. Thoughts, worries, doubts, confusions, and a whole lot of other endless mind chatter. In the Zen tradition this is called the "Monkey Mind."

Many of us talk about longing for "peace and quiet." We tell ourselves and others that one of the reasons we are so busy, so preoccupied, so noisy is that someday we want to live a life away from the rat race, a life filled with happiness, fulfillment, bliss and silence. Yet most of what we do makes and involves noise. Is it possible we have convinced ourselves that noise is some kind of preparation for silence? Is it possible we believe that by filling up all the spaces and places we will learn how to hear truth—our truth, God's truth?

There are other significant reasons that some of us are uncomfortable with silence. Silence is a kind of coming home to ourselves and some of us—at least half of us if the latest figures are accurate— have been traumatized in one way or another as children, either emotionally or physically. As a result of that trauma, there wasn't a safe place to be at home. Perhaps that is why so many of us don't feel it's safe to come home to ourselves as adults, and so we fill up the gaps and cover the pain with the noise of televisions and stereos and computers. We fill up the silence with thought. This scenario is played out not just in our individual lives, but in the world at large. No wonder there is so much noise. How can we feel safe and love silence when we violate and traumatize each other constantly as cultures and as nations.

A VERY DIFFERENT CHOICE

If you are not finding purpose and meaning in your life, perhaps it's time you begin looking for it where you can find it. Perhaps it's time to go beyond your habitual pre-occupation with noise, with other people's answers and opinions, time to finally put down the pretense that you will find what you are seeking somewhere out there and begin to remember that your best bet is to get quiet and listen, to remember that in the silence "you" show up. God shows up. Time, as Thich Nhat Hanh says, "to come back to the island of the self." Time to come home gently and safely, to come compassionately home. Time to remember that you do not have to do anything particularly difficult. You need only stop doing the things that make noise.

Experiment with this for just a few moments. Discover if it is true that the essential you, that wise and loving being who speaks through your heart, is only as far away as your next breath. Read the next few paragraphs and then give yourself the experience.

Here's what we suggest. As soon as you finish reading these instructions, lean back for a moment or two in your chair and surrender the weight of your body to its support. Feel how well the chair supports you. Feel how it, in turn, is supported by the floor beneath it. Experience how well cared for you are by your physical environment.

Now pay attention to your breathing. Take a few deep breaths and follow your exhales out. Breathe in and out. In and then out and follow your breath. If you feel a little warmth and tingling in your body, just enjoy it. Perhaps you can feel your shoulders relaxing. You might even let your arms hang at your sides and allow your lower jaw to drop.

Now direct your attention to your heart and breathe in and out through that area of your body. In and out. In and out. Inhale through your heart. Exhale through your heart. Just follow your breath. This is a simple key, a simple doorway to your own silence. Breathe in and out through your heart. And if you are so inclined, close your eyes and keep following your breath. In and out. In and out. Let your breath lead you. Follow it into the silence.

TODAY'S REFLECTION

My answers will not be found in the opinions and belief systems of others. They will be found in the stillness within me. So today I will remember that to get to the silence all I have to do is to follow my breath and be willing to listen. My breath is my doorway to the truest place within me called "home."

◆

Remember Energy Doesn't Care

A human being is part of the whole called by us 'universe,'
a part limited in time and space. He experiences himself,
his thoughts and feelings as something separated from the rest...
a kind of optical delusion of his consciousness.
This delusion is a kind of prison for us, restricting us
to our personal desires and to affection for a few persons
nearest to us. Our task must be to free ourselves from this prison
by widening our circle of compassion to embrace
all living creatures and the whole of nature in its beauty.

--ᵔ[Albert Einstein]ᵔ--

Although our species is beginning to explore more of the dimen-sions of our physical universe and to better understand the laws governing the physical sciences, when it comes to understanding and demonstrating the laws governing the human heart and true harmony and collaboration between the members of our human tribe we often appear awkward at best and quite backward at worst. And when it comes to understanding what path we can take to arrive at a more just, sane and sustainable way of life and a more elevated, positive level of human consciousness, we seem to stumble around pretending that life is a mystery.

Although we have given this seeming contradiction a reasonable amount of thought, we are still not sure if this pretense comes from our unwillingness to take responsibility for our true power as co-cre-ators, or if it arises from the fact that we our trapped in our minds and obsessively fascinated by our own egos. We are not sure if this pretense issues more from our refusal to turn the discerning spotlight of our intelligence on ourselves or from what appears to be our inability to separate what happens "out there" in the physical universe from what happens "in here" in the universe we call the "self."

Perhaps in the end it does not matter whether this pretense issues from our resistance, inability or from our unwillingness. What matters is that too many of us are missing the opportunity to make peace with ourselves and thereby to create a world of greater peace, stability and authenticity.

In this chapter we'll take a deeper look at the fact that you, the members of your family and the people you interact with each day at work, can contribute to a more just, natural and peaceful world. How? One answer lies in the fact that "energy follows thought and manifestation follows energy." Another is that this energy does not care how it is used.

Our scientists tell us that energy is the primary building block of the universe. Everything is composed of it, both animate and inanimate matter. Therefore, the only major difference between what we perceive as solid stuff, like rock, and what we perceive as less tangible stuff, like air, is the rate at which both are vibrating. In short, in our physical universe, the slower the rate of vibration the denser the matter and the faster the rate of vibration the less solid an object or element is.

If everything in the physical world is composed of energy, then it must follow that thought is also energy. And so when your thoughts create patterns of energy, and the more you think along similar lines and the more often you have similar thoughts about the same thing or person, the more of these patterns of energy you create. These patterns, in turn, create pathways, much like the pathway you create when you walk repeatedly through a field of grass. The more frequently you walk on that path (or think along the same lines) the more visible the path gets and visible paths attract more traffic until the path literally becomes a thoroughfare. Thoroughfares, as most of us know, tend to get busier until the traffic that moves along them has to slow down.

In short, thought becomes habitual and tends to follow the same pathways over and over. A particular concern, worry, fear, or judgment for example, tends to become habitual. A fantasy, like Hesse's summer house or your desire for a particular life partner or a different career or a home, becomes habituated. Your worry about not having enough, growing old, qualities in your life partner or children or your colleagues at work, they, too, become habituated. They, too, slow down and become dense.

Keeping this analogy in mind, let's go back and explore our original premise that we are powerful beings and that we may be avoiding our responsibility for bringing greater meaning and purpose into our lives. Let us also talk about another old adage: "Thoughts persisted in produce states of consciousness, and states of consciousness persisted in produce physical manifestation."

Whatever we think about, imagine, envision, consider, dwell on, reflect on, worry about, or obsess over becomes our physical reality. In fact, our thoughts are the means by which each of us gets to be a filmmaker who imagines a concept, writes a script, casts the parts, directs the action, and acts at least one of the main roles, in the production called their life.

These same thoughts get us involved in the editing and distribution of the film. They allow us to be part of the audience, and to also be the film's most demanding critic. In short, we produce the drama, or comedy or tragedy or epic that is called the story of our lives, and we do all of this on a regular basis and generally without much awareness by utilizing this stuff called "thought." In fact, it is the only way what we know of as our lives actually unfold.

When we both look back at our lives a few things are clear. The first is that at various times we have produced some really amateurish and embarrassing films. The second is that we have certainly produced a lot of films. Some of these films are definitely comedies while others qualify as tragedies. For example, Sedena made one of her films thirteen years ago at a time when her mother was dying and her first marriage was coming apart. At that time she realized it was necessary to craft a new script that would bring new meaning and greater purpose into her life.

In this case, the script involved envisioning a way of life that would include greater balance, harmony and inner peace. While working on the new script she realized that to make this film she would need a couple of things that were not present in her life at that time—a greater sense of awareness of what was possible and a greater willingness to roll up her sleeves and get involved in her own life.

With these realizations in mind and the pain of the challenges and chaos she was facing, Sedena began to discover some of the building blocks that would allow her to create the beginnings of a new life. They would eventually be forged into understanding and the unique healing practices and disciplines that today constitute the core elements that make up the transformational and personal development work she does with others.

ESSENTIAL SECRETS

We are spending this time on the relationship between thought and energy because we have noticed a few powerful clues in this topic that relate directly to creating lives and careers of greater meaning and purpose. The first is that thought is automatic and continuous and that it is the job of the mind to think. The second is that if we do not provide the mind with a positive focus, the mind will think about anything it attaches itself to. If it gets on a negative track it will stay on that track, doing its job, until we provide an alternate topic.

The third clue is that energy doesn't care how it is used, by whom it is used or when it is used. This building block of the universe—the stuff that places itself so constantly and willingly at our disposal and is the essential substance with which we create and run the ship of physical reality—is absolutely and completely neutral.

Anthropomorphize God until the cows come home; glorify, mystify or deny the energy that issues from God; utilize it for positive or negative ends, energy still doesn't care. Examine this premise for yourself. Ask yourself whether the energy you employ to create and deliver a positive and valuable service or product to your customers is the same energy that can be used to deceive or cheat them. Ask yourself whether the energy you call upon to express your love for someone comes from the same or a different energy pool you sometimes use to hurt that same someone. Ask yourself if the energy that allows you to create a work of art, invent a company, build a global company or start a volunteer group can or has been used to insult, abuse, deny, envy, betray, destroy or disregard others.

POSITIVE AND NEGATIVE ENERGY

For the sake of our exploration, let's agree that energy is neutral. If so, how does what we call "positive and negative" come into being? We believe that "positive and negative" result from the quality and character of the mind that thinks the thought from which this energy manifests. Just as a work of art, a child, an organizational system, an invention or discovery is ultimately determined by the skill, intent and character of the artist, the parent or the creator, so it is that the skill, intent and character of our minds determines whether the energy that places itself at our disposal is what we call "positive or negative."

Notice that energy lines up and serves your positive and negative thoughts. Notice that these thoughts affect the quality or absence of quality, the elevation or degradation of your life and your career and the lives of the people you interact with. Pay attention to the way you drain your energy by spending it on negative and destructive thoughts and how you harvest your energy by investing it in positive thoughts. Notice the connection between your thought and the manifestation of what the poet Mary Oliver calls "this one wild and precious thing called your life."

TODAY'S REFLECTION

Energy does not care. It is just the basic stuff of the universe that I get to use to create limitation or to lift myself and others to new levels of freedom. Energy is neutral. I either use it more consciously or it abuses me. Today, I commit to remembering that energy is the stuff through which I deny or create greater meaning and purpose in my life!

♦

Surrender to Surrender

All you have shall someday be given: therefore, give now,
that the season of giving may be yours and not your inheritors.
◦[Kahlil Gibran]◦

Author Idries Shah tells a wonderful Sufi story titled "What Is it
All For?"

The mulla Nasrudin lay under a mulberry tree one
hot summer's day, looking at some of the enormous
watermelons which grew on a vine nearby. His mind
turned to higher things.

How is it, he wondered, that an immense, impressive
tree like this mulberry brings forth such puny little fruits?
Look at the miserable, weakling creeper of a vine which
produces such huge and delicious melons. As Nasrudin
was pondering the paradox, a mulberry fell and landed
on his shaven head.

"Ah, I see," said Nasrudin, rubbing the spot where
the small mulberry had hit his head. "That is the reason,
is it? I should have thought of that before."

Whether it comes to us in a Sufi story about a mulberry rather
than a watermelon hitting Nasrudin's head or from the text of our
lives, the obvious is often our best teacher. And yet far too many of us
appear to overlook the obvious, spending most of our lives and a great
deal of our careers struggling against almost unbeatable odds to prove

we are "masters of the universe." It seems, in fact, that a lot of us believe that life and work are adversaries, things to be overcome or bested, and if we struggle hard enough and fight valiantly enough, we will eventually wrest success from them. We hope to win success and temporary security until Life enters wearing the disguise of Death and stakes its claim.

Success unattainable. Life hard. Career challenging. Where did these beliefs come from? How did we get on this path that keeps us circling around in the same loop? A cursory look at the majority of those we call "senior citizens" points out the faulty nature of such a strategy. Rarely does one find an older person who has been ennobled, empowered and renewed by their struggle to beat life. Instead, far too many seniors appear to be tired not only in body, but often in spirit from their attempts to do battle with life.

Perhaps you have also spent a large portion of your life thus far in struggle. Perhaps it is also true for you, as it is for us, that some of the things that you have struggled against and not bested, once surrendered to, have provided you with your greatest learning and reward. Perhaps, contrary to your expectations, you have also discovered that the degree of release we experience when we surrender is often in direct proportion to the degree of resistance we have previously exhibited.

Many of us have experienced this Law of Release and Resistance just as many of us are intimately familiar with the Law of Futility. And yet even in the face of this first-hand knowledge, even though we have been cautioned against this strategy of struggle in thousands of ancient and modern texts, we do it anyway. We continue to struggle mightily against life.

Most of us know that this struggling is futile, but every time a new challenge arises we seem to get amnesia. We live as though we have no idea that freedom and growth are most easily achieved by surrendering to the thing that we are resisting.

For example, for years George has been getting inner prompts to practice yoga. He also has had a lot of encouragement from people who know the benefits of the practice. The few times he took a class, however, he reported feeling awkward and clumsy, and so he turned away.

Recently, however, he was standing in the checkout line at a local health food store and overheard a conversation between two women in line ahead of him. One of them was raving about a yoga studio and the terrific classes. For some reason, the message landed and triggered all of those inner prompts and external invitations. As a result, he asked the women about the studio and then drove there immediately to investigate.

Now he is taking yoga classes two or three times a week. He's stretching and twisting through his awkwardness and discovering for himself how this practice relates to his next level of learning.

THE WHY OF STRUGGLE

It would be presumptuous for either of us to suggest we know why any of us struggles. But if you are willing, we can take a closer look at this subject together. Begin by recalling the first time you jumped off a diving board or rode a bicycle without training wheels. Do you remember the false starts, the trepidation, the anxiety? By comparison, do you remember your experience when you left that diving board for the first time or moved away from the guiding hand of a parent or friend to pedal the bike? Can you still feel some of the energy, excitement and exhilaration of that experience?

You might remember something else about that experience— the immediate and undeniable desire to do it again. And then what happened? Each time you did it, the degree of anxiety lessened and the degree of desire increased. In fact, after a few attempts you probably could not wait to jump, dive, ride, or do whatever you had previously been afraid and hesitant to do.

You learned that doing is often less difficult than anticipating, less difficult than the thinking and worrying about the doing. You learned that doing has a whole series of rewards you cannot obtain in any other way—rewards of greater energy, clarity, self-confidence and a sense of well-being.

And yet, even though most of us have had these experiences in our lives, when we are tested on a new lesson or in a new context or circumstance, we revert to old habits. Even though life presents us with opportunities to do and to learn something new each day, a lot of us opt out. When new opportunities arise, we resist and cover our fear and our anxiety with other more "acceptable" and "appropriate" feelings: anger, sadness, confusion or those old reliable partners, cynicism and judgment.

When confronted by the new, unknown and unfamiliar, many of us regress instantly to the little boy or girl standing on the edge of the diving board waiting for someone to tell us it's okay to avoid the challenge or better yet, for someone to come along and do it for us.

A THIRD ALTERNATIVE

There is a third alternative, however. We do not need to spend the remainder of our lives living in fear on the edge of the pool of life. Nor do we have to struggle with new challenges by attacking the water as if it were our enemy.

Test this suggestion against your own experience. Call to mind the image of someone learning to swim for the first time. Observe their process. Notice the anxiety they express before getting into the water, the awkward choppiness of their strokes. They flail at the water. Now contrast this image with that of an accomplished swimmer. Observe how they slide or dive willingly into the water and then move effortlessly through it. They seem to be in harmony with the water. No struggling. No fighting against. Instead, they appear to have "given up" to it, to have "surrendered" to it.

TO A HIGHER SOURCE

Now take a look at the phrase "give up." For most of us the concept of giving up represents something negative, something weak. It seems to signify a throwing in of the towel, a defeat. Yet on closer observation these are such harmless words. "Give" certainly does not have a negative connotation. Nor does "up." In fact, when the words are accompanied by a physical gesture of the hands raising up as if someone were presenting a gift, the real meaning for "giving up" becomes more apparent. Is it possible that to "give up" is to give over to something that is higher, something above us and around us? Something that we perhaps call God?

So rather than a weak experience, the act of giving up might allow you to experience something wonderful, something blissful. Have you ever "given up" to a tub of hot water when your body is tired? Ever "given up" to a soft bed when sleep is the thing you need most? Have you ever "given up" to belly-shaking laughter or to tears of joy that come from the center of your heart? Have you ever "given up" to someone's hands as they massage you or to the wonders of uninhibited dance? What about physical intimacy and orgasm? Isn't that a form of "giving up"?

If you have experienced any of these things, you have tasted bliss, so why fool around, even for one more day, with the notion that you have to struggle and resist life? Why pretend life and work need to be hard, that you have to beat or resist them? Why pretend that each encounter needs to be serious or threatening or that it has to have a perfect outcome, when right here and right now you have the option to surrender to whatever is next for you?

Whether the experiences we mentioned above are among your experiences or not, right here and now you can pick something to surrender to and surrender. Give up to a bath, to a lover, to a friend, to the experience of laughter, to dance, to moving effortlessly through the water or to doing whatever you are doing with one hundred percent concentration and commitment. Yes, put down this book and go in search of someone or something to give up to and to celebrate your authenticity and originality.

TODAY'S REFLECTION

Struggle and resistance are unnecessary and a lot of hard work. They are learned behaviors that arise out of my belief that life is something to be controlled and feared. By contrast, surrender is an expression of openness, of love, of courage. Today, I choose to give up to life. Today, I choose to be authentic.

◆

Know It Ain't What You Don't Know

When you do the thing you will have the power.
⊸[Ralph Waldo Emerson]⊷

Occasionally we both stop this whirlwind called everyday living long enough to consider how much time we have spent in the somewhat agonized, often frenzied and almost always frustrating search for "the answer."

In fact, we have spent years in this process, struggling, losing, gaining, falling, hoping, missing and grasping for some "key" we hoped would unlock a hidden doorway to some condition of being that is better and more perfect than whatever our lives offered at that particular moment. During our search we clung tenaciously to the belief that once we discovered the key, everything would be fine, terrific, outstanding and just plain wonderful.

We no longer believe in such a key. We don't think it's about what we don't know and don't have. We don't think it's about what we have not found, but rather about what we already have and what we already know. We no longer believe it is about finding the right teacher, formula, tablet, potion, position, or partner, but of recognizing and dealing with the potion, position, teacher and partner that life is offering us in this very moment.

We no longer believe it is about asking permission, waiting in line, graduating, finding the right direction, waiting until we retire, evolving slowly or discovering the right "path." Instead we are finally admitting the possibility that life is not about arriving and result, but about what a whole lot of wise people who have come before us have tried to tell us.

For example, a few weeks ago Sedena realized she had been "standing in line" regarding a new area of her work. For several months she had been involved in intense study, reading all she could get her hands on, listening to tapes, attending programs, working with healers who specialize in that particular field. While all of the studying was very valuable and contributed significantly to her understanding, her period of study went on longer than necessary. When she stopped to feel what was going on beneath the surface, she realized she was hesitant to begin applying what she had learned and was using 'studying' as a reason to avoid executing. As a result, she gave herself permission to start introducing the new concepts into her work.

For George, this kind of awareness happens around what he describes as his "spiritual journey." He finds that sometimes he avoids going deeply enough into the practice of any one spiritual technique by "shopping around" in some other practice that a friend or colleague claims is different or revolutionary.

Perhaps you can find examples in your own life of this constant quest for what you think you don't have or know. Perhaps your quests involve a particular aspect of your job you keep avoiding or your endless search for the latest driver or putter that will significantly lower your score or ensure that you hit longer, straighter drives. Perhaps your quest has something to do with finding the perfect technique to use in communicating with your child or making love to your partner or losing weight instead of just doing what you already know works well if you work it.

THE JOURNEY NOT THE DESTINATION

Our lives and our careers are intended to be about process, not perfection or result. They are about how we conduct the journey, about what we already know and about what we can practice along the way. Our lives and our work are not about our end game or destination. Please consider this possibility. We know you have probably considered it many times before, but take a few moments now and consider it again.

If your life and work are not about some future condition, result or possibility, if they are not about someone else's expectations or your anticipation, if they are not about what you don't have, don't know and have not yet achieved, then it is possible that your life and work may be about what you do have, now do and now know. It is possible your life and work are part of a remarkable journey of discovery and practice?

If this is even remotely true, you might be on the edge of the miraculous. Imagine a life in which you live each day knowing you are already "okay." Consider what every day could be like if you admit how much wisdom, ability and talent you already possess. Consider the possibility that the secret of life—your life—is not out there, in some future state or condition that needs to be won, but that the meaning and purpose for your life and your work are whatever is happening right here, right now.

Consider what would happen if your life and work ceased to be a frantic search for what you don't have and don't know and instead became a constant process of disclosing and practicing, inquiring and demonstrating what "already is," and being deeply grateful for what you "already have and know."

Every book then becomes the "right book." Every teacher becomes the "right and next" teacher. Every assignment, project or task at work becomes a means of expressing your talents, honing your skills, learning new competencies and enriching your life and the lives of people you work with and touch through your work. From such a perspective life and work become inventive, exciting, magical journeys in each "now." Each now has its own wonder, innocence, mystery and meaning.

Allow the possibility! Envision your life and your career without the boundaries of "I don't know how," and "I don't yet have." No more waiting to be better or more perfect. No more waiting for life to happen or for someone else to offer you another job or opportunity. Instead: a moving outside the concepts of lines, a going beyond waiting for permission to live, a stepping forward to take possession of your life and your career. No more waiting for your prayers to be answered, but a knowing that they are always answered at the moment of your request because you are entitled to a remarkable life, because you are a co-creator of your life. Each moment then is a stepping forward to celebrate your authenticity, a stepping into a "now" where you always have and always will be a divine partner with and an expression of God.

TODAY'S REFLECTION

I already have what I need. I already know what I am seeking to know. I already have achieved what I am trying to achieve. I am already full of aliveness and my authentic nature. My challenge today is to open to and celebrate all that I already have, all that I already know and all that I already am!

◆

Remember You Can Go Home Again

If you don't know where you are going,
you probably won't get there.

⊸[Anonymous]⊶

The expression "you can't go home again" refers to the futility of clinging emotionally to the past. It also suggests, as we discussed earlier in this book, that when we take risks and move beyond the boundaries of the familiar, we grow and can never return to the familiar as quite the same person we were before.

Looked at in another way, we can go home again. In fact, going home is what we have all come to the Earth to do. Each moment of our lives and our careers is part of a long adventure of awareness and learning leading us back to our home. As T.S. Eliot said so eloquently, "And the end of all of our exploring will be to arrive at the place from which we started and know it for the first time."

Why, then, do you think so many of us lead a bizarre existence denying who we are and the fact that we are going home? Why do we puff ourselves up and pretend we are separate and alone, that we are isolated and random occurrences in an uncaring universe? Why do we choose this as our battle cry when the truth is we are now and always will be destined to return to where we started—to the heart of God? If we make the connection between this awareness and some of the other topics we have explored in these pages, if we remember that everything and everyone is our teacher, and that each moment is another opportunity to learn and to remember that our lives are about discovering and demonstrating greater authenticity, then you will know that you can go home again. You will discover it is the only conclusion you can draw. And with this realization we think the jig, as they say, will be up!

Of course, those who want to keep the Dance of Illusion going can pretend that life has to be hard and can go on creating greater amounts of pain. But those who want to finish this awkward and stumbling dance of illusion, those who want to accept that we have a lot to do with both the outcome or the quality of our journey, can choose to return to a state of greater innocence, authenticity and trust. Indeed, for those who are willing to remember who we are and why we are here, life as we live it and work as we do it can become joyful, engaged experiences on our way home.

TODAY'S REFLECTION

Home is where my heart is. Home is where I am headed and where I have always resided. Today I will remember that I have already arrived. That I am home. Today I will remember that all I have to do is to open my heart and express my natural love for life and for this journey. Today I will remember that my reason for being here on the Earth is to celebrate the uniqueness, diversity and wonder in everyone I meet and in everything I do.

◆

Explore Etc.
(Eternally Traveling Consciousness)

When man rediscovers his loving he will,
for the second time, discover fire!
◦⟦ Pierre Teilhard de Chardin ⟧◦

Used as an acronym for Eternally Traveling Consciousness, "etc." becomes a much needed and gentle "whack on the side of the head." It becomes an obvious and yet effective way to remind us of a way to live and grow that is unlimited and ever expanding.

"Etc." A term designed to release us from a fantasy that many of us hold, a fantasy about a reward for the game of life, a reward for those of us who do good things and live a "right" life. Heaven, a place that is better, more valuable, more satisfying, more elevated than this one. Heaven or Nirvana, the place where some of us go when we graduate from the tumult of this thing called "life."

But with just these three letters ("etc.") we are reminded that this belief in "heaven" as a reward is another of those beliefs, like Hesse's summer house, that significantly limit us. We have a number of examples from our own lives in which this belief has proven to be a limiter, but we also each have an experience with one of our parents that stands our as particularly poignant.

Sedena's mother was a remarkable woman. She gave birth to seven children as the wife of a Navy chief petty officer who was often either at sea or moving the family from one home port to another. But even with all of the challenges, one of the things people who knew her always said was that Sedena's mother had the ability to turn lemons into lemonade.

Sedena's mother loved to travel. Even though it was not possible to travel to a lot, especially with seven children and on a chief petty officer's salary, she never lost her enthusiasm. "Well, one of these days," she would say. "Can't do it now, but time will come."

Sadly, the time the did not come, and Sedena's mother never got the chance to travel to the Holy Land sites in Israel she hoped to visit or to some of the European countries where her ancestors lived. Waiting until the kids were grown, waiting for an easier time, waiting until she and Sedena's dad retired, proved to be too long. The reward never materialized.

In the case of George's father, the story is a little different, but the outcome is the same. After a lifetime of very hard work and dedication to supporting his family and providing them with all of the things he never had, after working twelve- and fourteen-hour days at jobs he did not enjoy, after looking forward to the day he could travel and do all of the things he had never done, when that time came he had heart and artery problems that limited his mobility, preventing him from doing what he had worked hard for all of his life.

We are not suggesting that the dreams and goals we hold for the future are bogus or will never be realized. We are using these examples to show how our focus on future goals sometimes can preclude us from living in the "now." Our future goals can become fantasies, carrots that don't always turn out to be edible. We are also using these examples as a way of poking some holes in that old myth about rosy futures justifying unhappy, unpleasant and inauthentic present moments.

After all, as great as the possibility of some future states may be, most of us have never had a vacation that went on forever or a goal that once achieved remained forever satisfying. Have you ever felt that a task completed provided you with sufficient gratification to allow you to rest forever on your laurels? Have you ever had a vacation that went on forever or a goal that once you achieved it satisfied you completely?

How is it possible that this belief in a "permanent vacation at the end of the rainbow" has remained one of the major factors motivating humanity throughout much of recorded history? We know from personal experience, of course, that this is a hard carrot to give up, especially when we consider the amount of pain and suffering we have invested pursuing this belief. At the same time, if we are honest we have to ask ourselves some telling questions. What if our search for a "permanent vacation" is actually creating a lot more pain and suffering than it is relieving? What if there is a stronger and truer motivation for doing a good job and living a more aligned life? What if there is another belief that will not blind us to a greater truth or, in the end, rob us of our power, but instead will assist us in clearing our vision?

LIFE AS A CONTINUUM

How do you answer some of these questions? What if, instead of looking at your life and your career from a goal-oriented or prize-related perspective, you define life and work and whatever lies beyond them as a process, a never-ending experience, a kind of "evermoreness"?

We believe the concept of "eternally traveling consciousness" allows us to re-align our thinking about the purpose of life and work and even the meaning of death. For if there is a "neverendingness," then each thing we do becomes more than something to get through or to get done. Each activity, each encounter, becomes something to enjoy, to learn from and to experience. There is no "then" more important than this "now." There is no lingering anticipation or expectation of something next or more to come. Each now becomes a choice point, one of an endless number of moments in time in which we have the opportunity to select what we do and how we do it. Notice there is no "why do it" in this scenario. "Why" is goal-oriented. The concept of "etc." is all about "how."

This may seem like a very simplistic concept and it is! But who said that the underlying concept that motivates you has to be complicated? Why do you need to give in to the delusions of an ego that has been trained to inflate and measure its importance by the degree of conundrum it faces, the amount of reward that is associated with the conundrum's solution and the amount of expectation about what challenges need to be overcome next. Are we donkeys that need these carrots? Is it necessary that we be led around by our desire for a permanent vacation or a condo in a retirement community in the sky where there are no pets, no children and nothing to disturb the deathly quite of the place? Really, why would we want this kind of sterilized, sanitized existence when we can be living a natural process that comes from staying present in each moment and doing whatever needs to be done for its own sake, as joyfully, as authentically and, as well as possible?

If you give "etc." a chance, it will revolutionize not only your personal life but your career as well. "Etc." (eternally traveling consciousness) changes every aspect of life because the fundamental purpose and meaning of life changes. Suddenly the power games, the greed and lust games, the separation and acquisition games, the recognition and achievement games, the wealth and poverty games and all the other variations on the "superiority and inferiority game" become not only silly, but self-defeating.

Indeed, if we are all in a cycle of continuousness and each "now" is connected to every other "now," it becomes quickly and unarguably apparent that what each of us does in this "now" will affect what each of us does in the next.

NOT FOR OUR SINS BUT BY THEM

"Etc." is not a new concept. Many religions and spiritual sects have championed it under other names. Christmas Humphries, the Englishmen credited with bringing Buddhism to England, is reputed to have defined Karma as the condition in which we are punished by our sins and not for them. In our experience this is certainly true. And what are our sins but the errors and mistakes we commit primarily against ourselves and others often under the mistaken belief we are not connected to all things at all times?

Like children who commit blatant infractions of well-known rules, many of us move through our lives committing silly injustices and sins against ourselves and others in the belief that as soon as we get through it, "it" is over. Contrary to our limited consciousness, it is not even our job to declare "it" over. It's God's job or whatever you call the power that organizes and orchestrates this mystery we all reside within. "Over" occurs when all the related actions and interactions are complete or are somehow understood or declared complete. And since each action produces a series of connected and interconnected reactions, "over" is a very hard thing to determine.

Unless, of course, we use "etc." to help us remember that life is a wonderfully spiraling "ever-more-ness." Each part connects to the next. Each learning or failure to learn contributes to the next doing, to the next learning and opening. Each experience fully engages us in a statement of our readiness for the next. In this way, we are not rewarded by being allowed to go on to the next experience; we are simply following the natural order of things. In this way, we come to understand that each experience is simply another course credit in this giant university called Consciousness. And beyond Earth there are, no doubt, other universities and other courses. In "etc." there is never an end, always another step, another sharing, another expression of our loving.

With "etc." to guide us, we need never again complain of not having enough to do, of not being challenged, of not having value because this and all other universes are filled with more doings, more knowings. With "etc." there is never a conclusion, always a process bringing us into greater consciousness, greater fullness and joy, greater compassion, greater oneness, greater acceptance of what we have come here to demonstrate—that we are a more aware spark in the fire that is God.

TODAY'S REFLECTION:

This moment is not an end but part of a continuous process in which I am connected to all beings and all things through every thought, word, intention and action. I am a part of the never-endingness called God. Each "now" is my opportunity, one of an endless series of "nows" in which I can enjoy, learn, and demonstrate more of the wisdom and wonder that flows through me. When I stop looking for goals, results, and rewards and start being present, I am one with all that is. "etc," "etc," "etc."

Live Now and Forever

If not now when? If not me, who?
-[William Shakespeare]-

We have talked about many ideas in this book, and one of the most important is that we have the power to live out our dreams and to fulfill our destinies, to be who we have come here to the Earth to be in our personal lives, in our careers and in the world. Yes, this power is available to each and every one of us in every present moment.

We have explored the fact that each moment is a choice point and that in each moment we can we make truly valid, appropriate and aligned choices. Only in each present moment can we alter, upgrade, transform, align, test, explore, express, and experience our lives. All else is mind-full-ness and illusion. All else is a game we play that is not constructive or creative but is negative and repetitive. We also have determined that the amount of attention and awareness we bring to each choice determines not only the integrity and quality of that choice, but as a consequence, the integrity and authenticity of our lives.

We have agreed that there is an unlimited amount of learning and possibility available to us if we pay attention within each present moment. Living in this way and exploring these opportunities is not just refreshing, but rejuvenating, not just possible, but ultimately essential. When we are present in each moment, each moment is a new beginning.

We have explored ways we can find our way out of the prison of time or what Eckhart Tolle calls, "psychological time" and agreed that we do not have to declare an end to time. Instead, all we have to do is allow our attention to move naturally and effortlessly from one moment to the next. Each present moment carries with it an amnesty in the form of both a divine and a self pardon.

And we have learned that life is not so much being right or perfect or even about "doing" but about learning, curiosity, experimentation, and the day-by-day experience of being awake to our purpose and meaning.

So the present moment, what we call "now," is the only place any of this truly exists. By comparison "then" exists only as a conceit of our mind and to sustain this conceit we have to expend an enormous amount of effort and energy. We have to go away from all that is to some other place where a lot of things once were or to a place that some thing might someday be.

THE MAGIC KNIFE

There is a wonderful Zen story that talks about struggle. Once there was a humble man who owned a magic knife. In fact, the knife was so magical that people came from the farthest corners of the kingdom to visit him and discover the secret of why his knife never needed sharpening.

For many years a young man who lived in the same village as the man with the magic knife watched this procession of people gaze in wonder at this mystery. Finally, after building up his courage the young man, who had by now grown into his middle years, approached the man with the magic knife.

He said, "I have lived here in your village all my life and for many years have watched countless numbers of people come to learn the secret of the magic knife and none have discovered it. Would you grant this poor peasant a question?"

"Of course," said the knife's owner. "I will grant you as many questions as you wish."

"Is the knife made of some kind of special, secret material?"

"No."

"Do you sharpen it with a magic stone?"

"No."

"Then what accounts for the fact that it never gets dull? Do you practice black magic?"

"No," said the man who owned the knife. "There is no magic. I am a poor man, and I decided long ago that the time and cost of sharpening my knife would be too great. I also realized that each time I sharpen it, the knife becomes a little thinner. So instead, I decided to always cut between the bones not through them. In doing so the knife never encounters obstacles and never needs sharpening."

Obviously, in a world such as ours, where there are so many pulls and pushes, so much pressure to keep running—sometimes running just to stay in place—a lot of us forget this simple premise. As a result, the knife called our life gets dull. In fact, the more we rely on the promptings of our egos and our minds, the more we try to bully our way through our lives, the more we end up trying to cut through the bones of life rather than slowing down, breathing and staying present in all of the miraculous and wonderful spaces between the bones. Yes, a lot of us spend a lot of our time doing things the hard way, constantly looking for some magic or secret formula to save us and in the process overlook the simple, obvious and wise things we know work.

We also encumber our "cutting" by dragging the stuff of our past called memories and rules with us into each present moment and compounding this further by projecting these onto our future. As a result, we try to saw and chop our way through life with anticipation, worry and doubt as our companions and then we wonder why we are exhausted and our blade is dull. Most of us, in fact, are so occupied with all of this struggling, so entangled and committed to this illusion, we forget that difficult, complex and confused are not normal states.

By comparison, for those of us who remember who we are and what we are here to do, for those of us who let go of the past and avoid the temptation to anticipate or fret over the future, for those of us who live in the present, there can be a lot less pain, confusion and frustration and a lot more of the blade of opportunity.

"Energy follows thought, manifestation follows energy. Thoughts persisted in produce states of consciousness, states of consciousness persisted in produce physical actions." You know this is the way you create your life. This is the way you invent your future. And the remarkable thing is that you do not have to do anything to experience greater meaning and purpose in each "now." All you have to do is to stop trying to cut through the bone and gristle of life and start using the knife of your consciousness to wake up in this and every "now."

THE LAW OF THE OBVIOUS

This law demonstrates itself in many ways. To breathe in we must exhale. We must make room for the incoming breath. The next breath declares itself and demands our attention. We do not need to do anything special to breathe. It is a very natural process. In fact, God made it difficult not to breathe. We have to work hard to stop or limit our breath. By comparison if we pay attention, if we focus on our breath flowing in and out, we find we cannot think at the same time. To think we must take our attention away from this life-giving process.

Conversely, if we breathe fully, filling our lungs with breath on the inhale and contracting on the exhale, we bring greater clarity and power into our bodies and our brains. In fact, the average person takes over 20,000 breaths each day. If we breathe fully, that's over 20,000 opportunities to oxygenate our bodies each day, 20,000 times to remember to live in the "now." If we increase the number of breaths we take, increase them by only five per cent, then we will have approximately 2,700,000 more opportunities in our lifetimes to remember.

If you have difficulty breathing properly or feel a little unnatural breathing fully in the way we have just described, spend a few minutes watching a baby breathe. Notice how natural it is. Notice that it is possible to breathe fully, naturally and effortlessly and, when you do, to live life fully.

THE LESSON OF THE BREATH

If we live our lives exactly as we breathe and let each moment simply declare itself, we can discover that all we require is in the "now." We can remember that just as we do not try to hold on to a previous breath, or keep track of where it has gone or consider why it departed and what its departure means, we do not have to try to hold on to the past. Just as we do not spend a lot of time anticipating when the next breath will arrive, if it will arrive and what it will be like, we do not have to anticipate the future. Just as we do not spend time worrying about how we will appear to others when we take our next breath, if we are dressed properly to breathe or how our breath compares to the breath of another, we do not need to do any of this or any of the other silly things we do with respect to any other aspect of our lives or our careers.

Instead, all we have to do is to breathe and accept the living of each moment, and in the same way that we accept each breath there will be newness, and uniqueness, discovery and wonder, learning and knowing in each moment. Each moment will be unclouded and untarnished.

Explore this for yourself. Allow each moment to lead you to the next and in each moment do whatever you can to be awake and committed to your authentic and original life and a new forever will always be happening. And each forever is now. And each "now" can be joyful and innocent. In each present moment you can have as much meaning and purpose, as much bliss and contentment, as you choose. Now! Now! Now! Now and Forever.

TODAY'S REFLECTION

With each breath I take today I will remember that this is "now" and "now" is all that I require! Today I will breathe deeply taking in life in all of its fullness. Now. Here and Now. Now and Forever!

◆

It's as Simple as That, Olie!

*We don't experience the world fully
unless we are willing to give everything away.*

-◦[Pema Chodron]◦-

This short chapter is all about loving, about remembering to live in the present and to surrender to the harmony of your authentic self. It's about all the lessons you have explored in this book and are reminded of countless times each day in your own life. It's about finally putting what you already know into practice more frequently and with greater compassion and opening more courageously to what you do not know so that your life and your career reflect more of the meaning and purpose you are called to express.

Before closing we also want to revisit the agreement you made at the beginning of our journey together, the agreement not to pretend with yourself and with others that you do not have some things to learn and some beliefs to change. You've also been reminded of or introduced to beliefs and practices that can allow you to move beyond feelings of awkwardness and frustration, to let go of some of those limiting beliefs about not being worthy or competent enough and, as a result, not having enough success, love and joy in your life.

We trust you have found this to be an important agreement. You now know that to truly inherit greater meaning and purpose in your life you must willing to recommit to it every day for the rest of your life. As we have discussed many times, in order to stop all that huffing and puffing, the turning away from what troubles us and from those old and untrue stories about not knowing how we limit our lives, we have to commit anew each day to being who we truly are—one of the magnificent, wondrous instruments in this extraordinary orchestra called humanity.

Yes, the truth is—life is remarkable. The truth is—life is extraordinary. The truth is—life is simple. So please keep it simple. If you really want to be finished with the confusion and pain and with the complications that come from living everywhere but in the "now," then all you have to do is identify what is not working and start doing more of what you discover does work and to explore new options and strategies each day, the kind of strategies that keep you wide awake and moving closer to the edge rather than allowing you to go to sleep in the middle.

These few simple guidelines and, of course, some of the other recommendations and strategies we have explored, can assist you in creating more purpose and meaning in your life. As Laurel was so fond of saying to Hardy, "It's as simple as that, Olie!"

A LAST STORY

In an early chapter we mentioned an Egyptian legend about the Feather of Truth. We thought it fitting to close with another story about purity, the purity of our consciousness. This story is from the Zen tradition.

There was a wise old monk who for more years than anyone could count had been sought out by those who were looking for the secret to life's mysteries. The time had come, however, for the old monk to leave his body and pass into the other realms beyond this one. He had mastered his own life's challenges and had lived a life of long and true service.

As he lay on his pallet in a hillside meadow beside a bubbling stream preparing for his journey, however, a young fawn passed in front of him. "How beautiful," he thought, and almost allowed himself to hold this image. But then, just as the thought formed, he realized that as gentle and beautiful as the fawn might appear, it too was part of the illusion that his mind was creating and sustaining.

So with a smile, he bid goodbye to the fawn, turned his focus inward to his heart and his breath and in this way released his attachment to the Earth. With this the wise old monk let go into forever.

Just as the heart must be pure enough to balance a feather, so the mind must be free enough to be available to the truth. The Indian mystic Tilopa is reputed to have encouraged us to "have a mind that is open to everything and attached to nothing."

So we celebrate your courage and wish you a joyful and remarkable journey into greater and greater levels of your authenticity. Eternal vigilance. Eternal now. Eternally traveling consciousness.

God Speed!
God Bless!
God Is!

TODAY'S REFLECTION

Whenever I have enough of feeling limited and separate, whenever I get caught in feelings of lack and fear, all I have to do to remember who I am is to follow my breath, listen in the silence and keep my heart open. It's that simple! So today I will keep it simple! I will be stay in the present, express my gratitude for all that I have, all that I know, all that I can do, and participate fully in this extraordinary opportunity called my life.

50 Ways to Improve Your Authenticity Quotient

Here are some things you can do to live a more authentic life at work and at home.

1. Do whatever you do as if it were the most important thing you will ever do.
2. Love yourself, love what you do, love who you do it with.
3. Follow your passion and your heart with courage and commitment.
4. Trust in your Higher Power or spiritual connection.
5. Exercise your creativity in all that you do.
6. Trust yourself and others.
7. Seek to leave every circumstance and person better than when you encounter them.
8. Laugh more often and out loud.
9. Play more—with your children, friends, family, co-workers, and yourself.
10. Seek ways to be of service to life.
11. Allow yourself to make mistakes.
12. Express your concern for others.
13. Compliment and acknowledge others and yourself often.
14. Say yes to life, new experience, and new challenges often.
15. Be compassionate to others and to yourself.
16. Be grateful for all experiences, events and experiences in your world daily.
17. Practice open and honest communication.
18. Look for the primary learning in everything you do.
19. Lead by example.
20. Look for things to celebrate everyday in all aspects of your life.
21. Practice empathy and forgiveness.
22. Take a lot more risks.
23. Learn to listen to others and to yourself.
24. Stop procrastinating.
25. Ask others what they need and then do what you can to serve those needs.

26. Develop greater self-discipline.
27. Seek to understand, not to defend.
28. Be generous—with your time, your ideas, your energy, your resources.
29. Speak your truth with sensitivity.
30. Seek alignment with your truth above acceptance by others.
31. Learn the difference between knowing and believing.
32. Set good boundaries.
33. Express anonymous acts of kindness and generosity.
34. Mentor others whenever possible.
35. Give without fear of consequences or expectation of reward.
36. Support vulnerable beginnings—ideas, efforts, risks.
37. Do something just for fun every day.
38. Acknowledge others.
39. Contribute to the well being of your community.
40. Experiment with new behaviors and ideas.
41. Honor the earth and all life forms.
42. Be vulnerable.
43. Practice all things with a beginners mind.
44. Share what you know and admit what you do not.
45. Pay attention to your physical, emotional, mental, and spiritual needs.
46. Express your love more frequently and fully.
47. Be grateful for every opportunity, experience, object, and person in your life.
48. View life as a school from which you never graduate
49. Trust in the goodness of life.
50. Live each day as if it were your last day on earth.

Twelve Qualities that Contribute to Greater Authenticity in Individuals

Awareness

Understanding

Truth

Excellence

Neutrality

Trust

Intuition

Caring and Courage

Integrity

Tolerance

Yielding

Twelve Qualities that Contribute to Greater Authenticity in Organizations

Awareness of social responsibility

Understanding long-term needs of customers, employees, and financial stakeholders

Trust within the organization, between its leaders and employees, and its customers

Honesty at all levels within the organization and with the public at large

Employee satisfaction and retention

Nurturing of ideas, New Practices, New Products, and Services

Training and investment in employees

Innovation in products, services, strategies, and technology

Commitment to excellence in quality and customer service

Investment in the future

Teamwork development

Yield on investment in people, resources, products, and services

About the Authors

George and Sedena Cappannelli are a genuine Renaissance couple. As established writers, business consultants, political advisors, executive/personal coaches, and artists, the Cappannellis combine creativity and innovation with organizational change and self-development expertise to help individuals, families and organizations succeed. With over twenty-five years of experience with organizations and with individuals around the globe, the Cappannellis help redefine vision, develop new strategies, build strong teams and increase profitability and performance for organizations such as Boeing, NASA, Sun Microsystems, The Walt Disney Co., *The Los Angeles Times*, PepsiCo, TRW, The U.S. Navy, Hughes, Oracle, Pacific Bell and for thousands of people who attend their public seminars.

Under the banner of The Information & Training Company, an organization he founded eighteen years ago, George serves as an organizational consultant and executive coach to a number of Fortune 500 Companies, government agencies and national associations. Additionally, he has served as a special advisor in presidential and senatorial campaigns and has worked with a number of world leaders including Golda Meir, Lech Walesa, Desmond Tutu, Mother Teresa and the Dalai Lama. He also is an award-winning sculptor and film and television producer/director.

Sedena leads an equally dynamic life. In addition to the consulting and training work she does with The Information & Training Company, as the president of About Life, Inc., she creates innovative corporate and public programs focusing on empowerment and renewal for women. These programs and her personal coaching strategies are based on a unique combination of both Eastern and Native American practices as well as contemporary healing modalities. In addition Sedena is a talented actor and spokesperson and is the writer/producer of a series of story concepts for television that focus on personal and global change.

They live in Fountain Hills, Arizona.

BOOKS OF INTEREST

Jump Start Your Business Brain: Win More, Lose Less and Make More Money
By Doug Hall

Bestselling business author Doug Hall knows that in today's world, everyone needs innovation, inspiration, and illumination. You have to sell your ideas, your services, your products, and even yourself. In *Jump Start Your Business Brain*, Hall shares data-proven methods that can make sales, marketing, and business development measurably more effective.

All the methods detailed in Jump Start are backed by hard data. Grounded in statistical analysis of more than 4,000 new products and services and more than 6,000 business development teams, each method has been real-world validated during inventive projects with such leading companies as American Express, Johnson & Johnson, John Hancock Insurance, The Ford Motor Company, Procter & Gamble, Frito-Lay, Circuit City, and Walt Disney.

In today's competitive, time-compressed marketplace, *Jump Start Your Business Brain* reveals the impact of a back-to-basics, customer-focused approach to business, helping readers measurably increase their effectiveness—and the bottom line.

It's no longer enough just to show up. Nor is it good enough to follow the same old approach, year after year. *Jump Start Your Business Brain* contains big, bold, bright new ideas AND provides the proven measure of their likely success if implemented.

Life doesn't get any more straightforward than this—Jump Start today for increased revenue, recognition, and reward.

Paperback
Price $16.99   ISBN: 1-57860-179-7

To order call: 1-800-343-4499 / www.emmisbooks.com

Emmis Books   1700 Madison Road   Cincinnati Ohio 45206

BOOKS OF INTEREST

Defying Gravity: A Celebration of Late-Blooming Women
By Prill Boyle

It's never too late to pursue your dreams. The daring and determined women chronicled in *Defying Gravity* prove that it can take years for the right moment to arrive. But when that opportunity finally comes forth, when the right mix of courage and "it's now or never" bubbles up inside, the spirit overrides the fear and magic happens. Clearly, it's nothing less than life changing, a reawakening to the future.

Wini Yunker was a 65-year-old Kentucky woman who waited 39 years to fulfill her dream of joining the Peace Corps. Jo Fuchs Luscombe had never even run a PTA meeting before her mid-30's; at age 48 she won a seat in the Connecticut House of Representatives, and later became Republican Minority Whip. Patricia Symonds, a professor of anthropology at Brown University, didn't graduate from high school until her 40's. Jane Work began her career as a Gestalt therapist in her mid-60's and just retired last year at 84.

Every day, regular women are accomplishing extraordinary things later in life. Sharing these in-depth, inspiring accounts, author Prill Boyle pays tribute to women who discovered their gifts midlife and refused to let go of their dreams. Since writing the book, she's heard one question again and again: "Do you think there's still hope for me?" The answer is always an emphatic "Yes!"

Defying Gravity, in other words, is about hope. If you think you're too old or too weighed down to fly, these stories will dismiss your doubts.

Hardcover
Price: $20.00   ISBN: 1-57860-154-1

To order call: 1-800-343-4499 / www.emmisbooks.com
Emmis Books   1700 Madison Road   Cincinnati Ohio 45206

W9-BJM-664

Coping in a

DYSFUNCTIONAL FAMILY

CHAVEZ HIGH SCHOOL
LIBRARY
HOUSTON, TEXAS

Raymond M. Jamiolkowski

THE ROSEN PUBLISHING GROUP, INC./NEW YORK

Published in 1993, 1998 by The Rosen Publishing Group, Inc.
29 East 21st Street, New York, NY 10010

Copyright 1993, 1998 by Raymond M. Jamiolkowski

All rights reserved. No part of this book may be reproduced in any form
without permission in writing from the publisher, except by a reviewer.

Revised Edition 1998

Library of Congress Cataloging-in-Publication Data
Jamiolkowski, Raymond M.
    Coping in a dysfunctional family / Raymond M.
Jamiolkowski.
        p. cm.
    Includes bibliographical references and index.
    Summary: Discusses different causes of family problems,
including physical and emotional abuse, overprotection,
depression or mental illness, and perfectionism and suggests ways of deal-
ing with each situation.
    ISBN 0-8239-2715-6
    1. Problem families—United States—Psychological aspects—
Juvenile literature. 2. Self-help techniques—Juvenile literature.
[Family problems. 2. Parent and child.] I. Title.
HV699.J35 1998
362.82—dc20   93-13665
                                                            CIP
                                                             AC

Manufactured in the United States of America

About the Author

Raymond M. Jamiolkowski is a guidance counselor at Naperville Central High School, Naperville, Illinois. He holds a bachelor's degree in elementary education and a master's in guidance and counseling from Northern Illinois University, DeKalb, Illinois, and he did further graduate work at the University of Florida, Gainesville. Ray Jamiolkowski has taught grades two, five, and six at Edwin Aldrin Elementary School in Schaumburg, Illinois, and served as elementary school guidance counselor and testing and research specialist for the Marion County Schools in Ocala, Florida.

He lives in Naperville with his wife, Mel, his daughter, Jenny, and his son, David.

To Mel,
whose support and encouragement
have helped me to
understand what it means
to be a family

Contents

What's Wrong with My Family?

Karli recently turned down a full scholarship to the state university. She decided to stay home and go to the local community college. Karli had worked all of her life so that she could major in dance at the school three hundred miles from her home. She gave up her dream because she was worried about her little brother. She was afraid to think about what her mother might do to him if she wasn't there to protect him.

Michael has never lived up to his parents' expectations. His parents kept searching to learn what was wrong with their son. Their doctor prescribed one medication after another. Michael had seen three psychologists. Why didn't he try out for sports teams or the newspaper? Why didn't he do better in school? Michael knew how to get better grades, but what was the point? His parents would still never be satisfied. All Michael ever wanted to do was to draw cartoons. When his grades still hadn't improved, his parents forbid him to draw all summer.

Tawanda is afraid to go home. Her brother Tyrone might be there. When she is alone with him, he always makes fun of her. He likes to embarrass her.

1

Several times he has knocked her down or held her to the floor. Lately he has been grabbing her from behind and reaching across her chest. She begs him to stop, but he only laughs at her. Tyrone looks her in the eye and says, "If you even think about telling anyone, it'll be ten times worse."

What Is a Dysfunctional Family?

A dysfunctional family is one that fails to meet the basic needs of one or more of its members. These basic needs are survival, safety and security, love and belonging, self-esteem, growth, and development of skills for independent living. The psychologist Abraham Maslow identified these needs. Each must be met for an individual to function and contribute to society.

The structure of a family doesn't determine dysfunction. Single parents, stepparents, adoptive parents, foster parents, divorced parents, aunts, uncles, grandparents, and married parents are all able to contribute to healthy, functioning families. Families face significant hurdles after divorce and/or remarriage, but families regularly overcome those hurdles. If family members are committed to allowing other family members to meet their personal needs, a family will function in a healthy manner.

One would think that a family that does not meet the needs of its members would quickly disintegrate. In reality, dysfunctional families tend to stick together. Sadly, the sickness or the dysfunction binds them to one another. In the examples above, Karli is bound to her family by the fear of her brother's abuse; Michael's family is committed to the quest to find out what's wrong with him; and Tawanda is stuck by her fear of Tyrone. She is waiting for her parents to uncover on their own the horror she faces. These families have secrets. They would rather live with sickness than admit to outsiders that something has gone seriously wrong.

Members of dysfunctional families play a variety of roles. Sometimes one member is the aggressor, addict, abuser, or neglector. One or more members may play the role of the victim. Often one or more members may play the role of the codependent. A codependent is a generally well-intended person whose actions tend to protect the abuser, addict, or aggressor. The codependent, while trying to help, actually enables the dysfunction to continue. The codependent wife of an alcoholic makes excuses for her husband, calls him in sick to work, and generally tries to take the pressure off him. These actions make it easier for him to continue to drink. Eventually his disease consumes her. Codependents suffer silently throughout their family's dysfunctional behavior.

What Is a Functional Family?

A family is functional when each member has his or her needs met. As you have seen, these needs include: survival, safety and security, love and belonging, self-esteem, growth, and development of skills for independent living.

Needs, however, are not the same as wants, wishes, or desires. Being part of a family means cooperating so that every member is able to have his needs fulfilled. Each family member takes personal responsibility to contribute toward his own growth in every way possible. Functional family members are active. They rely on each other for advice and encouragement, but they contribute to the family, take responsibility for their actions, and solve their own problems.

Let's explore the needs of family members.

Survival

The most basic human need is survival. A family needs to provide each member with food, water, shelter, clothing, and health care. Without each of these, members could not live. Some homeless families meet these needs quite well by taking advantage of government assistance, food pantries, warming shelters, public housing, and free medical clinics. On the other hand, middle- and upper-class families may regularly and intentionally neglect these basic needs of their children. Some withhold food or medical care for long periods. Others neglect their teens' need for shelter by locking them out of the house during the course of a fight or an argument. Parents who neglect the survival needs of their children are breaking the law. Fortunately, states and counties have agencies to assist and defend neglected children.

Safety and Security

A family should be a place where every member feels safe and secure. Unfortunately, in many families, violence is a constant threat. Sometimes parents physically abuse children. Other times one sibling abuses another without restraint by the parents. Some spouses beat each other. In some cases, older teens beat their own parents or grandparents. When such violence occurs in a home, no one feels secure.

In some families sexual abuse, or incest, can occur. Any sexual contact between family members, other than the parents, is abuse. Sexual contact includes sexual intercourse; unwanted touching of genitals, breasts, or buttocks; or exposure to pornographic images. Incest is so strongly unacceptable to most people that victims are often ashamed to seek help. Incest often ends up becoming a lifelong family secret.

All states have laws to protect family members from physical and sexual assault. However, it is often difficult for victims to get the help and protection they need because they are afraid. They fear that a report to the proper agency will destroy the family, rather than treat the specific problem of abuse. Dysfunctional families continue to tolerate this sickness, unless family members have the courage to demand that it stop. Other family members need to support victims of abuse in order to bring a measure of safety and security to everyone.

Love and Belonging

People learn about love and belonging from their families. Every family member should feel accepted for who he or she is, rather than for accomplishments. A family's love should be unconditional. All members should feel valuable for being themselves. In a functional family, no one feels excluded from the family simply for doing something wrong.

Children learn to love through the example of their parents. If a child feels loved, he or she will learn to love other people. Without a parent's example, it is much more difficult to learn to love. Some children are fortunate enough to

5

have role models: aunts, uncles, and grandparents who are able to spend the time necessary to make a child feel loved. These cases are unfortunately too rare.

Self-Esteem

Self-esteem is the sense that one feels capable, valuable, and responsible. Families are very important in forming these feelings about ourselves. Most of the important things that people accomplish in life come about because they have the confidence and determination to succeed. People develop confidence and determination because they have a healthy amount of self-esteem. Self-esteem is not being proud, selfish, or conceited. Self-esteem is an understanding that you are a capable, worthwhile person. People with self-esteem treat others as they would like to be treated themselves. Self-esteem is what helps people have the courage to take an unpopular stand because they know that it is the right thing to do. People with low self-esteem find it difficult to make decisions, reach their own goals, or help other people.

Families differ in how much self-esteem is passed on to the children. A family has become dysfunctional when any of its members are regularly made to feel stupid, worthless, and incompetent. That doesn't mean that joking, teasing, or an occasional angry word is always unhealthy, but a family that constantly tears down the self-esteem of one or more of its members is not functioning in a healthy way.

Growth

Families promote growth. When a family meets all its members' needs for survival, safety, security, love, and belonging, the conditions are right for everyone to grow. Like plants that need rich soil, water, and sunlight to grow, a family must have its needs met before the members can grow emotionally.

Growth means change. For change to occur, everyone needs to communicate his or her needs and listen to the needs of the other members of the family. Everyone in a family has two major responsibilities. One is to express his or her feelings, both good and bad. The other is to listen to others to understand their needs as well. Communication is essential for a healthy family to function and to grow. The teen years tend to be a time of tremendous emotional change and growth. Sometimes teenagers need to take the initiative to open up the lines of communication within their families.

When a family is growing, every member feels support and encouragement. If a family's home is a constant battleground over schoolwork, friends, chores, or other responsibilities, growth stops.

Skills for Independent Living

One of the major responsibilities of parents is to give their children the skills that they will need to live on their own. Parents who do too much for their children can prevent them from learning to solve problems for themselves. Teenagers need to schedule their own time, to spend their own money, to take care of their own grooming, to prepare meals for themselves, and to make decisions independently. Parents who continue to do too many of these things for their children slow the growth process.

7

Perfectionism stifles growth as well, since no one can perform every task perfectly. Teenagers with perfectionist parents tend to give up, feeling that it is better not to attempt a task at all than to do it less than perfectly.

Overprotective parents try to shield their children from any kind of pain or discomfort. By protecting their children from teasing, school problems, and everyday difficulties, these parents tend to dominate them emotionally. Overprotected teenagers have great difficulty breaking away from parents who previously have solved every problem for them. People build up their coping skills by experiencing loss in childhood. Overprotective parents shield their children from the experience of loss. Suicide is common among overprotected young people, since they are unable to think of alternatives on their own when problems arise.

How Families Become Dysfunctional

Most families start out with hopes of functioning in a healthy, productive way. In some way, however, many of these families break down. Just as parents teach children how to live healthy, happy lives, they can also pass on their harmful, unhealthy traits. As teens mature, they adopt their parents' dysfunctional habits. Addiction, mental illness, and other health problems can also lead to dysfunction or can be the result of it. Sometimes parents' only desire is the good of their family, but good intentions can turn into fanaticism, perfectionism, overprotection, or emotional abuse. In other families one member cannot clearly express needs and emotions.

This inability leads to anger and frustration, which may result in physical abuse, sexual abuse, or neglect.

Dysfunctional families put teens at risk in two ways:

➥ They are in danger of being harmed by the dysfunctional family member.

➥ They risk becoming dysfunctional themselves.

The chapters that follow describe families in crisis. They suggest ways that teens can help bring about change and cope with that dysfunction.

It's true that functional families can become dysfunctional. But it's never too late for a dysfunctional family to become healthy.

Are We a Dysfunctional Family?

Families differ greatly in the ways that they solve problems, communicate, and meet individual needs. One family may allow their children to make many decisions, giving them an opportunity to learn to predict and accept consequences. Another family may be very rules-oriented; each individual knows his or her responsibilities and is expected to fulfill them. However, if in both of these families members have their basic needs met, and the children are developing the skills to live independently one day, the family is functioning in a healthy way.

There is no way of clearly dividing all families into two groups: functional and dysfunctional. All families vary in the degree to which needs are met. Dysfunction is more like a continuum scale. Each family theoretically could be placed somewhere between the two extremes.

Completely Dysfunctional
No one in the family is thriving.

Completely Functional
Everyone is growing
in a healthy way.

In reality, few families are at either extreme. At the completely dysfunctional end, few families could withstand complete emotional and moral sickness. Dysfunctional families tend to stick together when one or more members are still healthy. At the far extreme, when no one is functional, the family would fall apart.

The completely functional extreme is unlikely to occur as well. Life is filled with too many difficulties and challenges for a family always to meet every member's needs. Some parents do wonderfully with preschoolers but have a difficult time adjusting to pre-adolescents. Other parents don't adjust to parenting until their children's teenage years. Our psychological development makes it extremely difficult for families to function perfectly all the time. During the junior high and high school years emotional changes occur so rapidly that parents and siblings have difficulty understanding what is happening to the teen.

A Family Functioning Quiz

So the question really should be: How well is my family functioning? Below is a simple quiz to help learn how your family is doing. Check off each item that applies to you or your family.

1. I often go to bed hungry because there is not enough food in the house.
2. My clothes are not appropriate for the weather and do not fit properly.
3. My parent(s) do not care if I do poorly in school.
4. One of my parents or siblings is a drug abuser.
5. My parent(s) talk much more about my bad qualities than my good qualities.

11

6. My parent(s) work late or are away on business much of the time.

7. Our family finances are worsened by gambling debts.

8. I can't talk to one of my parents because he or she is having emotional or psychological problems.

9. I am ashamed of my family's political or religious beliefs.

10. Someone in my family has been sexually abused by another family member.

11. I worry that a parent or sibling will injure me.

12. I worry that a parent or sibling will injure someone else in my family.

13. One of my parents or siblings abuses alcohol.

14. The whole family revolves around my physically or mentally challenged sibling.

15. I don't try in school anymore, because I can never live up to my parents' expectations.

16. My parents know that I have been living with a medical or dental problem, but they won't take me to the doctor or dentist.

17. I feel hopeless. I can't talk to anyone in my family about it.

The purpose of the quiz is to determine a starting point for understanding your family. One family may have only one item checked, yet be completely unable to function. Another family may have several checked, yet be working together, communicating, and struggling to overcome difficulties. Cooperation, communication, and compassion for one another are measures that can tell how well a family is functioning.

This book is designed with a twofold purpose. The first is to help teens and preteens identify families with serious challenges and make changes where possible. The other purpose is to suggest ways to cope with life when change is unlikely.

Alcoholics Anonymous (AA) is an organization that has helped millions to deal with alcoholism. Members of AA have found this portion of "The Serenity Prayer" of St. Francis of Assisi to be helpful in learning how to cope with their difficulties:

> "God grant me the serenity to accept
> the things I cannot change,
> Courage to change the things I can,
> And the Wisdom to know the difference."

Types of Dysfunctional Families

Since every family is different, dysfunctional families come in many different types. These families' problems tend to fall into one or more of twelve categories. Each type of family requires a different approach if improvement is to be made. Each type also needs to make a decision as to when and from whom to seek help, and whether it is better to try to cope with the dysfunction rather than seeking to change things on its own. Let's take a look at the categories.

Emotional Abuse
When words or actions damage the self-esteem of any member of a family, that person suffers from emotional abuse. In a functioning family, children develop confidence and determination. Emotional abuse makes them less able to solve their own problems.

Neglect

In every family the adults must take steps to provide for the basic survival needs of all members. Even economically impoverished families must take advantage of the resources of the church or the community to meet the needs of every family member. Parents who ignore basic medical, dental, nutritional, clothing, or shelter needs are guilty of neglect.

Overprotection

At the end of their teenage years, people need to have developed the skills necessary to live on their own. Children need their parents' protection to be safe. However, when a child has always been protected from pain, tragedy, and problems, he or she can have great difficulty coping as an adult. Overprotected teens need to develop independence and responsibility.

Sexual Abuse

Sexual abuse is an abuse of trust. Any sexual activity between a parent and a child or between siblings is sexual abuse. It may consist of inappropriate touching, fondling, the showing of pornographic pictures, or having sexual intercourse.

Perfectionism

Children who are expected to perform perfectly by their parents often view themselves as failures. Since they are never perfect, they never meet their goals or fulfill their parents' expectations. Perfectionists often feel that they no longer belong in their family, since they have not been able to meet the family's expectations.

Substance Abuse

Whether it be drug or alcohol abuse, substance abuse damages a family. Often an addict abuses other family members emotionally, sexually, or physically. The abuser isolates himself or herself from the rest of the family. This isolation damages the family's ability to grow.

Religious or Political Fanaticism

Religious and political beliefs are important in any healthy family. When members become fanatics, however, or join a religious cult, emotional and intellectual growth within a family often stops. Healthy families accept and tolerate differences among people.

Workaholic Parents

Family must be a top priority to parents. When the demands of work regularly prevent one or both parents from being with their family, no one feels valued. Children of workaholics often feel that they don't belong to a family. Some workaholic parents try to make up for their absence with gifts or money. But what children really need most are their parents.

Depression or Other Mental Illness

Mental and physical illness do not cause a family to be dysfunctional if the illness is being treated. However, untreated illness, including depression, is a form of neglect. Left untreated, mental illness can destroy the health of an entire family.

Abusive Sibling

Physical abuse makes everyone feel unsafe and insecure.

Whether the abuse is at the hands of a parent or a sibling, a family is dysfunctional as long as it continues. Physical and sexual abuse are never acceptable, no matter what the circumstances are.

Physically or Mentally Challenged Sibling
Well-intended parents sometimes direct most of their love and affection toward the most needy member of a family. Other siblings can feel emotionally neglected when their brother or sister is getting all the attention.

Compulsive Gambler
Family members feel unsafe when the family finances are put in jeopardy by a compulsive gambler. Illegal gambling brings additional risks to a family.

Am I Safe in My Family?

Dysfunction ranges from slight maladjustment to unhealthy and even dangerous. Once you determine that your family is dysfunctional, you need to assess whether or not you are safe. Parents who demand perfection may be detrimental to their children's self-esteem and can be emotionally harmful, but they do not threaten the children's safety. In cases like these, teens need to work out issues with their parents to make the family more supportive and understanding.

Sometimes, however, the dysfunction is so severe that it poses a threat to a teen's safety and survival. These cases include dysfunctions such as substance abuse, sexual abuse, physical abuse, and other life-threatening situations. If you feel at any time that your family puts your safety in jeopardy, you need to leave immediately and go to a safe place. Turn to a trusted family member, a close friend, or a shelter for victims of abuse. Ask a school counselor, a coach, a clergy member, or someone else you trust if they know of somewhere that you can stay if you need to leave your home. It's not running away from your problems. It's beginning to solve them. Dysfunctional families cannot start to work on their difficulties until every member feels physically safe and secure.

Where Can I Get Help?

Sometimes families can solve their own problems. Other times they need the help of a professional. Once you know you are physically safe, you can look at your family's problem. Members of a very committed family may be able to change themselves. They can improve communication, encourage growth, and foster self-esteem. Family members can work together to help fix the dysfunction. You can talk to a parent, an older sibling, or a favorite aunt or uncle to get advice and assistance in working through your problems. Turning inside your family for help can be very effective when the dysfunction is not severe.

Sometimes parents don't realize that their children feel neglected because the parents spend all their time at work. They may not intentionally smother a physically or mentally challenged sibling with all their attention and ignore the other siblings. In these cases, making the family aware of the problem and agreeing to work on it can be the first step toward becoming a healthy family.

Other dysfunctional families have problems too serious to solve on their own. They need an outsider to help them.

If your family is dysfunctional because of an addiction, the addicted person needs to get help from a therapist or a support group such as Alcoholics Anonymous or Narcotics Anonymous. You cannot change the addicted person, but you may be able to persuade him or her to seek help.

If your family is dysfunctional because of abuse or neglect, your community has many agencies, including the police department, that can help and protect you. The best first step in these cases is usually to tell a school counselor, social worker, or other trusted adult with some training in the areas of abuse and neglect.

At the end of this book is a list of organizations that can help dysfunctional families. Dysfunction is just like any other illness: it takes time to heal. Things won't get better overnight. But eventually they will, and getting help is the first step in the healing process.

Living in a Dysfunctional Family

Some families strongly resist change. You may find that no matter what you do, the addiction or abuse continues. In such a case it is necessary to cope within the dysfunctional family. Three strategies that can help you cope in difficult situations are to surround yourself with positive, strong, healthy people, to confide your problems to a trusted adult, and never to give up hope.

A family should be a place where people feel that they are loved and that they belong. If this is not the case in your family, you will find it helpful to make friends who care about you and whom you trust. Such friends will stick by you during the hardest times.

A trusted adult such as a school counselor, a social worker, a youth pastor, a clergy person, or an aunt or uncle can be extremely valuable in helping you to cope. If you need to take action to protect yourself or a sibling from abuse, this adult can support you. If your parent is addicted, this person can help you confront the parent about the severity of the problem. If your family needs a change of attitude, the trusted adult may help you find the right words.

Finally, coping is hoping. As long as a person has hope, he has life. Never give up hope that you will survive to become a healthy, well-adjusted, productive adult. All of your dreams are still possible.

Emotional Abuse

"Your room is a pit again. But what should I expect? After seeing your last report card, I figure you'll never learn to operate complicated machinery like a vacuum cleaner." Luke looked up at his mother as she began to pick up his clothes. He thought about getting up and helping, but he knew that whatever he did would be wrong. He had learned that the safest approach was to wait until his mother left the room with his dirty clothes and then begin to clean up the mess.

Luke wasn't really bothered by his mother's yelling. He was used to it. Even her critical comments didn't hurt very much anymore. He felt he deserved them. After listening to them all his life, Luke believed that he really was lazy, selfish, and stupid. He was fairly certain that he would never amount to anything.

The night Luke brought home his first high school report card, his mother's reaction had bothered him much more than this. All through junior high Luke had gotten low grades. He got Cs in classes that he liked; Ds and Fs were more common in classes that he didn't like. Luke had decided on his own that high school would be different. None of the teachers knew him. He had no reputation to live down. This was his chance for a fresh start. In August, Luke had told his mother that he was going to get As and Bs in high school. She had laughed sarcastically and said, "Yeah, right. After nine years of school you're going to turn it all around and get good grades. I'll believe it when I see the report card."

But Luke was determined. The first week of school he really tried. He worked at being organized and spent hours on his homework. He seemed to be off to a good start in everything except algebra. Luke was embarrassed to ask his teacher for help, but somehow he found the courage. Mr. Mullins had explained several problems to him, but there just wasn't enough time during class. Luke asked if he could come back for more help, and Mr. Mullins replied, "Fine. Meet me before or after school tomorrow."

Luke felt the most optimistic he ever had about school. He was finally going to be able to keep up in all his classes. There was one little problem though: Luke rode the bus. To get extra help from Mr. Mullins, he would need a ride to school in the morning or home in the afternoon. He asked his mother to give him a ride.

She responded, "Am I your personal chauffeur? You want me to get up extra early just because you can't learn math. Should I be punished because you were too lazy to do your homework? I don't think you're being fair to me, Luke." Luke dropped the issue and tried to figure out algebra on his own.

The third week of school, Luke came down with a stomach flu and missed three days of classes. He had a hard time making up the work when he got back. Some of the teachers suggested that he meet with them to catch up, but Luke knew that wasn't possible.

21

CHAVEZ HIGH SCHOOL
LIBRARY
HOUSTON, TEXAS

Discouraged, he continued to go to classes, but he was now lost in several of them. Everything seemed to build on the work from earlier in the year. Each day Luke seemed to understand less. Before he got his report card, Luke thought he was failing algebra. He was pleased to see that he was not. He wasn't really surprised, though, by the other three Ds.

He dropped the report card on the kitchen table and walked toward his room. His mother glanced at it. "Nice job, Luke. So much for all As and Bs."

For a moment Luke hated his mother. He wanted to scream at her at the top of his voice. But the feeling only lasted a moment. What good would it do to shout at her? He wasn't going to do any better next time. She would just make fun of him for "pretending" that he would. Luke went up to his room and turned on the stereo extra loud.

Luke's father worried that at this rate his son would have trouble graduating. He proposed a deal. If Luke got all As and Bs on the next report card, he could take driver's education, and if he had all As and Bs for the rest of the year, his father would buy him a car that summer.

This sounded great to Luke. He started calculating the possibilities of improving his marks. That night he overheard his parents arguing about the plan. His father said, "We have to do something to get the boy started. If we don't, we'll end up supporting him for the rest of our lives."

Luke was surprised that his mother didn't respond strongly to this pronouncement. She simply said, "There's no point in arguing with you about this. It's not as if there's a chance he'll ever do it."

Luke began the second quarter hopeful, but heavy-hearted. He wanted so much to be able to drive, but driving his own car was something he had not dared to dream. Luke worked diligently. He stayed up late studying. He risked ridicule by asking his friends to help him with his homework. His grade averages slowly came up. Two weeks before finals Luke's grades were: English B-minus, world history B-plus, earth science C-plus, and algebra C-minus. He was climbing a mountain, and the summit was in sight.

The earth science final would be a take-home test. Luke could check, research, and verify all the answers. His B was assured. Math was going to be tough. He would spend the rest of his time studying for that final. Luke had already figured out that he would need an A-minus to bring up his grade.

The tests were hard. World history turned out to be an essay test. Luke wasn't a great writer, but he worked right up until the time limit. There was nothing he could do now but wait.

Finally, ten days later, the report cards came out. Luke's grades were:

Course	Final Exam	Grade
Algebra	95%	B
English	82%	B-
Earth Science	88%	B
World History	79%	C+
PE	N/A	A-

Luke was caught completely off guard. He had worked so hard. He had earned an A on the algebra final. He had brought every one of his grades up. But the world history final dropped his grade to C-plus. His father was encouraging. Luke was sure that he remembered their agreement, but he didn't bring it up. He simply said, "Son, these are the best grades you've had in years."

His mother scanned the card and flipped it toward Luke. "I guess driver's ed will just have to wait until next year."

Luke was crushed, discouraged, disappointed, exhausted, and hopeless. He went up to his room. This time he didn't turn on the stereo. He sat on his bed and stared out the window with his hands balled into tight fists on his lap.

Options and Alternatives

To grow emotionally, people need encouragement the way flowers need sunshine. Without sunshine, a plant withers and dies. Without encouragement, a person's dreams and hopes die as well. The most important ingredient missing in Luke's life is encouragement. It is difficult to hope if you don't believe in yourself. Believing in yourself starts with someone else believing in you.

Luke's mother not only withheld encouragement, but she went out of her way to discourage her son. A lifetime of predictions that he would fail had led Luke to believe that failure was his destiny. After having been called lazy, selfish, and stupid since he was a toddler, Luke felt that the descriptions fit. People tend to live out the expectations of their parents. A child who is expected to do well in life usually does. A child who is expected to be a failure usually lives up to that expectation as well.

Luke must have a deep reserve of hope inside of him. At the beginning of high school, completely on his own, he decided that he had what it took to be successful in school. His self-image was shattered a few weeks later by the first-quarter grades. Even after that, Luke was able to use his father's incentive to pull himself together and bring up his grades. His improvement was phenomenal, but it was not good enough to satisfy his mother. Few people would be able to withstand all those defeats and still continue to struggle.

Luke's family is dysfunctional because it does not contribute to the self-esteem of all family members. Luke's mother not only is negligent in failing to build self-esteem in her son, she is actively causing damage with her comments to him. Without self-esteem, a person is not able to grow emotionally.

It is not uncommon for young people faced with emotional abuse like Luke's to consider suicide. In fact, suicide is the third leading cause of death among young people aged fifteen to twenty-four. Among people who attempt suicide, all share a common feeling: hopelessness. Emotional abuse leads to hopelessness. Although Luke's situation is not hopeless, his feelings are. For him to survive in his family, Luke needs to find hope, strength, support, and encouragement.

How Can I Cope?

Teenagers in a situation like Luke's need encouragement. Since he is not being encouraged at home, Luke needs to turn elsewhere for help. Everyone needs support. The support and encouragement of others help us feel safe and secure and know that we are loved and belong.

Seek Support

If you are experiencing feelings like Luke's, you may want to talk to a guidance counselor, social worker, trusted teacher, or youth leader at your church, temple, or mosque. It is rare for people to pick themselves up one day and say, "I have always thought of myself as a failure, but today I am going to become a success." Finding an older, more experienced person can be a good first step toward rebuilding self-esteem.

Family counseling is the quickest route to healing the hurt. If your parents have suggested counseling, don't fight it. Insist that they participate as well. If necessary, bring up the idea of family counseling yourself. Even if they are reluctant to try, you will have communicated your need to build your self-esteem. You can go to counseling on your own if they refuse. You will still be helping yourself.

Experience Success

Once you have begun to rebuild your confidence, a next step might be to start experiencing success. The best way to find success is to ask yourself what your talents are. Maybe you like drawing, talking to people, playing a musical instrument, horseback riding, or playing a particular sport. If you like to draw, join the newspaper or yearbook staff. If you enjoy talking to other people, become a peer tutor or peer counselor. If you enjoy playing a musical instrument, join or start a band. If horseback riding is your thing, con-

26

sider taking a job at a local horse barn or training for competition. Joining and getting involved will widen your circle of friends. True friends provide support and encouragement.

Encourage Others

Another way to build your own self-esteem is to encourage other people. People with low self-esteem are likely to put others down. These people don't believe that they will ever be happy. Oddly, they take a small amount of pleasure in making people around them miserable. That pleasure is seldom lasting. Putting down other people usually invites retaliation. This can only make you feel worse in the long run.

On the other hand, encouraging and supporting other people makes you feel better about yourself. As an added bonus, it can often turn an antagonist into a friend. The person that you encourage may be there to back you up when you need support.

Avoid Negative People

Still another approach is to avoid people who bring you down and to seek out people who encourage you. Luke cannot avoid his mother, but he can seek out other people who will give him hope. Often people who have experienced emotional abuse seek out others whose self-worth has been damaged as well. You would be better off spending time with people who have healthy levels of self-esteem while you are tying to rebuild your own.

Never Give Up Hope

Finally, never give up hope. No matter how dismal a situation looks, things can get better. The situation may not be perfect, or even as good as your friends have it, but you can become healthier. Hope often springs from appreciating the good things that you do have. Health, clean clothes, food to eat, and a warm bed to sleep in all can help you appreciate your life. Remember, where there is hope, there is life.

Neglect

Jake Robinson asked Mary Ellen Springer to marry him the summer after he finished high school. Mary Ellen was a junior at the time. She had never planned on going to college anyway, and she was so much in love with Jake that she said, "Yes!" They were married that August.

Jake had already started a job at the local garage. Mr. Fischer, the owner, had promised to pay for classes on brake and automatic transmission work. Jake thought this would be a pretty good opportunity.

Jake and Mary Ellen figured that they had it made. Jake had a talent for fixing cars, and as far as they could tell, there would always be cars that needed repairing. They were both surprised when Mary Ellen became pregnant just two months after the wedding. But it was okay. They both wanted kids eventually, and now seemed as good a time to start as any.

Jake signed up for the automotive classes, but they were much harder than he had expected. High school had never been easy for Jake, and these classes at technical school moved just a little too fast. But Jake was both proud and stubborn. He told everyone that he was wasting his time taking classes. After all, he needed to work more hours at the garage so that he could save enough money to be able to open his own garage someday.

Mr. Fischer was able to keep Jake busy doing oil changes, repairing flats, and making other simple repairs. Mr. Fischer's business was growing since he had bought a computer to analyze newer cars. Jim Ferguson, the new automotive technician, operated the computer and directed Jake and the other workers to make the repairs that the printouts advised. Behind his back, Jake laughed and called Jim Ferguson "the college weenie."

Jenna Robinson was born in May. It was noisy in their one-bedroom apartment. Baby Jenna seemed to cry most of the time. Mary Ellen's mother said it was normal, but Jake found that hard to believe. It frightened Mary Ellen when he shouted at her to keep the baby quiet. She was very frustrated when Jake would walk out at any hour to get away. It seemed as if she could never get a break from the noise.

Soon after Jenna was born, Mary Ellen found herself expecting another baby. Jake seemed less pleased than the first time. He was working long hours now, trying to save up some money. Jake Thomas Robinson, Jr., was born on June 11. Jake Thomas would be known as JT.

It was four years before Mary Ellen became pregnant for the third time, but there were complications with this pregnancy. She had to stay in bed for the last two months before Sarah's birth. Mary Ellen's mother helped quite a bit with Jenna and JT. But the medical bills were growing.

Sarah was born with some fairly serious health problems. Medications and frequent visits to the doctor were necessary for the first years of her life. Jake and Mary Ellen found that his salary was just enough to pay for rent, groceries, clothes, and the payments on Jake's truck. Jake begrudged Sarah's doctor bills. When Jenna and JT started school, Jake told Mary Ellen to put down that they had a religious objection to the required immunizations. This was not true; Jake just didn't want to pay for the shots.

Jake wanted a better life for his family and for himself. He offered to work as many hours as Mr. Fischer would let him. But, still, there was little left over at the end of the month. Jake told Mary Ellen that she would just have to cut back. The kids had older cousins who could give them used clothes. Shoes could last a long time. A winter coat wasn't really needed when two sweatshirts would do. Mary Ellen found that she could stretch the grocery budget by buying cheap starchy foods like macaroni instead of fresh fruit and vegetables. The kids at school from low-income families, who got free lunches, ate more and better food than the Robinsons.

When Jenna was in fifth grade, she told her parents excitedly that she had a chance to join the school band. It would only cost $50 to rent a clarinet. Mary Ellen sadly told her no. The other boys in JT's class were starting Little League baseball. Jake told JT that Little League was for sissies and that he could spend his time fishing or doing chores around the house.

At last, Jake's bank account was beginning to grow. He figured that in three more years he would have enough for a down payment on his own shop. In the meantime, Sarah was beginning to develop ear infections. Mary Ellen begged Jake to let her take Sarah to the doctor, but Jake said to just let the earaches run their course. That's what his mother had always done. The earaches did eventually go away, but the next year the school nurse found that Sarah had suffered a 50 percent hearing loss. Her teacher let her sit in the front row of the class. The nurse told Mary Ellen that Sarah would probably need glasses. She also asked when Mary Ellen had last taken the children to the dentist. Mary Ellen had to admit that the children had never been to the dentist. She thanked the nurse for trying to help.

After the school nurse had called three times, Jake finally allowed Mary Ellen to take the children to the eye doctor. Jenna's eyes were fine, but JT and Sarah both needed glasses. Sarah didn't seem to mind the new glasses—she thought that her blue frames were pretty—but JT was embarrassed to wear the inexpensive frames. His father said that the kids would call him four eyes if he wore glasses. The other high school kids already made fun of his hand-me-down clothes. The black-rimmed glasses would be just too much. JT never got glasses.

Jake was frustrated and angry that he had to go into the bank account to buy glasses for Sarah. He decided that if he had to spend money on that, he might as well buy a new truck. The garage could wait. JT forgot about the teasing for a little while, though, when his dad took him for a ride in the "king cab."

Mary Ellen was excited to see Jake spending money for the first time in so long. She hoped it meant that they might stop being quite so thrifty and start enjoying *their savings. Unfortunately, the only difference she saw was that Jake now spent money on accessories for his truck. Money for clothes, snacks, books, or movies was scarcer than ever.*

JT and Jenna were both finding it harder and harder to fit in at school. They had never played any organized sports, so it was difficult to begin in high school. Both enjoyed music, but lessons and instrument rentals were out of the question. Jenna was becoming discouraged. JT was turning angry and sullen. They both knew kids whose families were poor. But their father owned an expensive new truck and had money in the bank for "someday."

Options and Alternatives

When the adults in a family do not provide for their children's survival needs, those children are suffering from neglect. Withholding necessities, as Jake has done, threatens his family's health. Jenna, JT, and Sarah are in a situation that they cannot resolve on their own. They need to receive health care. They need dental work and regular checkups. They have never received their immunizations. JT will have trouble keeping up in school if he doesn't get glasses soon. Their nutrition has never been good, making it hard to compete with healthier classmates.

The options available to the Robinsons include: changing their father's attitude toward money either by themselves or with outside help, finding ways to get health care and food within their budget, or finding ways to earn money to ease the financial strain.

Jake's attitude will be very difficult to change. He has set a goal of owning his own business. He will not let anything he does not consider important—even his family's health—get in the way. Mary Ellen has not been able to change her husband's mind about the way household money is spent. Jake has control over the bank account, and Mary Ellen is not able to persuade him to change his thinking.

Jenna, JT, Sarah, and Mary Ellen could all sit down with Jake to discuss the family's finances. That may seem like a difficult plan, but it might work if everyone stuck to the subject. It might be helpful to point out gently to Jake that everyone in the family needs better health care and nutrition. It would definitely not help for Jenna and JT to accuse their father of being selfish or cheap. Name-calling and accusations never bring a family closer together.

Another way to attempt to change Jake's attitude would be to find someone outside the family to help. First, Jenna and JT should discuss any such ideas with their mother. Some people who might help are Jake's parents; Jake's brother, sister, or a close cousin; a clergy person whom Jake respects; or the school counselor or social worker. JT and Jenna would need to explain the situation fully and ask the outside helper to avoid strong accusations and harsh criticism of their father.

Several ways are possible to obtain health care and more nutritious food at a lower cost. One place to start is with the county government. Many counties employ home economists whose main job is to help families live more comfortably and enjoy better health within their budget. Clinics may be available that provide checkups and immunizations at little or no cost. Medical and dental colleges often provide free services to give their students an opportunity to perfect their skills. If you find yourself in a situation like the Robinsons', your school counselor or social worker should be able to point you in the right direction.

A third plan that may ease the strain is to find ways to bring more money into their home. Even if you are under sixteen, there are many ways to make money: by baby-sitting, mowing lawns, shoveling snow, walking pets, handing out flyers for new businesses, delivering newspapers, and many other activities. Be sure to discuss any money-making plans with your parents. Be careful to avoid unsafe situations, such as working with unfamiliar equipment, accepting a job a long distance from home, or working long hours or late at night.

How Can I Cope?

The conditions that the Robinson children are experiencing are familiar to millions of people. They are living as if they were in poverty. Neglect is child abuse, and it is illegal. Jake is neglectful because he has the means to provide his children with better nutrition, clothing, and health care. He chooses instead to ignore these problems, and consequently they worsen.

One of the Robinsons' problems is that they do not qualify for public assistance. If they did, they would receive food stamps, free medical care, and financial assistance. Jake's earnings and savings disqualify them for these programs. Many homeless families meet their children's needs far better than Jake does by taking advantage of government and charitable assistance. If you think that your family may be eligible for assistance, look in the Government section of your local phone book for programs that can help you. Such programs include welfare, public housing, Medicaid, and job training.

Getting Help
It is essential that health and nutritional needs be met. If your family is not providing these, you must look for assistance outside your family. The school nurse, guidance counselor, or social worker would be a good person to ask. A coach, teacher, or religious leader may help as well. A trusted grandparent, aunt, or uncle, whom your parents respect, may be able to talk to your parents for you.

Recovering from Years of Neglect
Even if parents stop neglect, problems usually still persist. Neglect diminishes self-esteem. As discussed in the previous chapter, you may be able to improve self-esteem by: seeking adult support outside of the family, family counseling, experiencing success, encouraging other people, and avoiding the influence of people who have negative ideas and personalities.

Remember, the key to ending neglect will likely come from outside your family. If your first attempt is not successful, try again. Don't give up until you find someone who is willing to help you and the rest of your family. Neglect, like any type of child abuse, is not your fault. However, by making others aware of your family's neglect, you can help to end it.

Overprotection

Mrs. Karatowicz has always been there for Ben. His earliest memories are of Mom feeding him, taking him to the park, reading to him, buying him clothes, walking him to and from school. Ben Karatowicz and his mother have always been close.

Ben didn't have many friends in elementary school. He had a daily ritual to his life. In the morning Mom selected his clothes, fixed his breakfast, and walked him to school. After school she was always there to see him home and to ask about what had happened in class. Mrs. Karatowicz often seemed more interested in the details than Ben was himself. After a snack, homework, and piano practice came dinner. After dinner there were card games, reading, TV, or some activity at church. Weekends were for piano recitals, concerts, theater, and more church. Ben was allowed some time to play, but usually he played video games or read.

Ben's father was around, but not often. A successful lawyer, Mr. Karatowicz left for the office before Ben woke up and often got home after Ben had fallen asleep. When he came home for dinner he always brought a briefcase full of papers, which he worked on right after eating. Mr. Karatowicz was a stern man who seldom found time to be with his wife and son, but he did provide them with a substantial home and luxuries that many of Ben's classmates' families could never afford.

Since Ben was usually asleep when his father got home, Mr. Karatowicz got into the habit of asking his wife how Ben was doing. Mrs. Karatowicz always pointed out Ben's successes. Any failures and limitations were downplayed. Occasionally, on weekends, Ben's father would tell him how proud he was of him. In the back of his mind, Ben always wondered how his father could possibly know what was happening in his life.

By seventh grade Ben seemed to have found his niche. His grades were good, his homework was always done, and any permission slips from home were always signed and returned the next day. Ben was liked by his teachers because he never talked during class, was always on time, and was respectful and courteous. Ben seemed to be dedicated to school and piano, with few other interests. The music teacher, Mrs. Levine, gave him permission to practice during the lunch period. Ben would eat his lunch by himself and hurry to practice while his classmates laughed and gossiped in the cafeteria.

Eighth grade started out as had most years. Mrs. Karatowicz had purchased all of Ben's new school clothes and supplies by mid-August. Ben arrived at school on the bus, picked up his schedule, and went to his first-period class, English. The teacher was Mr. Majewski, an institution in the school. He had been there forever. This was his twenty-seventh year of teaching. He was gruff, loud, and very demanding.

On the second day of school, Mrs. Levine stopped Ben in the hall to ask him about a music festival in which he had participated during the past summer. Knowing that most teachers were not too strict the first few days, Mrs. Levine didn't even think about giving Ben a pass. Arriving in English class thirty seconds late, Ben drew Mr. Majewski's wrath.

"Mr. Karatowicz! Do you feel that your command of the English language is so strong that you need not arrive on time to my class?" Mr. Majewski demanded.

Ben slithered toward his chair, his face red, praying he might suddenly become invisible. "No, sir," he mumbled quietly.

When Ben got off the bus that afternoon, his mother "just happened" to be walking the dog near the bus stop. They walked home together. Ben didn't speak of the embarrassing moment in English class. Mrs. Karatowicz sensed that something was not right, but she let it drop.

The first week of school went well in all of Ben's classes except English. In that class, every paper that Ben turned in was returned with errors bloodied in red ink. Mr. Majewski seemed to enjoy reading Ben's latest run-on sentence aloud to the class. He smiled when he pointed out the mistakes, but few of Ben's classmates dared to join in for fear their paper might be the next one used as an example.

Ben kept all this to himself. One evening when Mrs. Karatowicz brought a snack to Ben's room, she noticed that his wastebasket was half full of attempts to begin his English assignment. Ben was sniffling, *and his eyes were red. He told his mother every-thing. The next morning Mrs. Karatowicz went to school and demanded to see the principal. She insisted that Ben be removed from Mr. Majewski's class and that action be taken against the teacher for his treatment of her son. The principal was reluctant to make a change. He pointed out that although Mr. Majewski was tough, his students scored higher on the final writing test than any others in the district. Mrs. Karatowicz replied that if she could not get sat-isfaction here, she would speak to the superinten-dent. The principal relented. Ben was transferred to Mrs. Millikan's class.*

Mrs. Karatowicz was very encouraged by her abil-ity to force a change for her son. Ben was just happy to be out of Mr. Majewski's class. He felt now that he should tell his mother about any problems at school, and she would be able to make them disappear. It was strange, though, that the only C Ben received all year was in Mrs. Millikan's English class.

High school became difficult. Ben felt left out socially. With no close friends, few people seemed to notice him. Ben noticed girls in his class and wanted to meet them, but he didn't know how to get started. The only dance he went to was the senior prom. He went to that only because his mother told him that Aileen Menninger's mother had said that her daugh-ter didn't have a date yet. Aileen had told her mother that she would be willing to go with Ben if he asked her. Ben did ask her. Then Mrs. Karatowicz made all the arrangements for a tux, flowers, and dinner.

Ben was accepted at several prestigious universi-

ties. But he decided to go to the local junior college, because he didn't know what he would do at a university far away from home.

Options and Alternatives

Ben Karatowicz has never been neglected. He has all the material things anyone could ever want. He has a mother who loves him deeply and is sensitive to his feelings. She always does whatever is necessary to protect and assist her son. As far as Ben is concerned, his mother is the only important person in his life. Mrs. Karatowicz has gone beyond simply ensuring that her son is safe. Her actions are overprotective.

In families, all members need to feel that they are loved and belong. In the Karatowicz family, Ben's mother's needs were not being met by her husband. Ben's father was an emotionally distant man who seldom connected himself to the rest of the family. His career fulfilled most of his emotional needs for belonging, self-esteem, and growth. Ben's mother turned to her son as a way to feel connected to another person emotionally. Ben became her career and her sole focus. He was her only means of feeling that she was contributing to the growth of something or someone important.

Ben didn't need to make decisions. When a difficulty arose, he knew that his mother would tell him what to do. Thus he never developed the ability to make decisions for himself. By the end of high school, Ben was too dependent on his mother to make a breakaway to college.

Ben's dependence on his mother gave him security and

comfort, but it deprived him of the opportunity to develop friendships. Often as he was growing up, Ben sensed that he should have friends his own age. All through junior high, he felt disconnected. He didn't have to face the aloneness at lunchtime because his well-meaning music teacher let him practice instead of sending him to join his classmates. Ben never learned how to get along with his peers and to solve problems. By the time he entered senior high school he was so isolated that he usually ate lunch alone.

In many dysfunctional families one or more family members engage in behavior that is dangerous or destructive, such as physical abuse, sexual abuse, or addiction. In other families there is extreme neglect of emotional or material needs. The Karatowicz family has none of these problems. The family is not functioning in a healthy way because Mrs. Karatowicz is using Ben to fulfill her own needs for growth, love, and belonging. Ben, as a result, stopped growing emotionally at a very young age. His mother dominated him and protected him from pain for so long that Ben could no longer make decisions or develop relationships with peers without his mother's help.

Families have several purposes. One is to meet the needs of members. Another important purpose is to provide a place where children can develop the skills needed to live independently. The moment a child is born, he begins the journey out of his or her home. A very important goal of a family is to allow children opportunities to break free and choose their own lives as adults.

Often the process of becoming independent is painful. Ben felt safer in junior high when he was allowed to practice piano at lunch time. At the same time, however, he was not practicing social skills. When Mrs. Karatowicz demanded that Ben's English class be changed, she kept him from learning ways to cope with the harsh treatment that most people experience as part of everyday life. People learn to cope by living through difficult times, rather than by avoiding them. Ben was not able to face leaving home to go to college because he had never been allowed to cope with any difficulties as he was growing up.

What Can I Do?

If your parents are protecting you from dangers and difficulties that you should be able to handle on your own, there are several things you can do to help your family to function in a healthy way. A first step is to evaluate yourself. Are you so dependent on one or both of your parents that you have trouble making even the smallest decisions? Do one or both of your parents rescue you from problems and protect you from even minor difficulties? Do you feel uncomfortable and unsure of yourself with people your own age?

If your answer to any of these questions is yes, you need to decide that you want to make some changes. It will not be easy. If your parent has been protecting and rescuing you all your life, you probably feel a large degree of comfort in this. Getting your parent to allow you to experience the pain of everyday life calls for courage, but it is a step that you need to take if you are someday to live independently. You don't need to make a complete break, but you do need to start moving toward taking responsibility for your own problems, rather than allowing your parent to solve them for you.

Once you have decided to become less dependent on your parents, you need to take action. The next step is to talk to the parent who has been dominating you emotionally. This will be difficult for you as well as for your parent. Try to be calm. Show confidence. You are asking to be given more adult responsibility, so you need to show that you are ready for it.

When you attempt to persuade your parents that a change is needed, stay focused on the issue. Talk about your feelings. Focus on what you need your parent to do differently to help you to mature into an independent, responsible adult.

> Ineffective statement: "You treat me like a little kid."

> More effective statement: "I feel that I'm not given enough freedom to make decisions."

> Most effective statement: "I feel as though I'm not good at making decisions. I would like to talk to you about letting me take more responsibility for making my own decisions."

It may take several discussions to reach agreement. Both of you may occasionally break your agreement. Your parent may slip back into dominating, overprotective patterns, or you may find yourself slipping into dependency. If you persist, however, there is a chance that you can break the cycle.

If it is not possible to break the emotional domination, it may help to talk to your other parent. Again, stay focused on your feelings and needs. You may feel neglected or shunned by this other parent. Try to put those feelings aside and work together to establish healthy relationships in your family.

If you are not able to break the emotional domination on your own, it may be necessary to get help from outside. A close relative, the school counselor, a social worker, or a trusted teacher may be able to help. Talk to people who may be able to confront your dominating parent with you in a gentle and understanding way.

How Can I Cope?

If you are unable to find someone to speak for or with you, at least try to find someone in whom you can confide. Talking about your feelings helps you to understand them. It is healthy to talk about "bad" feelings. It enables you to deal with them and work toward a solution. If they are buried inside you, you cannot resolve them.

Always remember that it is normal during the teen years to want to be with your peers rather than with adults. You need to make and keep friends your own age. Choose friends who are trustworthy and who care about you. Stick with friends who seem to be making good decisions. You may be able to improve your decision-making skills by observing the choices that they make.

Sexual Abuse

Alice Anderson felt dirty all the time. She wore clean clothes. She bathed every night. She brushed her teeth and washed her hair regularly. But still she always felt dirty, smelly, and disgusting.

Alice never talked to anyone about the way she felt. How could she? If she talked about how awful she felt, she might have to say why. And Alice could never tell anyone her terrible secret.

Alice's father was well respected in their suburban community. Mr. Anderson was a certified public accountant. He did the taxes for many of the wealthiest people in town. Businesspeople trusted him with all their financial affairs. He had proved himself to be an extremely capable tax accountant.

Mrs. Anderson was quiet, a bit too quiet, perhaps. While Mr. Anderson worked, Mrs. Anderson maintained their proper suburban home. Everything was neat, organized, and orderly in the Anderson household. Everything had its place, and everyone knew where things belonged. Even though Mrs. Anderson was an excellent cook, they seldom entertained. As a matter of fact, few people outside of the family had ever been in their house.

Alice seemed to take after her mother. She seldom had much to say. She had only a few girlfriends. She was pretty and friendly enough, but most people thought she was shy. Actually, Alice wasn't shy; she just didn't want to get too close to other people. She knew that the closer people got, the more likely it was that they would find out her secret. That was a chance that she simply would not take.

At the beginning of her freshman year Alice met Carli. They became friends instantly. Carli was funny, outgoing, and carefree. Going anywhere with her was an adventure. She would go up to total strangers and say the most absurd things. Once she walked up to a man sitting on a bench at the shopping mall and carried on a fifteen-minute conversation with him in a thick French accent. She told him that she was broken hearted because she had lost her pet ferret in Gina's Boutique.

Another time Carli persuaded the manager of an ice cream shop to give her a taste of all thirty-one flavors. After she had tried every single one, she said, "I guess I'm not in the mood for ice cream after all."

Carli liked Alice because she was quiet and a good listener. Carli was almost always able to make Alice laugh, a feat no one else had ever been able to accomplish. While most people thought that Carli and Alice were opposites, actually they fit together like pieces of a puzzle. Each one's good points brought out positive qualities in the other.

After much pleading by Alice, her parents finally allowed her to sleep over at Carli's house. Late at night, after hours of talking and laughing, Alice let her guard down a bit. She confided, "There are some things that you'll never know about me."

Carli responded innocently, "What do you mean? What things?""Never mind what things!" Alice exploded, "I don't want to talk about it! Don't you dare ever ask me about it again!"

Carli was surprised that Alice was cool toward her after that. But, never one to be dismissed easily, she teased, joked, and passed notes to Alice. When one of the girls on the basketball team made fun of Alice's clothes, Carli called out to her in a German accent, "Do we now need to get an approval from the fashion police?"

Soon Alice and Carli were back to laughing together again. One night when they were talking on the phone, Carli asked, "What was the big secret that made you so mad at me when you slept over at my house?" Suddenly, the phone went dead.

The next day Alice tried to pretend that nothing had happened, but Carli could feel a difference in their friendship. It hurt her feelings to have Alice hang up the phone on her. Alice seemed to be closing her out. Carli was beginning to wonder if having such a moody friend was worth the trouble.

The first evening of that spring was warm and clear and wonderful. Carli went over to Alice's house to see if she wanted to hang out. She found Alice sitting on a swing, curled up into a ball, whimpering to herself. Approaching cautiously, Carli put her hand on Alice's shoulder. Alice pulled back. "Don't touch me! Don't touch me! Don't touch me!"

Alice's pleading was so pitiful that Carli was torn between wanting to console her and wanting to run away. She stuck by her friend. "What happened?

What's wrong, Alice?""My father ..." The rest was nothing but Alice's sobbing and tears.

Carli sat with her for nearly an hour before Alice's mother came out to call her in. Although Alice's eyes were all puffed up and her cheeks were clearly stained with tears, Mrs. Anderson appeared not to notice that anything was wrong.

What Alice just could not tell Carli was that her father forced himself upon her sexually. He had started when Alice was little. It hurt. He was stronger than she. She could not stop him from forcing her to have sexual intercourse with him. Mr. Anderson usually seemed to feel bad about it later and gave her gifts. Alice always hated his gifts. Mr. Anderson told her that if she told anyone what he had done, even her mother, she would be taken away and put into a school for bad girls. Alice has never told her mother or anyone else all this. She is hanging on dearly to her terrible secret.

Options and Alternatives

Alice needs to know that what has happened to her is not her fault. Many girls and boys who have been sexually abused feel a terrible sense of guilt. They believe that the sexual assault was their fault, that they should have fought harder, run away, or hidden. None of these are possible when a young child is assaulted sexually. Some victims of sexual abuse tell themselves that they were too attractive or cute. They blame themselves. They, of course, are not the ones at fault.

Sexual abuse is the most extreme abuse of trust in a family. Young children naturally trust adults. When this trust is used by an adult to gain sexual gratification at the child's expense, extreme emotional damage to the victim is the usual result. Alice's first step toward escaping her terrible nightmare must be the realization that her father's abuse is in no way her fault.

Many victims of sexual abuse feel worthless. The attack on their body makes them feel dirty and disgusting. This feeling of worthlessness diminishes their self-esteem. They think that no one will ever want them. People with a healthy self-concept feel good about themselves. Sexual abuse makes people feel bad about themselves. But it is something over which they have absolutely no control.

Sexual abuse always makes a family dysfunctional. For one thing, each family member becomes isolated. The sexual abuse is a secret that most victims feel can never be told to anyone. The abuser—whether it's a father, a mother, an uncle, an aunt, a brother, a sister, or a cousin—knows that the sexual abuse is wrong and will seldom speak of it, except when threatening the child or teenager. The victim is usually ashamed and unable to confide in anyone. This isolates the family members from each other and from outsiders. An important part of a healthy, functioning family is communication. Sexual abuse blocks communication in every direction.

Victims of sexual abuse are angry, but they feel powerless to express their anger to their abuser. Often their anger is expressed in unexpected ways or toward people who don't deserve it. Alice became angry at Carli on several occasions without justification. She screamed at Carli because she was unable to scream at her father.

Many sexually abused children feel helpless. They feel that control of their bodies has been taken away from them. They view themselves as incompetent. Since they cannot fight the major trauma in their lives, they feel that they cannot accomplish anything. Often these victims become passive. They react to people and events, rather than taking control over their own lives.

Finally, many victims of sexual abuse feel hopeless. Seeing no escape from their problems and pain, they often consider suicide as an alternative. However, people can overcome tremendous difficulties as long as they have hope. Continued sexual abuse combined with the guilt, low self-esteem, isolation, anger, and helplessness diminishes a victim's hope.

How Can I Cope?

Both males and females can be victims of sexual abuse. Boys who have been sexually abused by an older male often fear that the experience has made them homosexual. This is not true. The factors leading to homosexuality are not completely understood, but one thing is certain: Aggressive forced sex does not turn a heterosexual into a homosexual.

Another myth about sexually abused boys is that the abusers are homosexual themselves. This is also not true. Sexual abuse is an act of aggression and anger. Many men who sexually abuse boys are actually heterosexual. Their abuse of young boys is an act of power and control over another person. They are generally people who feel powerless and controlled themselves, so they take out their anger on weaker victims.

It is rare for victims of sexual abuse to be able to escape from their situation without some kind of outside help. Victims of sexual abuse need three kinds of help: help to escape the isolation, guilt, and fear; help to keep them safe from repeated attacks; and help to rebuild their self-esteem and hope.

Alice was looking for an escape from her isolation. Her mother was not any help. Actually, Alice's mother seemed to be aware that something terrible was going on, but she did nothing to stop it. Often when children are being physically or sexually assaulted by one parent, the other parent does nothing to prevent the abuse. The human mind is able to protect itself by ignoring things that are too difficult or painful to deal with. Often the non-abusing parent simply will not allow herself to know what is happening. Sometimes the non-abusing parent feels that no matter how dysfunctional the family is, she cannot face life outside of it. Alice's mother may have feared that if she stood up to her husband, she would lose him, her daughter, and her home.

Alice was lucky. She was able to trust Carli. Alice tested their friendship on several occasions, and each time Carli stood by her. Confiding in Carli would be an important step for Alice to take to escape her father. Even if she is able to confide in Carli, they will need help from a strong and capable adult such as a school counselor, school social worker, teacher, minister, priest, police social worker, or other person familiar with sexual abuse.

The first step they need to take is to report Mr. Anderson's actions to the local police or the state or county agency that deals with sexual assault. This is a frightening step for most victims for several reasons. They fear that the abusive parent will be put into jail, which would result in the family's being broken apart. They fear that no one will believe them, that it will anger the abusive parent and invite further abuse. They fear that word of the abuse will become known in the community, causing them great shame and embarrassment.

In the worst case, all of these fears can become realities. Still, community agencies and the courts try to provide confidential help for the sexual abuser through psychological therapy.

The courts provide protection for the victim of abuse, but only in the worst cases is the victim removed from the home. Usually the abuser is required to leave the home while undergoing therapy. Victims can be granted an order of protection by the courts, which forbids the abuser to contact or harass them.

Once Alice is able to escape her isolation and find protection from her father, she will need counseling for herself. This can be provided by the school, her church, a mental health center, a psychologist, a psychiatrist, a social worker, or a women's support group. The therapy is needed to help Alice see herself as strong, capable, worthwhile, and in control of her body and her life. Alice's image of herself and her self-esteem need to be rebuilt. She needs help to feel both lovable and loved.

Perfectionism

Josh lives in a beautiful home. His parents work hard to provide it. Mrs. Wilson is a tax attorney for a big firm downtown. She works long hours, but is allowed to do her work at home some of the time on her computer. Mr. Wilson recently left his legal practice when he was appointed a county judge.

When they were in school, both Mr. and Mrs. Wilson were excellent students. They met while attending the state university, where they both graduated with honors. Mrs. Wilson had been the valedictorian of her high school class. She waited until she was thirty-three before she became pregnant with Josh. Because they had always demanded so much of themselves, the Wilsons waited until they were financially able to give their son a very comfortable life.

At Roosevelt Junior High, Josh excelled. In eighth grade he was invited to take high school-level science and math classes. Everything seemed to go well, with one exception: history. Mr. Maxwell, the history teacher, did not seem to care much about his subject. He assigned readings and then told the students to use class time to answer the questions at the end of the chapter. Some of the movies he showed were interesting, but most days were spent simply looking up

*answers and writing them down. In all his other class-
es, Josh found it easy to motivate himself, but in Mr.
Maxwell's class he just did what he had to do to get by.*

*Josh wasn't surprised when the report cards came
out. He had As in all of his classes except history. His
grade in that class was B-minus. That didn't bother
Josh. He told himself, "I haven't really learned anything in that class. An A would make it seem as if I
had learned something. To me, a B is an indication of
what a poor teacher Mr. Maxwell really is."*

*When Josh's parents saw the report card, however,
they hit the roof. "B-minus in history! You've been
telling us that history is your easiest class. This grade
is a disgrace. It's an embarrassment." They restricted
him from using the phone and from visiting friends
until he brought home three consecutive As in history.*

*Josh really resented this punishment. He knew he
could have gotten an A with little effort. His successes in his high school classes were being ignored. He
was working harder than he had in his entire life, only
to be punished for getting a B in a class he did not
even consider important.*

*Josh complied with his parents' orders, but his writ-
ten work in history took on a sarcastic tone. Each
essay took a point of view that Josh knew was exactly opposite to Mr. Maxwell's opinion. Many teachers
might appreciate this lively interplay of ideas. They
would enjoy teaching a student who could think for
himself. Mr. Maxwell, however, was not like most
teachers. Instead of acknowledging the thought and
creativity in Josh's answers, he marked them wrong.
Josh's next three test grades in history were all Cs.*

Josh's ongoing battle to do things his own way was beginning to have an effect on his other classes. The high school classes required his full attention. He was spending too much time on ways to oppose Mr. Maxwell and too little on his other classes. As a result, his grades in the rest of his classes started to fall off.

On his next report card Josh had a C in history and Bs in math and science. The Wilsons met with the school counselor to ask how they could motivate Josh to do better work. The counselor tried to assure them that Josh was doing fine and that they should be pleased with his progress. She agreed reluctantly to send them regular progress reports so that they could monitor his grades.

The first progress report seemed to show a step in the right direction. The C was now a B. The B in math was up to an A-minus. The Wilsons told Josh, "We know you can do better than this."

That infuriated Josh. To bring up his C to a B, he had had to do A-plus work. He was writing essays that required no creative thought whatsoever; all he was doing was giving Mr. Maxwell's own opinions and biases right back to him. He felt he was betraying his own values and beliefs just to get an A. He told himself. "Never again!"

Josh became difficult and argumentative in all his classes. Whatever opinion a teacher presented, Josh argued the opposite view. Since the teachers liked Josh, they seemed to enjoy the interplay at first. Soon, however, most grew weary of his challenges. The more Josh battled, the more his grades dropped.

The Wilsons went back to the counselor to ask for the name of a psychologist who might be able to help straighten out their son.

Options and Alternatives

From the time he was born, Josh's parents gave him every opportunity to excel. All his life Josh heard the message: Be proud, be the best, be the first. The expectations were extremely high, but so were Josh's abilities. Until eighth grade, he had been able to overcome every obstacle and meet each challenge that had come his way.

Capable students succeed in school for a variety of reasons, such as to please their parents, to avoid punishment, to please a teacher they like, and to please themselves regardless of the expectations of others.

Most elementary school students who do well want to please their parents. They are praised when they learn a new word, color a picture, learn a song, or participate in a play. The parents' praise is usually enough to motivate these young children. Some students continue to work for parental praise through high school and college. These students tend to be emotionally dominated in unhealthy ways. An emotionally healthy teenager appreciates his parents' approval and encouragement but does not rely solely on that to provide motivation for success.

Some parents use punishment and withdrawal of privileges to motivate their child. Occasionally this approach is effective. Healthy, functioning families have high standards and expectations. A family becomes dysfunctional when the element of communication is missing. The

Wilsons didn't talk to their son; they reacted by punishing him. They never talked to him when his grades dropped further. They got the advice of a school counselor without talking to Josh about it. The Wilson family is suffering from their perfectionism, but the root of their problem really is ineffective communication.

Also, the Wilsons' love for Josh is based more upon his performance than on his identity as their son. Their affection is not consistent. Rather, it is conditional upon good grades and good behavior. Josh's family became dysfunctional when his parents' desire for him to succeed became more important than their love for him.

During the teen years many students tend to ignore their parents' approval or disapproval. Partly this is a healthy desire to develop the needed skills for independent living. Many teenagers consider school their private domain and schoolwork their job. Some test their teachers carefully. If they like and respect a teacher and feel that the teacher likes and respects them, they work harder in that class. If they don't respect a teacher, they may be more likely to slack off. This approach to school is extremely shortsighted. A student has a particular teacher only for a semester or a year. Grades, however, stay on a transcript for many years. Students who choose not to work for a teacher they don't like may find doors to college programs or jobs closed to them.

Many successful students do their best work simply for themselves. They meet their own high expectations because they wouldn't have it any other way. These students are able to put off immediate enjoyment in order to reach long-term goals. It is important for all teenagers to ask themselves what gives them their motivation. It may come from family, teachers, or ethnic or racial heritage. But for true success, the most important source must be from yourself.

How Can I Cope?

Josh has always worked hard at school, but he has not yet reached the stage where he is motivated to work just for himself. You may be in a similar position. You may be battling your parents and teachers over grades that they consider unacceptable. You may feel that no matter what you do, you never seem to please your parents or teachers.

You need to ask yourself for whom you are working. Whom are you trying to please? Who benefits when you succeed? You may need to rethink the ways you motivate yourself. If you are motivated by a need to please other people, you will often find yourself disappointed. But if your motivation comes from within, you will always be able to succeed.

The Wilson family is dysfunctional partly because they have lost the sense of belonging. Family members need to respect and accept each other as they are. When they don't, communication is blocked. The Wilson family will continue to be dysfunctional until one of two things happens. Either the parents will come to understand that Josh is motivated by their approval and begin to recognize his successes—or Josh will come to realize that his successes are all his own.

Substance Abuse

A few years ago, Karl and Lisa Franklin celebrated their fifteenth wedding anniversary with a trip to Acapulco. Their first night out on the beach, a couple nearby offered them a drag on their joint. The sweet smell of marijuana took the Franklins back to their college days, and the scent was too tempting to refuse. Marijuana was cheaper than alcohol, and they preferred it anyway. When they returned home a week later, Karl and Lisa stashed a bag of pot in their suitcase, sprayed with perfume to disguise the odor.

For Lisa, the thrill of marijuana wore off a few months later. She had too many others thing to do, she reasoned. Between her job, her son, and managing their home, she needed to be alert and awake. After all, she wasn't a college kid anymore. Karl, on the other hand, said that the marijuana helped him to relax. It eased the stress of his job and took the edge off after a long day.

Then, when their son Jason was fourteen, a friend offered to let Karl try cocaine. "Why not?" thought Karl, and he agreed to snort some lines. He found that he liked cocaine much more than marijuana. Although pot helped him to relax and made him feel mellow, coke gave him extra drive and energy. He could excel at work and keep Lisa and Jason happy at home. Karl enjoyed the coke so much that he offered to let Lisa try *it too. But she wasn't interested. "Just don't let Jason see you with that stuff," she warned him.*

As the months went by, Karl paid more and more attention to his cocaine habit and less to his job and his family. His boss had given him several warnings about his poor performance, but Karl just couldn't seem to concentrate at work anymore. He thought that maybe he needed a new job. Maybe he was just bored with this one. He spent hours alone or with his friends, who were also into coke. Karl needed the drug at least once a day, and he couldn't snort when Jason was nearby. So he started spending time away from home and staying out late at night.

Karl knew that Lisa disapproved of his drug use, but that was simply because she hadn't tried coke. She never complained, though, and she always covered for him. He'd heard her make excuses to Jason about why Dad wasn't going to his baseball games anymore. Besides, she'd been working longer hours. Cocaine was expensive, and Karl didn't have as much money for the family as he once did. Lisa's extra hours helped them to make ends meet.

One night, the mother of one of Jason's friends called the Franklins. Furious, she demanded that they come and get their son immediately. Jason emerged from the house with a big, goofy grin on his face. Both he and his friend reeked of pot smoke. Karl noticed immediately that their eyes were bloodshot.

Karl grabbed his son by the arm. "Get in the car," he shouted. "You're a disgrace. How many times have I told you to stay away from drugs? I would have thought that you were smarter than this."

Jason pulled away from his father and glared at him. "I may be a disgrace, but you're a hypocrite. At least I'm only smoking pot. Not like you."

"What's that supposed to mean?" Karl demanded.

"I found your stash of coke," Jason replied. "So don't think that you're fooling anyone. You aren't."

Options and Alternatives

When the use of alcohol, prescription drugs, or illegal drugs stops a member of a family from growing, sharing, and supporting the rest of the family, that family becomes dysfunctional. Substance abuse by teens may be the cause of dysfunction or it may be a result of it.

Alcohol is the most common addictive drug among adults. An estimated 6.6 million children in the United States live with an alcoholic parent. Although it is legal, alcohol can be an extremely destructive force in a family. Many alcoholics are physically or emotionally abusive at times. Parents who would never dream of harming their spouse or children when sober may inflict tremendous damage while under the influence of alcohol. Siblings may abuse each other when drunk, and children may even threaten or abuse their parents. An alcoholic family member may experience blackouts, not remembering what happened after he or she has had a few drinks.

Some alcoholics use drinking as an escape from everyday life. They may not abuse family members, but they neglect them emotionally. They spend time in bars or drink at home in front of the TV. These alcoholics do not contribute to the self-esteem and growth of the other members of their family.

Not all people who drink are alcoholics. But when drinking interferes with any family member's safety, security, sense of belonging, self-esteem, or emotional growth, alcohol is becoming a problem. When a person loses control of the amount or frequency of his drinking, that person is an alcoholic. The consequences of alcoholism can be severe. Studies show that, in the general population, about 20 percent of suicide victims are alcoholics.

Alcoholism is a physical disease. It is not curable. Once a person loses control of his use of alcohol, he cannot be cured. An alcoholic who has stopped drinking is called a recovering alcoholic and will be one for the rest of his life.

Alcoholism may develop immediately or gradually. Some people lose control over their use of alcohol with their first drink. Others develop alcoholism over a period of years.

It is impossible for a son or daughter to bring an alcoholic to recovery, just as it is very difficult for parents to force an alcoholic teen to become sober. Some children of alcoholics believe that if they can be good enough, achieve enough, or do everything their parent wants them to do, the parent will stop drinking. Similarly, parents believe that if they were better parents their child would not be a substance abuser. Neither belief is true.

Another myth is that alcoholism is strictly hereditary. It's true that the way your body responds to alcohol is likely to be similar to the pattern of your parents. But the choice to begin to use alcohol is your own. If you choose never to use alcohol or illegal drugs, you will never develop a problem with substance abuse.

Most alcoholics need a great deal of help and support during their recovery. Alcoholics Anonymous (AA) has been the most effective program to help alcoholics. Meetings of AA are held in nearly every city and town in America, nearly every night of the year. Recovering alcoholics go to these meetings to obtain the support and encouragement that they need and to offer help to others.

Drug-abusing family members run additional risks. Whether the abuser is using marijuana, cocaine, LSD, heroin, or other illegal drugs, she is risking arrest and imprisonment for drug possession and use. Her present or future career is at risk, since few employers will hire convicted drug users. An even worse risk for drug abusers who share hypodermic needles is AIDS (acquired immunodeficiency syndrome), a disease for which there is no cure. In addition, an AIDS-infected woman who becomes pregnant is likely to pass the virus on to her unborn child.

Effective programs are available for abusers of illegal drugs. One is called Narcotics Anonymous. Another, Cocaine Anonymous, has helped thousands of people addicted to cocaine. These programs are similar in approach to that of AA. Many hospitals have both inpatient and outpatient clinics for treatment of substance abuse. Like alcoholics, drug addicts cannot break their addiction. A drug addict remains an addict for the rest of her life. With a single return to drug use, she risks losing control.

In the Franklin family Karl and Lisa abused marijuana. Karl started doing cocaine, and Jason abused marijuana. The dysfunction in this family came partly from the fact that communication about substance abuse had broken down severely. Jason disapproved of his father's drug abuse but had never confronted him. Neither had Lisa. Instead, she had helped to make it is easier for Karl to support his cocaine habit. Karl disapproved of his son's drug use but wasn't honest with him. This failure to communicate has created a great deal of distance between the Franklin family members.

How Can I Cope?

There are two important elements in coping with a parent's or sibling's substance abuse. These are understanding the addiction and seeking help outside of your family. So many myths surround substance abuse that some factual information is necessary. Also, the process that allows a person to become addicted is so complex that help from someone outside of the family is generally needed for the family to function.

Understanding Addiction

Sharon Wegscheider-Cruse and her husband Joseph Cruse wrote in their book *Understanding Co-Dependency* that three conditions are necessary for a person to become chemically addicted:

1. Genes that result in the person's being susceptible

2. An agent that can cause the disease, such as alcohol or drugs

3. A permissive or even promotive environment or society for the person and the chemical to get together

Karl, Lisa, and Jason were all susceptible to addiction. Our society is permissive about substance abuse, as was the Franklin family atmosphere. Alcohol is still advertised widely, promoting its use. The Franklin family was permissive about drug abuse. Prior to the confrontation between Karl and Jason, no one spoke about substance abuse. Their silence encouraged continued use. Because no one had ever clearly communicated thoughts about substance abuse, the problem continued to worsen.

Codependency

Many families affected by substance abuse have one or more persons who act as codependents. In her book *Codependent No More,* Melody Beatty defines codependency as follows:

> You are a codependent if you let someone else's wrong actions affect your life so that you feel that you must control the bad things that person does.

Codependents are usually well-intended people who are just trying to be understanding and supportive and to help the addict to relieve stress. Lisa was a codependent to Karl.

In *Strong Enough for Two,* Jim Mastrich outlines five steps for overcoming the type of codependent behavior that nurtures and enables addiction. They are:

1. Stop the denial and acknowledge the dissatisfaction in yourself with yourself and loved ones

2. Recognize the ways in which you enable

3. Understand what you feel when you enable

4. Gain insight as to how you first developed your pattern of enabling behavior

5. Begin to practice attitudes and behavior that characterize healthy relationships

Enabling often feels and looks like coping, but it is quite different. Enabling actually makes the situation worse. Codependents become less healthy themselves because of another family member's addiction. Their own social relationships suffer. Their hopes and dreams are set aside by the substance abuse.

Seeking Help Outside the Family

Everyone in the Franklin family needs help. Karl needs help to control his addiction. Jason may be addicted or may simply need help to get control of his own life and learn to deal with his father. Lisa has to confront Karl's drug problem and stop being a codependent. Many community programs exist to help substance abusers like Karl and Jason.

A program for the spouses of alcohol and drug abusers is called Al-Anon. Members can receive advice and support from men and women who are married to substance abusers. Al-Anon is listed in the business section of the phone books of most towns and cities in the United States.

The program for teenage children of alcoholics and drug addicts is called Alateen. Alateen has helped hundreds of thousands of young people to cope with their parents' substance abuse. Younger children can join Alatot. In many communities Al-Anon, Alateen, and Alatot programs are coordinated so that parents and children can attend their own meetings at the same time. Adults who grew up in a dysfunctional alcoholic home can find support in the organization Adult Children of Alcoholics.

You may also want to consider family therapy. Often substance abuse is a symptom of other problems within the family. Or it causes severe family difficulties. Family therapy can help pull a family together. It can help them deal with their dysfunction as a group.

If you are growing up in a substance-abusing home, seek help. See your school counselor, social worker, or other helping professional. Find out about Alateen programs and attend their meetings. Millions of children grow up with substance abusers or are abusers themselves. Finding support in others will help you cope.

Religious or Political Fanaticism

More than the other six children in the Johnson family, Jonas feared his father. Or at least he thought it was his father that he feared. Perhaps it was the church itself that frightened him. Jonas was the oldest boy in a family that was the centerpiece of a small but tightly knit congregation. While the church members looked to his father for truth and guidance, they looked to Jonas to be an example of the preacher's best work.

The Most Reverend Obediah Johnson, Jonas's father, had founded the Divine Light Apostolic Missionary Church just a year before Jonas was born. People in the inner-city neighborhood were impressed by the strength of his preaching. He stood against drinking, drugs, gangs, and guns. He stood for daily prayer meetings in a rented storefront that served as a church, families combining all their money and property for the use of the entire congregation, and rejection of all the ways of the world. Currently the DLAMC comprises twenty-one families. The heads of these families, fifteen men and six women, serve on the council of elders.

Church members meet daily. The personal funds of all of the members are held in common. All decisions about money matters are made by the elders. At first the council approved increased allowances to families only for such items as food, rent, and medical

69

expenses. *Several years ago, however, Obediah Johnson proclaimed that the choice of which college to attend, trips of more than two days' duration, automobile purchases, and marriages must be approved by the elders. This was acceptable to the people, since nearly all of their requests were approved. When a few requests for major purchases were rejected, the members didn't really complain. They just stopped asking and accepted what they had.*

Last year the Reverend Mr. Johnson announced the "Year of Holiness." He asked the congregation to take one year to reject the ways of the world. Members turned off their televisions and radios; stopped dancing, listening to rap music, and playing competitive sports; and broke ties with all godless people who might lead them into temptation.

To replace those activities, the church was kept open longer hours. Members of the congregation were encouraged to fast regularly, read scripture, and pray. Those with jobs were encouraged either to work longer hours or to take a second job to increase the income of the congregation. The community funds were growing dramatically. Since no one wanted to appear greedy or selfish during the Year of Holiness, requests for special purchases and expenses were down. This circumstance greatly encouraged Obediah Johnson and the council of elders.

The younger members of the community, however, had a hard time adjusting to the Year of Holiness. If a child was caught watching television or listening to music, the council of elders assigned a "correction." First corrections consisted of memorizing Bible verses and cleaning up around the church. Second offenses were punished by withholding food for short periods and restricting the offender to one room. Third offenses, and there were very few of these, incurred physical punishment: twenty-one blows with the "rod and staff of righteousness." The hardest blows were generally delivered to the child by the offending child's parent and by the Most Reverend Obediah Johnson.

To his high school classmates, Jonas was known as Johnny. Because of his calm confidence, he was generally well liked. Johnny was a talented athlete, and basketball was his first love. All through elementary school and junior high, he completed his homework, chores, prayers, and services as efficiently as possible so that he could go down to the schoolyard and work on his jump shots, free throws, and lay-ups. Basketball was his escape from the cheerlessness of the Divine Light Apostolic Missionary Church.

The Year of Holiness took away Jonas's escape. Competitive sports were forbidden, and Jonas was told specifically that basketball was not allowed. Jonas was deeply disappointed. He had counted on trying out for the freshman team this year, and he dreamed of being moved up to junior varsity by the beginning of the season and making the varsity team by season's end. The Year of Holiness had snuffed out that dream.

For the first month Jonas did not play basketball at all. It was only twelve months. It would be hard, but he would stick it out. Anyway, he was watched so carefully by the congregation that he could never get away with breaking the rules. He was, after all, the Reverend Obediah Johnson's eldest son.

Jonas was assigned a paper in World History class. The school library did not have adequate resources to research the paper, so Jonas went to the public library several miles away. His work finished, Jonas waited for a bus. In the schoolyard behind him, nine boys were playing basketball. What would it hurt to watch? Jonas walked over just to take in the game. He barely noticed when the bus passed by; another one would be along shortly. The four-against-five game continued, lopsidedly in favor of the five players. One of the four spotted Jonas watching.

"C'mon, get in the game," the player called.

Jonas hesitated for just a moment. The player asked, "What's your name?"

Jonas blurted, "Johnny. Okay, let's play some ball!"

Mrs. Johnson became very concerned when Jonas missed the evening prayer service. But it took his father only a few seconds to figure out why Jonas had come home two hours late. The council of elders assigned Jonas a harsh physical correction. After all, he was the eldest son of the Most Reverend Obediah Johnson. They believed that Jonas should be an example to the entire congregation.

Options and Alternatives

Religious Fanaticism

Jonas Johnson is a PK, or Preacher's Kid. As such, he is held to a higher standard of behavior by members of the community. The preacher's leadership is judged to a certain extent by the actions of his children. Obediah thinks the congregation will infer that if he is unable to rule his own children, he is not a fit leader for the church. There is tremendous pressure on all six of the Johnson children, including Jonas.

Preacher's kids are not the only ones who feel this pressure. Children of all kinds of people—principals, teachers, police chiefs, day-care workers, politicians, psychologists, pediatricians, and similar professionals—often feel that they are being watched carefully. The children's parents feel that their own work is being judged by the actions of their children. Any person whose job involves the care of others is continually being tested. Parents leaving their toddler at a new day-care center want as much information as possible about the workers. They often ask the workers questions about their own children as a means of judging their fitness. A day-care worker whose children have had trouble at school or with the law is less likely to be trusted with the care of other children.

Despite that, it is important for teenagers to know that they are not responsible for their parents' success (or lack of success) in the workplace. They are not responsible for the inferences that people draw. One of the needs that a family fulfills is the opportunity for personal growth. If a young person is pressured to conform to standards designed merely to improve a parent's standing in the community, that teenager will not grow as a person. Fulfilling someone else's dreams and expectations instead of your own is the opposite of growth.

The pressure to conform to imposed standards often makes young people rebellious, particularly if the standards are not reasonable. It is unreasonable to ask a

73

teenager to conform to expectations that benefit only the parent. Most people are willing to do what is "right" because they know that it will benefit them in the long run. We save money, stay physically fit, and do our homework because we believe it will be good for us at some future time. It is not reasonable to ask a teenager to do these things because not doing so will make his father look bad in the eyes of the community.

Rebelling against such a situation is understandable, but it is equally limiting to personal growth. Rebelling is simply reacting to someone else's standards. Rebelling is saying, "You can't make me do things your way." Conforming and rebelling are opposite sides of the same coin. Both stifle growth. Real personal growth comes from knowing yourself and making choices of which you can be proud.

Another issue in Jonas's life is the church itself. The Divine Light Apostolic Missionary Church (DLAMC) is not really a church. It is a cult. The difference between a cult and a church is this: A church focuses outside of itself on a supreme being for support, wisdom, strength, inspiration, consolation, and the like. A cult does not focus outside of itself. Its focus is inward and local. Members of a cult surrender control of their behavior, belongings, or money to the cult. Once control has been given over to the cult, it is difficult for cult members to break away.

The DLAMC is a churchlike cult. It is easy for people to be attracted to such cults. The members are committed to the scriptures and reject evil. They are kind, compassionate people. But the DLAMC has control over every aspect of its members' lives.

Other cults are not churchlike. Some are antisocial, such as street gangs, Satan worshippers, and witch covens. In these antisocial cults, members are usually initiated by being required to perform some act that is either illegal or morally repulsive. After initiation, members dare not leave the cult for fear their actions may be revealed.

Political Fanaticism

Political fanaticism can create dysfunction in a family as well. Political fanaticism involves holding so strong a belief about how society should conduct itself that a person is unable to put the needs of his family before his commitment to the cause.

The Ku Klux Klan and the Neo-Nazis are two examples of political groups whose members are often fanatical about their beliefs. Members of these groups keep their affiliations private. Because some members of these groups have committed illegal acts such as killing African Americans or destroying Jewish synagogues, members are highly secretive about their activities. It is difficult for a family to function in a healthy way when one or more members are leading a secret life. Politically fanatic parents often try to influence their children to adopt their beliefs. As a result, they pass on their dysfunctional behavior to their children.

How Can I Cope?

Breaking away from a cult, or a fanatical political organization is very difficult, particularly if your own father is the leader. The first step is to recognize the situation for what it is. Jonas is being asked to behave so that he does not harm his father's reputation. He is also being asked to conform to unreasonably restrictive standards. One way to cope is to accept the situation as it is and conform. As long as this decision is made with full awareness of the consequences, conforming will not totally stop personal growth. In this churchlike cult, conformity may be acceptable to the teen as long as he or she recognizes that it is a free choice and not done out of fear.

Another choice is to reject the organization. This would be extremely difficult for Jonas, since his family life is centered around the DLAMC. For Jonas to play basketball would require either defiance of his father's authority or a bending of his father's will. After experiencing severe physical punishment, Jonas is unlikely to defy his father's authority. As leader of the council of elders, Obediah is unlikely to back down. For Jonas to make any progress, he will need help from his mother, a trusted member of the council of elders, another preacher respected by his father, an aunt or uncle close to his father, or perhaps the basketball coach at school. Any of these people might be able to find a way for Obediah to lift the restriction on basketball and to save face at the same time.

Breaking away from any group that has so much influence on one's life can take years. Former members of the group then need years of supportive therapy to reassure them that they were not to blame for ritualistic activities that their parents imposed on them. It takes a long time for them to realize that they did not betray their family when they rejected the cult.

For Jonas to discover who he is and what he believes will be a difficult process. He will need to untangle the expectations of the DLAMC from his parents' real concern for his well-being. Jonas will need help to to do this.

There are many places where Jonas can go for assistance. In the Yellow Pages of the local phone book there are community agencies to help young people. Often there are agencies whose purpose is to help people break away from cults; their expertise is equally applicable to political groups. They will be able to help you deal with the cult or political group. Contacting them can be the first step in coping with the dysfunction in your family.

Workaholic Parents

Aimee was used to being alone by now. Six weeks after her birth, her mother went back to work. For the first few years Aimee's baby-sitters were other moms who took care of her to supplement their incomes. At three, Aimee was enrolled at the Rainbow Connection, a preschool. Aimee never thought too much about the twelve hours she spent there each day. She had caring teachers, and her mom always brought her something special that she could eat in the car before dinner.

When school started, Aimee split her day between Armstrong Elementary School and the Rainbow Connection. Each day the kids were divided into walkers, bussers, and special bussers. The walkers and bussers got home by three o'clock. Special bussers had to stay longer at school.

By fourth grade Aimee begged her mom to let her take the regular bus home. The other kids teased the special bussers, calling them "babies." Aimee promised to do all her homework and chores before anyone got home. She would call Mom each day the moment she got home. She would never let anyone into the house.

Both Mom and Dad were pleased with how responsible Aimee was becoming at home on her own. Although they were often in meetings, most days she was able to reach one of them as soon as she got home. Now, instead of doing art projects and quiet time, Aimee went right to her homework. That is, right after she got a snack and turned on the TV to watch reruns of "Gilligan's Island," "The Beverly Hillbillies," or whatever else was on that afternoon.

Things started to change when Aimee entered junior high school. Dad was traveling more often. It seemed that he was out of town most of the time. Mom had more responsibilities at work as well. It was becoming unusual for her to get home before seven o'clock. Aimee's responsibilities changed too. Many of her school assignments were group projects. She never contributed much to group projects, because no one was home to drive her to wherever the meetings were held.

In eighth grade Aimee made the basketball team. Dad came to one of her games. Mom came to two. Aimee called Mom at work right after the city championship game, just to let her know that they'd won.

When Aimee wasn't playing basketball, she was hanging out at school, hanging out at the park, and hanging out at her friends' houses. She couldn't keep track of her dad's trips and her mom's meetings well enough to be able to get in touch with them, even if she had wanted to.

High school was becoming a blur. Aimee's friends had other friends who could get beer and wine anytime they wanted. The drinking started on the weekends, but pretty soon Aimee couldn't wait for school *to end so she could have a few glasses of beer. By the time her parents got home she had brushed her teeth and used mouthwash to cover the odor. When she started missing school so that she could drink during the day, her grades began to slip drastically.*

Surprisingly, her parents didn't even notice that Aimee didn't produce the first-quarter report card. Aimee simply forged Dad's signature. When the semester grades came back all Ds and Fs, however, her parents sat down together with Aimee. It was the first time in a long time that Aimee could remember their taking the time to do that. "Who cares now?" she reasoned. "It's too late to do anything anyway."

Options and Alternatives

Families need to do much more than meet basic survival needs. Everyone in a family may be safe, well fed, warm, and nicely dressed. They may have all the material things that are needed. But even in homes with a VCR, big-screen TV, CD player, and microwave oven, every member of the family needs to feel that he or she belongs.

Aimee's parents have set firm goals in their careers and seem to be achieving them. Working with others toward a goal gives a person a sense of being on a team, a feeling of belonging. Both parents feel that they belong at work. They are able to have lunch, exercise, even take a few moments off to share what is happening in their lives with their coworkers. But they never have any time at all for their daughter.

Aimee's parents are more than merely ambitious and hard working. They are workaholics. Workaholics are addicted to their work, and the rewards that it brings them, in the same way that compulsive gamblers are addicted to their habit. In Aimee's family both parents have put their jobs ahead of their family's needs. Both parents feel that they are valued and have a sense of belonging at work. Workaholics are often too busy with their work to notice what's happening at home.

Aimee first felt that she belonged when she made the basketball team. Winning the city championship was an experience that she and the other girls had gone through together. Unfortunately, when the season ended Aimee was left feeling more adrift than ever. She wanted to belong but no longer had a team to which she could belong. She could not turn to her parents because they were never available.

In high school, Aimee's friends became her family. Being with them made her forget her loneliness and isolation. Aimee may have known right away that drinking was not for her, but she didn't want to turn away from people who liked and accepted her. Her parents were too busy to see that Aimee was in trouble. She couldn't confide in them. By the time they realized she was abusing alcohol, it was too late to prevent it.

People need to belong. When they don't feel important and valuable at home, they seek a sense of belonging from other people. Some teenagers become sexually active at a very young age. Both guys and girls want to be loved and accepted. Afraid that saying no will cost them acceptance and love, many teenagers are willing to risk pregnancy and disease. Because they don't get attention and affirmation at home, they have to turn to other sources, many of them harmful.

Many others turn to gangs or other groups just to end the isolation. Being in a group that steals, vandalizes, or intimidates creates secrets. Everyone involved in the illicit activity is willing to protect the rest of the group. These secrets bind teens tightly to the gang and isolate them from everyone else. These groups then become a substitute for a family.

Some young people think seriously about suicide or running away from home. They hurt because they feel so empty. Wealthy teenagers attempt suicide more often than those living in poverty. Many who have been rescued from suicide attempts say that they just couldn't stand being so alone.

Families in which both parents are strongly attached to their careers at the expense of their children are not really families at all. Aimee's family is more like a group of people who live in the same house but seek to meet their needs for belonging, self-esteem, and growth outside the home. They have never had to support each other through difficult times, because times have never really been difficult (until now).

Young people in workaholic families often find themselves burning out at a very early age. They see how hard their parents work for economic advantage and decide that it's just not worth it. You have to give up too many things. Belonging and love are more basic needs than self-esteem and growth. If the need to belong is not being met, it is very difficult for someone to set goals and to succeed.

What Can I Do to Help?

Talk to Your Parent(s)

Stop and think about what you need from your family. Which specific need is not being met? If you are like Aimee, you may feel that you don't have your family's support. Without arguing or accusing, try to explain to your parents how you feel.

Be prepared if along with support a few new limits are set. Many workaholic families do not know each other well. Everyone is coping by ignoring what is happening. Aimee's parents may have smelled alcohol on Aimee's breath or, more likely, they just weren't around to notice her drinking problem. Working together requires compromise. You and your parents need to compromise and to see each other's point of view.

Be prepared to get help as a family. Workaholic families are more likely than others to seek professional help to resolve problems. They are used to going to experts for help in their own careers and treat their families as they do their jobs.

Unfortunately, they often have the greatest difficulty accepting suggestions for change. Aimee needs more help than her parents can give her right now. Her drinking has gotten to the point where she needs to work with a counselor or support group. Although the entire family is dysfunctional, Aimee needs the most immediate help. She will do much better if the family can work together toward her recovery.

Be prepared to try more than once. Aimee's family developed its pattern over fifteen years; they are not likely to be able to change it on the first try. It will take a great deal of patience and compromise for them to learn to support and care for one another.

Talk to Other Trusted Adults

What adult do you trust most? You may want to confide in your school counselor, social worker, youth minister, aunt, uncle, scout leader, club advisor, or coach. You may want to tell this adult immediately that all you need is for him or her to listen. Talking to other adults may help you to clarify your own thinking. The first time you talk to your parents, they may dismiss your position as an exaggeration. After all, they have seen all the changes you have gone through in your life. Or your parents may feel so threatened that they cannot really listen to you.

Try to use your trusted adult as a way to bring your family together. When you have been listened to and understood, it is easy to think that the talk has resolved the problem. Don't let your adult friend take the place of your parents, but allow him or her to lead you back to them.

What Can I Do to Cope?

Sometimes no matter what you try, things just won't change. You have been patient, open-minded, and willing to compromise, but the family is still functioning badly. What are some things that you can do to help cope in a workaholic family?

Find Healthy Groups to Join

Sports teams, clubs, the school band, scouts, church youth groups, antidrug groups, and community action groups are all good groups to try. This is a time to keep an open mind. Even if you have already dismissed the people in these groups as geeks, jocks, or weirdos, give them another look. If you can accomplish something together, they may help you develop self-esteem, set goals, grow, and achieve. These groups can not take the place of your family, but they can help you to cope when your family is unavailable.

Find a Mentor

A mentor is any adult to whom you can turn for advice and counsel. Older brothers or sisters, aunts or uncles, grandparents, teachers, coaches, counselors, scout leaders, priests, rabbis, ministers, and club advisors all make good mentors. Sometimes you can learn about making decisions just by observing a healthy adult. Your mentor need not be exactly the kind of person that you hope to be, but should be someone who understands life and who seems to have common sense.

Set Goals for Yourself

Start with small, one-day-at-a-time goals and work your way up to this week, this month, this quarter, this semester, this year, and finally, high school graduation. Long-term goals are the hardest to set and can easily slip away. If you can set and achieve daily goals, long-term goals will come easier.

Don't be too hard on yourself if you cannot meet these goals. If you don't succeed, set easier goals. If today's goal was to finish all your homework, but actually you went to the movies and hung out with friends, don't give up.

Tomorrow set a more reasonable goal, such as completing your math homework and spending one hour working on your history paper.

Keep Talking to Your Parent(s)

Even though you may be coping by meeting your needs outside your family, you should still try to share your hopes, your dreams, and your accomplishments with your parents. Keep an open mind. Just as your life is changing, your parents' lives change as well. Try to be there when they are ready to belong.

Depression and Other Mental Illnesses

Sarah Fernandez was embarrassed about her mother. It wasn't the usual embarrassment that most teens feel if a mother is uncool or hopelessly out of date. Mrs. Fernandez acted crazy. She was becoming more and more unpredictable. Some days when Sarah came home, her mother would be singing and dancing through the house. Mrs. Fernandez was filled with energy and life on those days. She would try to get Sarah or her brothers to dance or sing along with her, but they never would. It was just too strange and overwhelming. Inevitably, Mrs. Fernandez would become angry with her children for not joining her. She would scream at them, sometimes calling them ungrateful, selfish, or just plain boring.

Other days would be just the opposite. It would be obvious that Mrs. Fernandez had not even got dressed that morning. All the lights in the house would be off, and her mother would be in bed or on the couch. Sarah and the boys had learned the hard way never to disturb their mother on these days. The mildest request would lead to her crying and carrying on about how no one ever did anything for her. She would go on about how she would be better off dead or if she had never gotten married or had kids.

Mr. Fernandez had learned to adapt to his wife's mood swings. When she was happy and lively, he would smile and joke with her. He could calm her without angering her. They could talk for hours about their plans, hopes, and dreams for their children. These times were bittersweet for Mr. Fernandez. He knew that during the depressed days to follow, his wife would forget, deny, or simply refuse to go along with most of the plans they had made.

On his wife's depressed days, Mr. Fernandez simply let her be. He had learned to ignore her self-pity. Either he or Sarah would prepare dinner. They would do whatever cleaning was needed around the house. Both Sarah and her father made sure that the boys didn't disturb their mother. Often during these dark periods, Mrs. Fernandez would attack her husband verbally in tirades about how little money he made, how lazy and worthless he was, how he could never make any woman happy. Mr. Fernandez did not bother to argue back. He tried to calm her as best he could. Then he went about taking care of the children, making repairs around the house, or doing the necessary yardwork.

Mrs. Fernandez had not always been so erratic. When they were first married, she was warm and loving. She occasionally had days when she was down or depressed, but no more than normal. She had worked as an X-ray technician until Sarah was born. Later she went back to work part time, but she lost her job because her work was inconsistent. Some days she performed perfectly; other days she made serious errors and her work had to be redone. Her supervisor simply could not trust her. Mrs.

Fernandez went on a few job interviews but soon became discouraged and decided to be a stay-at-home mom.

Mr. Fernandez knew that something was wrong with his wife, but he felt helpless to do anything about it. Once when she was at her worst, he suggested that she see a doctor. Mrs. Fernandez erupted, "I'm not crazy. There's nothing wrong with me. Who wouldn't feel bad with a lazy husband and worthless children? You'll never get me to a doctor! Absolutely never!"

He tried a few more times, with the same result. When Mrs. Fernandez was down, she refused to see a doctor. When she was feeling well, there didn't seem to be a need.

Mr. Fernandez explained to Sarah and the boys, "I love and accept your mother just the way she is. You all must do the same."

Accepting her mother was becoming more difficult for Sarah. Her chemistry teacher had encouraged her to enter a project in the district science fair. Sarah found a suitable project and worked on it for months. Unfortunately, the night of the fair was one of Mrs. Fernandez' energetic periods. Sarah's mother arrived at the fair in her brightest dress, wearing far too much makeup. She walked up to total strangers and told them that her daughter had the best project in the fair. She described hours of tireless work that she and Sarah had spent together preparing for this evening—hours that Sarah certainly could not remember: Her mother had shown no interest whatever in the project, at least not until this very night.

A few of Sarah's friends asked her quietly whether her mom was okay. Most of the others stared at her or made comments behind her back.

The announcement of the winners was the worst. When Sarah's project was awarded second place, Mrs. Fernandez came unhinged. She screamed hysterically, "This is an outrage! Everyone knows my daughter had the best project. The judges are stupid, ignorant fools!"

The ceremony stopped for a moment while a security guard and the assistant principal escorted Mrs. Fernandez from the building. She argued briefly, told them not to touch her, then strode out of the building by herself.

Sarah felt humiliated. As she walked home, she thought of all the things she wanted to scream at her mother. She wanted to tell her mother that she was a sick, crazy person who needed a psychiatrist. She was ready to give her a tongue-lashing. When Sarah entered the house, Mrs. Fernandez was lying on the couch. She obviously had been crying. Her red-rimmed eyes seemed to look through her daughter. Pathetically, she mumbled to her, "Baby, yours was the best."

Mental Disorders

Mental illness is a disease of the mind. It often affects the way a person thinks and feels. When the way a person thinks or the emotions that he experiences differ greatly from reality, the person is said to be mentally ill. Some common mental disorders are depression, bipolar disorder, anxiety disorders, psychoses, and addictive behavior.

Depression

When people have suffered a loss, a traumatic event, or some other tragedy, they may feel depressed. This is called situational depression. A person grieves for the death of a loved one. For a time he or she may avoid other people, say that life is meaningless, and appear gloomy and sad, but eventually he or she feels better. The loss of a job, reaching middle age, the birth of a child, the death of a parent or child, and similar events can lead to situational depression. The person needs help, support, and encouragement. Good friends, a minister, a counselor, or a psychologist or psychiatrist may help to ease the intensity and shorten the duration of the depression. But situational depression is usually easily treated. It is a temporary form of mental illness.

Major depression differs from situational depression in important ways. Persons suffering major depression feel grief, sadness, loss of appetite, and lack of interest in activities, but there is no obvious trigger, or cause, for their depression. No specific event has occurred. People suffering from major depression often sleep poorly, are either very irritable or hopeless, think or speak of suicide, and sometimes have hallucinations or delusions.

Psychiatrists are able to treat depression effectively with antidepressive medication and individual or group therapy. Talking to a therapist or a group can help a depressed patient control his thoughts and feelings and check them against what is really happening around him.

Bipolar Disorder

Mrs. Fernandez is suffering from bipolar disorder, sometimes called manic-depressive disorder. It differs from major

91

depression in that the manic-depressive person alternates between low, depressed feelings and high, excited, energetic states. These mood swings may last hours, days, weeks, or months. Bipolar disorder is harder to treat than depression because medication that relieves the depression also makes the hyperactivity worse, and medication to calm the excited phase deepens the depression. It is very difficult for a physician to adjust the medication to even out the extreme emotions.

Untreated bipolar disorder can lead to accidental death in the manic stage or suicide in the depressive stage.

Anxiety Disorders

Many things in our daily lives create anxiety: worries about money, popularity, reputation, safety, acceptance by peers, and many others. Anxiety becomes a problem when it causes us to retreat from healthy activities, or when our physical health is affected by our worries. Three common types of anxiety disorder are panic attacks, phobias, and obsessive-compulsive disorders.

Panic attacks are severe feelings of nervousness, fear, or tension that occur for no particular reason. Some people panic in enclosed places such as elevators; others panic in wide-open places such as parking lots or sparsely populated shopping malls. Panic attacks can cause a person to faint, vomit, or break into a cold sweat. Medication is effective in treating panic attacks. Sometimes relaxation techniques can help. Providing support while gradually introducing a person to a place where his or her panic attacks tend to occur can help to control the anxiety.

Phobias are unrealistic or excessive fears of a certain situation or object. People may fear cats, spiders, crowds, enclosed places, or even leaving their own home. Psychologists usually treat phobias with talk therapy, which helps the patient understand where the fear came from, and relaxation therapy, in which the patient learns to relax while facing the feared object or situation. The person is led to imagine himself in a situation with the feared object, in order to develop confidence. Then the feared object or situation is introduced slowly and with another person's support.

A third type of anxiety disorder is obsessive-compulsive disorder. Obsessions are recurring thoughts about violence, infection, death, or other themes that a person cannot seem to put aside. Recurring thoughts are common, but if the thoughts persist over months they present a problem. Compulsions are actions that a person cannot stop repeating, such as hand-washing, checking to see that car and house doors are locked, or counting objects. Antidepressant medications can be very helpful in treating people with obsessive or compulsive disorders.

Psychoses

Psychoses are disorders of thinking so severe that the person cannot distinguish thought from reality. In schizophrenia, a common psychosis, people may have a grossly inflated opinion of their own importance. They may have beliefs with no basis in reality (such as that aliens have placed an antenna in their head that is transmitting bizarre thoughts into their mind) or hallucinations.

People suffering from schizophrenia usually need long-term intensive treatment. Most patients must spend some time in a hospital. Medication can be extremely useful. Untreated schizophrenics have great trouble adapting to everyday life.

Addictive Behavior

Addictive behavior can involve drugs, alcohol, tobacco, gambling, caffeine, or even food. Any addiction can cause a dysfunction in a family. When an addict's need threatens the safety, security, feeling of belonging, self-esteem, or growth of any of the family members, the addiction is a problem for the person and the family.

Doctors or psychologists can effectively treat addiction, but the key to treatment is that the addict must want to break free.

How Can I Cope?

The Fernandez family is dysfunctional because the members choose to let Mrs. Fernandez's mental illness go untreated. For real change to occur, they must confront Mrs. Fernandez and insist that she go for treatment, or take her to treatment against her will.

People with untreated physical diseases usually get sicker and sicker. It is likely that Mrs. Fernandez's mental health will also become worse until she receives help. The sooner she starts psychological therapy and medication, the easier it will be for her entire family to begin to function in a healthy way.

She most likely needs to see a psychiatrist, but a medical doctor, social worker, psychologist, or similar professional may see her first and refer her to the specific help she needs. Some promising research is being done currently that links body chemistry to mental illness. Changes in diet and in supplemental vitamins and nutrients can lead to a dramatic improvement in many people with mental disease.

Abusive Sibling

Jim and Kate had always understood why their parents were so proud of their older brother. After all, William was a star high school athlete in football, wrestling, and track. The Roundtree family had attended William's sporting events ever since he was in grade school. Now everything the family did seemed to revolve around his sport seasons.

Roger Roundtree would tell Jim and Kate how Native Americans had lost their heritage, and how the Cherokee people had been swallowed up by a European society. So many Cherokee traditions were lost; their way of life had been destroyed. But when Roger Roundtree watched his son on the athletic field, he saw a Cherokee warrior facing overwhelming odds. More often than not, William Roundtree was victorious. In his father's mind, William's victories on the athletic field were also a vindication of the Cherokee people.

Neither Jim nor Kate shared William's athletic prowess. Kate had tried cross-country running and basketball but failed to make her junior high school teams. Jim preferred books and music to athletics, but in his freshman year he did try out for the football team, with disastrous results. The coach had expected great things from William Roundtree's younger brother, but found him lacking speed, strength, and intensity. Out of respect for the family, the coach kept him on the team a week longer than he probably should have. Mercifully, he cut Jim two days before the first game.

Jim was relieved to be cut from the team. He had already discovered that he was not suited for football, but his father forbade quitting. Jim was already planning to try out for the marching band. He began thinking about his challenging high school classes.

When Jim told his parents about being cut from the team, his mother was sympathetic, and his father said he understood. What Roger Roundtree didn't say was that he had known all along that Jim was not the athlete his older brother was.

William's reaction, however, took Jim off guard. William was furious. He had been so busy with the varsity squad that he hadn't realized how badly Jim was doing with the freshman team. Varsity players who had watched Jim joked about his ineptness, but none had dared to say anything to William.

William was determined to help Jim express his Cherokee heritage. He would make his brother tougher, stronger, faster, and more focused. He would turn Jim into a warrior. To William, Jim was an embarrassment. William would make him into a man.

William pushed Jim out of bed the next morning at 4:45. "We're going for a run." Jim didn't dare to disagree. He dressed, and they headed out into the predawn darkness. It seemed unnatural to Jim to be running before his body was fully awake. Football had him in the best physical condition he had ever been, but that was not enough to keep up with William. William pushed, prodded, and commanded him to keep running, to keep going. When Jim fell breathless to the ground, William called him a wimp, a baby. When William gave him a swift kick in the ribs, Jim finally got up and dragged himself home as best he could.

William forced Jim to run for several days, but despite his punching and kicking, Jim's endurance did not improve. William decided to make his brother a fighter. Since he held that only weaklings fight with gloves, they fought with bare fists. William told Jim that the black eye he inflicted was a badge of honor. He said Jim should wear it proudly and tell anyone who asked about it that it was none of their damn business.

Mrs. Roundtree noticed the black eye right away. She gave Jim an ice pack to put on it and told William that he should be more considerate of his younger brother. William did not respond.

Roger Roundtree seemed not to notice. Jim wondered whether his father was too occupied with his own affairs, or whether he approved of the discipline that William was attempting to instill in him. Either way, Jim felt helpless and betrayed.

In the meantime, Kate was going out with another member of the varsity team. Carl Mitchell had always liked to brag about how far girls would go with him, but he watched what he said when he started dating Kate. Carl already knew that William didn't like him. William had got on him before for being lazy in practice and had lectured him about letting the team down by not doing his best.

In the locker room one afternoon, Carl noticed that William had gone into the coach's office and shut the door. He took the opportunity to huddle a group of players around him and describe in vivid detail his date with Kate Roundtree. What Carl didn't notice was that William had emerged after only a moment and was standing right behind him.

Although it would take a while for Carl's injuries to heal from William's beating, the coach only suspended William for one game. In his judgment, Carl had provoked the beating.

Kate was startled when William came in and began slapping her face, leaving bright red welts. He called her a disgrace to the family. Kate had no idea how far he would have gone if her mother had not come in and ordered him to stop. William stomped out of the room, still fuming.

Options and Alternatives

One of the basic needs that a family meets is providing safety from physical danger. A family becomes dysfunctional when one of its members harms or abuses another member. Bruises, welts, black eyes, burns, cuts, or broken bones are all physical abuse, no matter what the abuser's intentions are.

William Roundtree wants the best for his younger brother and sister. He wants his brother to develop physical strength, endurance, and confidence. He wants his sister to keep her reputation intact. He seeks to accomplish these aims through physical abuse. William's methods are more likely to cause lasting emotional problems.

Jim Roundtree is already more fearful and less confident. The likelihood of his trying out for another sport is very small. The only thing his fights with William have taught him is to avoid further fights. Jim, a capable student and musician, is forced to take time and emotion away from the things he does best.

Kate Roundtree may fear her brother's abuse, but her resentment of William is likely to lead to unwise actions. People filled with resentment often react by making poor choices to spite the person they resent.

Neither Jim nor Kate can feel secure and loved or have a sense of belonging and self-esteem in a home where they experience physical abuse. They will have trouble achieving personal growth if they do not feel safe.

William Roundtree was given great leeway by his coach and teammate. Carl could have charged him with assault. Carl's comments about Kate were despicable, but they did not deserve a brutal beating. Had Carl pressed charges, the Roundtrees would probably have been responsible for all of his medical expenses. It is likely that William would have been found guilty of assault.

Besides the physical abuse, the Roundtree family is dysfunctional for two other reasons. First, William has power and influence that should be exercised only by the parents. Neither parent interceded in time to prevent him from doing harm to his brother and sister. A family should have a balance of power and control. As the children mature, they need to be given additional freedom to develop skills for independent living. But primary control over the family must remain in the hands of the parents. In the Roundtree family, this is no longer true. William has been permitted to inflict physical harm on his siblings. Their mother seems unable to control William, and their father is unwilling to do so.

The second dysfunction of the Roundtree family is that the focus of their attention, admiration, and aspirations is on William and his athletic career. All of the family's activities revolve around his activities. All efforts seem to be focused on nurturing his success. This imbalance makes Jim and Kate feel undervalued and unwanted.

It will be difficult for Jim and Kate to help reorganize their family. Their first step is to try to persuade their parents to take control of the family and stop William's physical abuse. Jim and Kate could work together to speak with their parents. They might talk to their parents separately or together. For the family to function healthily, Mr. and Mrs. Roundtree need to recognize and value the abilities of all three children. They also need to control William.

Jim and Kate might argue that William needs to be stopped for his own good. William was lucky not to end up in trouble with the police over his assault on Carl. If the Roundtrees are not willing or able to stand up to William for them, Jim and Kate need to take their own measures to protect themselves.

How Can I Cope?

In some dysfunctional families, members know that they cannot change the situation and must learn to cope as best they can. This is not the case with physical abuse. It is not permissible for teenagers to be subjected to physical abuse. If you are being physically abused, you need help.

First, it is important to define physical abuse. Physical abuse is not routine spanking, restriction to a room, or a slap on the cheek after a disrespectful remark. Physical abuse is not rough play between siblings of about the same size and age. Physical abuse is any exchange between family members that results in bruises, welts, broken bones, cut skin, burns, or similar injuries inflicted by one person who has power over another. Usually physical abuse is inflicted on children by parents. Less commonly parents allow abuse by one sibling over others.

Physical abuse is not to be tolerated. If you are being physically abused, get out of the situation. First, use all the resources at your disposal within your family to improve the situation. Try to talk to your parents or sibling.

If that fails, get help from outside the family. In most states, teachers are required to report abuse to child protection agencies. A teacher, counselor, or social worker would be a logical person to tell. Any of them should be able to connect you with people who can help.

If school personnel are not available to you, try a clergy person. If you feel that you are in immediate danger, call the police. Most police departments have youth officers who can help. Some police departments have social workers specially trained to deal with such situations.

The most important thing is to take steps to get help. The situation may become difficult before it improves, but it will only get worse if you accept it as it is.

Physically or Mentally Challenged Sibling

Paul Martin was hoping that his dad would be able to make it to his wrestling meet. If they won this meet, his team would clinch the top spot in their division and be assured of an invitation to the state playoffs. Unfortunately, his brother, Ryne, had to practice for next week's Special Olympics. Mr. Martin would have to make it another day.

Everyone knew that little Ryne Martin had a difficult life. Having Down syndrome made it hard for him to learn things that came easily to others. His severe hearing loss made it even harder. Mr. and Mrs. Martin tried to make up for his disabilities by giving him every possible advantage. Mom volunteered at Ryne's school. Dad seemed to spend all his time organizing and fundraising for the Special Olympics.

The parents and kids at Ryne's school really appreciated the Martins' tireless efforts. Mrs. Martin was honored at a luncheon for the faculty and staff. A local community group awarded Mr. Martin a plaque for outstanding humanitarian work with the Special Olympics. These small recognitions almost made up for the sacrifices necessary to raise a disabled child.

When Paul was younger, his parents asked him to help Ryne and try to teach him things. But no matter how hard he tried, Paul inevitably ended up becom-

103

ing frustrated with his brother. He never meant to snap or yell at Ryne, but he couldn't help himself.

Paul felt that he worked hard keeping up with schoolwork and doing his own chores. He had to admit that he resented a brother whose main chores consisted of dressing himself, brushing his teeth, and finishing breakfast in time for the minibus that took him to school each day.

The Martins eventually gave up trying to make Paul help Ryne. They told him that they would be satisfied if he just kept up with his own responsibilities. Paul was able to keep his end of that bargain just fine, at least for a while.

Then the Martins joined a group devoted to winning greater rights for physically and mentally disabled people. The time they spent working for the group began to seem continuous. Both parents were so deeply involved that the general maintenance and routine of the home broke down. Paul was needed to buy groceries, cook meals, figure out ways to make repairs, and, once in a while, to keep an eye on Ryne.

Paul had planned all year to try out for the soccer team. On tryout day Mom had a meeting with the group's lawyer that ran longer than she had expected. Paul was stuck watching Ryne. He thought of leaving him alone and going to the tryouts, but he knew he couldn't do that. He never thought of taking Ryne with him. What kind of impression would that make on his soon-to-be teammates?

When Mrs. Martin finally arrived, Paul exploded at her. Normally, Paul wouldn't talk to his mother that way. If he hadn't been stuck watching his "retarded" brother, he would never have done it.

Paul was twenty minutes late and still furious. Coach Johnson did not appreciate Paul's sarcastic tone of voice. He was very patient when Paul told him that he was teaching the wrong way to kick a soccer ball for distance. But the coach had to act when he screamed at another player for missing an easy pass. He ordered Paul to leave the tryout. Needless to say, Paul did not make the team.

This had to be somebody's fault. Paul knew that he was a better player than at least five of the boys who made the team. It wasn't Paul's fault that he was late. And who wouldn't have been angry after having to watch his brother for all that time. Paul didn't know if it was his parents' fault for being so involved or Ryne's fault for just being Ryne. He did know that he himself had done everything right. He had been responsible. His parents almost never came to his wrestling meets to support him. But he was the one who got cut from soccer. Paul felt like hitting someone. He just couldn't figure out whom.

Options and Alternatives

Many families with mentally or physically disabled children function very well and meet the needs of all members. Such a family becomes dysfunctional when all of the family's energies are focused on meeting the needs of one member while others are neglected. Special children do require a lot more time, effort, and patience from every family member. Nevertheless, each member needs to feel loved and part of the family.

Teenagers with mentally or physically disabled siblings often find it difficult to express their anger. When everyone in the family is asked to sacrifice for one person, resentment is understandable. But although life and nature can be unfair, families must try to be fair with each other.

When you find yourself feeling angry with your family, it is important to determine exactly what is making you angry. Ask yourself: When did I first feel angry? Is the person or situation capable of changing? At whom or what am I directing my anger? Did another person hurt me intentionally or maliciously? What did I do that may have led to the problem?

1. When did I first feel angry?

Anger often builds slowly. We find ourselves treating other people with sarcasm, criticism, or hostility without knowing what is bothering us. It helps to stop for a moment and think: When did I start feeling this way? What happened just before I started acting differently? It's surprising how often we shove the circumstance out of our memory and then take out our anger on someone else. Paul was not angry with his coach or the other players. But he took his anger out on them, costing himself an opportunity to make the team.

2. Is the person or situation capable of changing?

It is a waste of energy to stay angry at a person or situation that cannot change. People become angry at weather, illness, the price of a movie ticket, even the arrival of their birthday. This is common but not very helpful. Paul knew that it made no sense to resent his brother for having Down syndrome, but he resented Ryne nevertheless. When you know that the object of your anger cannot change, it is best to accept the situation. Paul needs to understand that although Ryne cannot change, his family can.

3. At whom or what am I directing my anger?

After Paul thinks about his situation for a while, he will probably realize that his anger should be directed toward his parents. This is a situation, too, that many young people find hard to express. The Martins are well regarded because of their efforts with Ryne. It is hard for Paul to be angry with them when the community considers them wonderful parents. Paul's anger and resentment, however, arise from the fact that the family gives priority to Ryne's success and expect Paul to succeed on his own.

4. Did the other person hurt me intentionally?

Paul may consider his parents at fault for the family's imbalance, but he should think about whether they are hurting him intentionally. Did Paul's mother maliciously try to keep him off the team, or was her lateness simply an accident? If Paul's parents knew the effect that their volunteer work was having on Paul, would they change?

5. What did I do that may have led to the problem?

After Paul has sorted out all of this, he has to face a tougher question: whether his own actions may have led to his failure to make the soccer team. Did Paul make it clear to his mother that he needed to

be on time for the tryouts? Could Paul have controlled his temper and kept his opinions to himself
at the tryouts? Did Paul explain or apologize for
his actions to the coach?

Parents of mentally or physically challenged children
often spend much of their lives trying to make it up to the
child. They feel guilty, thinking that something that they
did may have caused the disability. Or they may be motivated by a sincere desire to make up for everything they
believe that the child will miss.

Both of these kinds of thinking lead to dysfunction in a
family. In most cases a mental or physical disability cannot
be prevented. Even if one was preventable or was caused by
an accident, there is nothing that a family can do to change
their situation. Children who are blind, deaf, wheelchair-
bound, or mentally disabled generally remain so for life.

The disabled cannot be given the same advantages as
everyone else. They are disabled. They can be given
reserved parking spots and elevators, closed-captioned TV,
Braille books, special classes, and the like. But none of
these privileges alter the fact that they have a disability.

A key to living with disabled persons is accepting and
appreciating them for exactly who they are. Whatever
their limitations, every individual has talents and
strengths. A family needs to focus on these rather than a
person's weaknesses.

Most parents of disabled children would like to have a
normal family life. But their preoccupation with the disability doesn't allow them to focus on the growth and
strength of every family member.

If you are in a family like the Martins, the first step to take is to identify your needs from your family that are not being met right now. You might make a list of what your disabled sibling needs and how those needs are met. Then make a second list of what you need and how both your needs and your sibling's can be met in a way that is fair to all family members.

The second step is to communicate your needs to your parents. This may not be easy. If you speak of their preoccupation with your brother or sister, they may simply say that everyone in the family needs to make sacrifices. You will have to persist, but always be sure to focus on your feelings and your needs. The chances are good that in your parents' preoccupation they did not realize what was happening to you.

Remember, most parents hoped for a healthy, happy, and problem-free family. The presence of a disabled child makes this goal much more difficult to achieve. You may have trouble communicating with them if they are holding in feelings of guilt, anger, and resentment because their family is not turning out in the way that they had hoped. Communication goes both ways. It is important that you listen to them.

Remember, a functioning family needs a balance so that every member can experience love, belonging, self-esteem, and growth.

If you have tried communicating with your parents to no avail, you might try talking to a close aunt, an uncle, or a friend of the family whom your parents respect and trust. Such a person may be able to express your thoughts to your parents for you or with you. Again, be sure to listen while you are expressing your thoughts. You may come to understand better what is happening to your family if you can get the perspective of an adult who knows your family well.

What Can I Do to Cope?

Many families with disabled children remain focused on the needs of the special child in the family. The other members need to find their own ways to develop self-esteem and to cope. If you are in this situation, there are several things you can do.

1. The first step is to be honest with yourself and with others. Many siblings of disabled children are teased or made fun of. When people ask you about your "retarded," "crippled," or "weird" brother or sister, tell them the truth and set the facts straight. Don't just smile and ignore them or go along with their hurtful comments. You'll find yourself feeling guilty about your behavior and regretting your own words.

2. A second step is to keep the lines of communication open. Be honest with your parents or some trusted adult. Let them know when you are feeling anger, resentment, or guilt. You never know when your parents will be ready to change priorities in order to put the family's needs back into balance. You may find your sibling difficult to communicate with on an equal footing, but keep trying to find common ground or activities that you can enjoy together.

3. A final step is to accept your disabled brother or sister just as he or she is. You cannot change your sibling's special needs. Acceptance means understanding that he or she is not responsible for the drain of your family's time and money to make his or her life more comfortable. Your sibling is not to blame when your peers make remarks about you or your family. You have every right to express your feelings to your parents and to try to work through them. However, acceptance means realizing that your parents must spend more time with your sibling than with you and that you need to take some responsibility for your sibling's experience of love, belonging, and growth.

Compulsive Gambler

Roger Stahl loved sports. Any activity involving a ball or a puck was fascinating to him. He read sports newspapers and magazines. He watched an all-sports TV channel and listened to an all-sports radio station. Roger cheered for the home teams in baseball, football, basketball, hockey, and soccer. He also followed professional tennis, golf, and bowling. It didn't matter whether the sport was professional, college, or amateur, Roger Stahl loved it.

Roger competed a little when he was growing up. He went in for baseball, basketball, football, and wrestling. Never the best player on the team, he still knew what it was to face competition. Roger didn't just think that sports were like life; he believed that sports were life.

Roger had an amazing memory for sports. Considering how little actual playing time he had had, Roger had hours and hours of stories about his games. He could list the winner of every Super Bowl ever played, the World Series champs for the past two decades, every National Basketball Association champ since 1962, and the Stanley Cup winners for every year since the NHL expanded to his area.

Cheryl Stahl enjoyed sports too. She liked the championship games and the classic rivalries. She didn't follow the teams day to day, but she enjoyed attending the big games with Roger. For the first few years of their marriage, most of their free time was spent at sporting events.

When the twins were born, Roger cut back a little on his sports to spend time with his daughters. Martina and Steffie needed both parents to keep them warm, fed, and happy. Roger found that he could feed the babies and watch TV at the same time. He discovered that many games were rebroadcast late at night so he could watch them when the girls woke up for a late-night bottle.

A couple of years later, the Stahls had a son. They named him Robert, after Cheryl's father, but they called him Bo. Roger knew from the beginning that his son would be an athlete. Everyone thought little Bo was so cute in his team shirts, jackets, and caps. Roger was already planning the sports training that he would provide for his son.

Over the next few years Cheryl's interest in sports dwindled. She continued to tolerate Roger's interest in the games but was bothered by one aspect: He was putting money in just about every sports betting pool at his office. He told Cheryl when he won, but she assumed that he lost many more times. She was disturbed one day when she overheard Roger giving a friend one hundred dollars to take to Las Vegas and place as a bet on the Super Bowl game. When Roger won the bet, she didn't know whether to be happy or not. The extra money would come in handy, but she didn't really want their young children to know that their father was betting such large sums of money.

Word of Roger's skill at picking winners spread around the office. A guy in another department approached Roger with a proposition: Roger would pick Saturday's basketball games and the coworker would place a bet for them with a bookie. Roger said no thanks to the offer. He didn't know the man very well, but he did know that placing bets with bookies was illegal.

In the meantime, Roger was having a pretty good run of luck. His five- and ten-dollar bets with friends were turning into twenty- and fifty-dollar bets. Roger figured that overall he was ahead. Even when he lost, he was only losing money that had been won.

It seemed no time had passed at all when the twins turned fifteen. Both girls enjoyed volleyball and swimming. They played volleyball mostly for recreation, but swimming was competitive.

Roger was getting to be known around the office and the neighborhood as a betting guru. He knew the Las Vegas odds for every game every weekend. He made his predictions, and bet on some of them. He won some, lost some. Overall he was about even. But Roger really wanted to get ahead. He dreamed of being able to buy Martina and Steffie a new car for their sixteenth birthday. He decided to place a bet with a bookie on the World Series. Roger felt that the bet was a sure thing. Most people were surprised that the Cleveland Indians had made it to the Series, and few gave them a chance against the Atlanta Braves. But few people had the statistics that Roger had compiled. He calculated daytime versus nighttime, grass versus Astroturf, right-hander versus left-hander, and other stats so obscure that only another sports statistician could understand them. Roger was confident that Cleveland would win.

He withdrew three thousand dollars from the twins' college savings account and bet it at seven-to-one odds. As everyone remembers, however, the Braves won the Series that year. Roger couldn't tell Cheryl about the loss. He had to get even. He began to use more of the college fund to make more and more bets. The longer the odds, the better he liked them. Roger had been betting for fun. Now he was betting out of fear of discovery. The local bookie was taking his bets on baseball, basketball, golf, and tennis. He was even betting on college games. But it seemed that Roger's luck had turned. He was losing far more than he was winning. Cheryl hadn't noticed the savings account balance yet, but she had noticed that money was becoming very tight.

Bo was a freshman at Springfield South High School now. He made the junior varsity baseball team and played second base. Roger was proud of Bo. He never missed a game. Cheryl and the twins seemed to enjoy the games as well.

One night at dinner Bo mentioned that three of their best players had come down with chicken pox and would miss the next two games. Roger asked Bo a few questions about the boys, but didn't seem to show a particular interest.

Two days later the police showed up at the Stahls' home. They wanted to ask Roger about a slip they had seized during a bust of an illegal betting parlor. The slip read: "Roger Stahl, $200, Highland to beat

Springfield South, May 3." Bo was so ashamed that he couldn't even look at his father as Roger drove off with the police.

Options and Alternatives

Roger Stahl was obsessed by sports. Psychologists define an obsession as any persistent thought on a particular theme or idea that a person cannot get out of his mind. Most obsessions involve themes like death, violence, or sex. Roger's obsession was sports.

Although Roger's obsession was extreme, it didn't make his family dysfunctional. Each member of the family had an interest in sports in his or her own way. Sports did not interfere with any member's survival, safety, security, feelings of love and belonging, self-esteem, or personal growth. In many ways, sports drew the family together rather than pulling them apart.

What made the Stahl family dysfunctional was Roger's compulsive gambling. A compulsion is a repeated behavior that cannot be controlled. Common compulsions are ritualistic behavior such as repeated hand-washing, continually counting objects, or checking over and over again that doors are locked. These behaviors are relatively harmless. Their only negative consequence is wasted time. Compulsive gambling, however, has many obvious problems. Roger's problem had escalated to the point where he was betting and losing his children's college fund. He was keeping his gambling a secret, which was separating him from his wife and children. His name on the slip taken at the gambling raid may lead to legal problems. It has already led to embarrassment and loss of respect on Bo's part.

Many psychologists look at compulsive gambling not as a compulsion, but as an addiction. To a person addicted to drugs or alcohol, the need to get drunk or high on drugs overrides any problems that may result from the substance abuse. Legal problems, hangovers, marital difficulties, or job loss are not enough to make an addict stop his destructive behavior. The compulsive gambler reacts to gambling the same way addicts react to alcohol or drugs. The gambler is addicted to the excitement of the risk that he is taking.

The most effective treatment for compulsive gamblers has come from an organization called Gamblers Anonymous. Gamblers Anonymous is a twelve-step program similar to that of Alcoholics Anonymous. Compulsive gamblers provide support and encouragement for one another. They attend regular meetings to help them break their habit.

Sports gambling is not the only type of gambling in which parents participate. Risky business investments and stock purchases or get-rich-quick schemes are all forms of gambling. Such risks become compulsive for many people. The challenge of thinking up an easy way to make money takes up a great deal of their time.

One of the major problems with Roger Stahl's gambling was that it put his family's financial security at risk. For some people, compulsive spending does the same thing. Compulsive spenders are people who are unable to control how much money they spend. They buy things whether or not they have the money to pay for them. As long as the family income remains the same, these families manage, but if one of the parents becomes ill or loses a job, their home, car, and belongings are all at risk.

How Can I Cope?

If you are in a situation like that of the Stahl children, you need to take some steps to protect yourself. The children of an alcoholic or a drug addict fear for their physical safety. They learn to keep a low profile or hide when their parent has been drinking or using drugs. Children of compulsive gamblers need to protect themselves financially.

If your parent is a compulsive gambler, protect your own money. Don't enter into loans cosigned by your parent. Don't obtain credit cards that can be used by you and your parents. Better yet, don't get a credit card at all. Maintain your own savings account for college, an automobile, or other large purchases. Keep the account in your own name or in joint name with the parent who is not a compulsive gambler. This will help protect your credit rating.

As you become a young adult and consider purchasing a car and, later, a home, you will find that a good credit rating is an extremely important asset. If a parent has ruined your credit rating, you can seek help from an attorney to fix it. If you are worried about paying for college, there are things you can do. You can declare yourself an independent student, which means that you are supporting yourself financially. The college will likely help you to pay for your education if you do so. You can also obtain student loans to pay for college.

Remember that to a compulsive gambler, credit is what a supply of drugs or alcohol is to an addict. But some people who would never dream of giving money to someone to purchase illegal drugs will lend money to a compulsive gambler without a second thought.

To cope in a family with a compulsive gambler, you need to realize that financially you will have to do many things on your own. College money may be lost, money for a car may be unavailable, money for simple everyday pleasures may be gone. You will be better able to cope if you can find ways to earn your own money to get the things you need. You may need to take control of your own financial life to meet your personal goals.

Single-Parent Families

A family is not dysfunctional simply because it is headed by a single parent. Many single-parent families thrive and flourish. Today growing up in a single-parent family is a common experience. More than 16 million teens currently live in single-parent families. Whether created by the death of one parent, out-of-wedlock birth, or divorce, a single-parent family can meet family members' needs.

It is, however, a greater challenge for one parent to meet his or her children's needs alone. There are unique pressures upon single parents. Single-parent families have lower incomes. It is more difficult for a single adult to find the necessary emotional support outside of marriage. In some places out-of-wedlock births are still met with disapproval from some people.

The average single parent earns considerably less than married wage earners or single nonparents. It is easier to meet a family's needs if money is not a constant problem. If there is enough money for food, housing, and medical care, there may not be enough left over for clothing, participation in sports, school pictures, and other common experiences. In some single-parent families, each member works for the common good of the others. This can be a healthy way to build confidence and self-esteem for everyone in the family.

Some single parents find it overwhelming to work and meet the needs of their children at the same time. For these families welfare and other community services are available. Some believe that accepting government assistance can diminish a person's self-esteem. Welfare recipients often feel weak and powerless because they are unable to meet their children's needs on their own. This way of thinking can be very unfair. It makes sense to use whatever means are available, including welfare, to meet a family's needs. It is essential, however, to emphasize that the ultimate goal of a family is to develop skills for independent living. Parents should give children the tools to earn their own way if they are physically, emotionally, and psychologically able.

Emotionally it can be more difficult for single parents. Adults also need support. It is unreasonable for parents to rely on their children to support them emotionally. A good friend, a close sibling, or a person with whom the single parent has developed a loving relationship can be vital to the health of a family. People find it very difficult to give emotionally without occasionally receiving love, caring, or affection in return. Romantic love may not be necessary for all single parents, but a close supportive friendship with another adult can be very important. That is not to say that children of single parents should become matchmakers for their parents, trying to find them a mate, but children need to tolerate and accept the adult relationships of their single mother or father.

Each year more than one million babies are born to unmarried women. Children born outside of marriage often feel different from children of married parents. But many children born out of wedlock are wanted just as much as those born to married parents. A mother who chooses to bear and keep her child outside of marriage generally has good reasons. The father may have abandoned her; she may have known that marriage between them would be miserable; she may simply have felt strongly that she wanted to raise a child on her own. It is essential for teenagers who were born out of wedlock to discuss this with their mothers. How people come into the world is not important. It is what they do once they get here that matters.

All single-parent families are unique. Whether created by death, divorce, or the mother's being unmarried at the time of the birth, all of these families have an opportunity to be healthy and functional if the needs of all family members are a priority.

Death of a Parent

One of the most painful traumas that any family can suffer is the death of one of its members. Losing a parent can be especially troublesome because of the economic and emotional support that the parent was providing. Families in which one parent has died are not necessarily dysfunctional. In many cases, they are stronger, tighter, and more committed to each other's needs than two-parent families. It is important to understand the grieving process and to know what to expect after a parent's death. This helps keep communication open. It is only when communication breaks down or a family member turns to drugs, alcohol, gambling, or compulsive working to cope that a family is in danger of becoming dysfunctional.

The loss of a parent is usually followed by an intense period of grief and sadness. Coping during this time is very difficult. Some family members need support from outside the family. Relatives may spend more time with them and assist in the day-to-day operation of the household. Friends may assist with carpools, cooking, or yardwork. In some cases clergy may provide some support. Many families take advantage of counseling to get them through this difficult period.

Families encounter many difficulties after the death of a parent. One tendency is to try too hard to be strong and capable. Family members sometimes feel that they have to get on with their lives and try to bypass the grieving process to do so. Ignoring their feelings, family members return to school, work, and regular activities as if nothing has happened. This simply prolongs the grief. The sadness and the loss will be felt eventually. It is important to go through the grieving process with the support of your family. Ignoring your loss will only make it harder when other family members have moved on to another emotional stage. Most people endure pain more easily in a supportive environment. Family members should not be afraid to cry. Crying is a healthy way to relieve emotional distress.

The year following the death of any family member is especially traumatic. Each holiday, birthday, anniversary, and special occasion focuses on the past and celebrations with the one who died. Many families try to establish new traditions and ways of celebrating during this year. It is essential that the entire family participate in planning these occasions so that no one feels that the memory of good times in the past is being cast aside.

Eventually the family is ready to move on. The remaining parent has established supportive friendships. Often the single parent considers dating and remarriage. It is important that the children tolerate and accept this turn of events. No one can replace the lost parent. No one will live up to the memories that a child holds. Children and teenagers often strongly resist the thought of someone's taking the place of their deceased parent. It is important to discuss these feelings, but to set them aside. Each person who becomes part of a family needs to be accepted for who he or she is, not as a replacement for someone who is gone. Families who come together to support, encourage, and help each other after a death usually become even stronger.

Divorce

Fifty-six percent of all children in America live or will live in a family that has gone through divorce. This is more than 10 million people. Sixty percent of all single-parent families are created through divorce.

Divorce has a dramatic effect on a family. During the time surrounding a divorce it is common for all family members to undergo a period of intense sadness, anger, frustration, and even grief.

Family members tend to fall into some of the same traps as families who have experienced a death. Some ignore their own feelings and pretend that nothing significant has happened. Others make the divorce the defining issue in their lives for years, using it as an excuse for all of their personal failures.

Divorced families are not automatically dysfunctional, but there are some major challenges to keeping a divorced family healthy and functional. Following many divorces, child custody is shared. A typical arrangement is for children to spend weekdays with one parent and weekends (or every other weekend) with the other parent. In other families children switch homes every evening, every week, each month, every six months, or in the summer and on major holidays. None of these arrangements is easy. Married parents often disagree on approaches to setting limits, spending money, and granting privileges. Following a divorce many of these problems are magnified.

Some divorced parents use children as a means of communicating with or gathering information from their ex-spouses. This is unfair to the children. If you find yourself in this situation, ask your parent to speak to the other directly. Some young people use the friction between their parents to their own advantage. They play one parent against the other or ask one parent for a privilege or purchase that they know the other would deny. This is a tempting trap, but it is short-sighted. You may get what you want today, but in the long run the increased animosity that you create will be disadvantageous. Eventually it will make life more difficult for you in both homes.

Stepparents and Blended Families

When single-parent families become stepfamilies or blended families, they add new people to the family. This addition changes the dynamics in the family and impacts communication. Family members have to work hard to keep talking to each other. But, instead of becoming dysfunctional, blended or stepfamilies can become stronger and more functional after the addition.

In his book *Step by Step-Parenting*, James D. Eckler describes two myths that children and adolescents often hold about stepparents. These myths often block growth and communication because young people may be unable to see their new or potential stepparents for who they really are.

Myth of the Wicked Stepmother

Fairy tales and young adult literature often portray stepparents as selfish and without consideration for the children. When a child is born he or she is the center of the universe. Parents set aside their schedule and their own needs to meet the infant's needs. Children grow up feeling that they play a central role in the family. A stepparent enters a family with a relationship with the single parent. That relationship usually is developed before any relationship with the children starts. It is natural for children to feel pushed away by this relationship. Many children and adolescents are jealous of the time that their single parent is now spending with someone else. The wicked stepmother (or stepfather) image is created because it is easier to dislike someone that you don't know well than to realize that your parent needs someone besides you.

It is important to recognize what is happening if you start believing this myth. Try to get to know your new or potential stepparent. Find out what he or she is really like before making a judgment.

Myth of Instant Love

Another attitude toward a new or potential stepparent is to see the person as the answer to all the family problems. Some children imagine that once their single parent is remarried everything will be wonderful.

This is unfair to the stepparent. Blending a family, especially if other stepsiblings are involved, is hard work. In the long run it is worth it, but everyone in the family needs to make compromises and adjustments. Children or adolescents who expect instant love often find themselves disappointed. They soon come to resent their new stepparent. It is better to keep your expectations realistic. It takes a while for a family to blend. The key to making it work is for everyone to communicate honestly.

How Can I Cope?

Many single-parent or blended families function in a healthy way. Others, however, suffer from the unique stresses listed above. Most school counselors or social workers offer counseling or support groups following divorce, death, or remarriage of a parent. Seek them out for help. If you have a member of the clergy or a relative with whom you feel more comfortable, he or she would be a good source for assistance.

Recent statistics show that about half of all American marriages end in divorce. This results in millions of children being raised in single-parent homes. Adding to that parents who have died, parents who have abandoned their families, and children who were born to single mothers, quite a few teens are going through major family reorganization. The best way to cope is to be patient and tolerant. If each member of a family clearly maintains open lines of communication and a willingness to listen, the family will function well for everyone.

Remember that for a family to function, each member must meet the needs of the others. Whether you are in a small single-parent family, a two-parent family, or a large blended family, you share in the responsibility for making the family function.

What Can I Do?

There are many kinds of dysfunctional families; we have discussed only a few examples. The one thing all dysfunctional families have in common is that they do not meet the needs of all their members. A family should provide the basic necessities of life such as food, shelter, and clothing; safety and security from danger; love and belonging; self-esteem; growth; and the skills needed for independent living. If any family member is significantly lacking in any of these factors, that family is dysfunctional.

If you are in a dysfunctional family, ask yourself three questions: What is making my family dysfunctional? Can I make a difference? Can I cope if change is impossible?

Families Resist Change

All families, including dysfunctional ones, have a balance. Each member has his or her role. In the family of an alcoholic, each member knows how to react when the alcoholic member has been drinking and when he is sober. Each person understands how the family works, who makes decisions, what everyone is allowed to do and not allowed to do. No matter how bad a situation becomes, it is usually predictable and understood by all family members. Often fear of the unknown keeps people from taking steps to make a change. A very old (but untrue) saying is, "Better the devil you know than the devil you don't know." It is untrue because the unknown can often be better and healthier than your current situation.

Many adults choose to live in horrible situations because they fear living alone. Both men and women often tolerate humiliation and abuse because they can't bring themselves to imagine a life that is different. One explanation for this is that a family enhances the self-esteem of each of its members, but dysfunctional families tear down self-esteem. Without self-esteem, a person is unwilling to take risks. He or she lacks the self-confidence to begin a new life.

Other dysfunctional families resist change because all of the members love one another even while they hate the words or actions of one. It is hard to separate one's love for a person from his or her actions. For the spouse of an emotionally abusive parent to say, "I love you, but I can't tolerate the things you say," is very difficult, but it can be very effective in making a family healthier.

A final reason that dysfunctional families resist change is pride. People hate to admit that they need help. Most dysfunctional families find it difficult to change without the support of a person or organization outside the family. Many people who would give their last dollar to help another are sometimes unwilling to accept help for themselves. It is often said that the first step to recovery is admitting that you need help.

What to Do If Change Seems Possible

If you think it is possible to make changes for the better in your family, take action. Find out all you can about the situation that is harming your family. Read about the problem. Your public library has books that focus on each of the twelve types of families discussed in this book. You can also find information about other personal and family problems there.

Talk to people who are experts in helping. Throughout this book we have suggested that you talk to a school counselor, school social worker, police social worker, clergy person, teacher, aunt, uncle, or close friend of the family. These people can help you think things through and work out practical considerations.

Make a plan of action. Think it through carefully. Many families of alcoholics confront the alcoholic together in a supportive environment. If you are being physically or sexually abused, police and social workers are trained to help and protect you once you report it. If your family's dysfunction comes from an attitude of overprotection, perfectionism, religious fanaticism, or other ideals gone haywire, you may have to confront them subtly and in small steps. Perhaps you can join with the healthiest members of your family to confront the problem.

See your plan through. If it does not go exactly as you had hoped, think about what happened and try another approach. Talk over the roadblocks that you hit and problem-solve ways to overcome them next time. Be patient. Dysfunctional families take years to develop the balance that keeps them together while remaining dysfunctional. It will take time to change. If your family becomes committed to change, expect periodic setbacks. Often a family takes two steps forward and one step back, but even that pattern moves you in the right direction.

What to Do If Change Seems Impossible

If you cannot change your family, you must protect yourself. In the process you may be able to help younger siblings. If your family is dysfunctional, but you feel that you have a healthy level of self-esteem and are growing as a person, you may be able to help younger brothers and sisters. Teaching them how you have learned to cope and listening to them when they are in pain will help both of you. Some people have survived in very sick families because they had an older brother or sister who loved them and made them feel that they belonged.

If you have older brothers or sisters, talk to them. They may be able to tell you how they survived their teen years in spite of the problems at home. If you are an only child, grandparents, aunts, uncles, or cousins may give you strategies for survival.

Most important, never give up hope. Even when change seems extremely unlikely and escape seems years away, you always have hope. Stay close to healthy friends and other adults who can support and encourage you.

Many people who grew up in dysfunctional families have accomplished great things. Several presidents of the United States used the determination that they developed during a troubled childhood to keep them focused on their goals. If you have hope, you too can see your dreams come true.

Who Can Help?

There are two safe and healthy ways to approach any dysfunctional family. The first is to try to change the situation that is making the family dysfunctional. As discussed in the previous chapter, families can strongly resist changes, but if you take small steps toward change, you may well reach your goal. When change is possible, it usually takes courage and patience to make it happen. Some family situations require you to report wrongdoing to outside agencies. This can be very difficult for teenagers, but if physical or sexual abuse is occurring it must be reported. Families in which such abuse is happening are in crisis, even though they may not know it. Everyone in the family will need help to recover from the abuse.

The second approach to a difficult situation is to accept the situation as it is. Disabilities, low income, illness, and other problems often occur in families. Often the most effective approach is to make the best of your situation. Coping in a dysfunctional family means keeping up the hope that you will eventually live a happy, fulfilled life even though your natural family has problems. Coping is being conscious of the dysfunction in your family and taking steps to make sure that you don't repeat the same mistakes.

How to Help Yourself

One way to decide the best source of help is to think about which of your needs is not being fulfilled. Your approach to coping should be related to that need.

Survival

Young people need adequate food, shelter, clothing, and health care. If your family has enough money to meet those needs, but for some reason your parents do not provide the money, you are suffering from neglect. If you cannot persuade your parents to provide it, you should talk to a school counselor, social worker, child welfare worker, or similar person who will work on your behalf to make sure your needs are met.

If the problem is low income or no income because of your parents' unemployment, help is available. States, counties, cities, churches, and synagogues all have funds to assist people needing food, shelter, clothing, or medical care. You can help your parents to get information about these agencies or get the information yourself. The phone book may be a good place to start. Again, your school counselor or social worker may have helpful information.

Safety and Security

People are not safe and secure when they are being physically or sexually abused. The abuse may be inflicted by parents, siblings, stepparents, or live-in boyfriends or girlfriends. This abuse must be reported. If you are aware that a family member has been abused, you must help him or her to report it. After the abuse has been reported, seek and accept further help to understand what has happened and to allow your family to reorganize in a healthy way.

Love and Belonging

If you feel unloved and unwanted in your family, it is possible to meet these needs in a healthy way outside your family. Unfortunately, many young people try to meet these needs in unhealthy ways. Some engage in sex with many partners, hoping to feel loved. Others join gangs or other antisocial groups to feel that they belong.

You can feel love and belonging outside your family in safe and healthy ways. Most churches and synagogues have youth groups, which are excellent places to feel you belong and learn to understand yourself at the same time. Some people feel more comfortable with school clubs, sports teams, Boy Scouts, Girl Scouts, student organizations, theater groups, or other organizations in which people work together for a common goal. First, think about what you like to do. Then find a way to share your interests with other people.

Self-Esteem

If you feel that you are dumb, ugly, clumsy, or incapable, you need to boost your self-esteem. People can do that through accomplishments. They are proud of themselves when they have done something well.

A good way to work toward a sense of accomplishment is to set goals. At first, your goals may be small, such as to say hello to someone new, to get to your first-period class on time, or not to eat snacks between school and dinner.

As you accomplish each small goal, you can set harder goals. As you challenge yourself, little by little you will begin to feel better about yourself.

Another way to raise your self-esteem is to help other people. Talk to someone who is more lonely than you. Volunteer to help elderly, disabled, or very young people. Helping others will make you feel good about yourself.

Growth and Developing Skills for Independent Living

If you find it difficult to grow as a person in your family, you may need to develop more responsibility. The first step toward developing responsibility is to talk frankly to your parents about your feelings. If you feel overprotected or dominated, let them know that you are capable and ready to be given a chance to try new things. Ask them for more opportunities that will allow you to prove that you can take on greater responsibility.

If your parents are unwilling to grant you the freedom you need, try to demonstrate your independence at school or in other settings. Take a leadership role in a club or an organization at school. Do the job without your parents' help, while demonstrating your capabilities for everyone to see. Such leadership will help you learn to work with other people, which will be very useful in the workplace in the future.

Resources in Your Community

When you have decided what kind of help you need, the next step is to decide where to go to for help. The first places most teens turn for help are their schools and their churches, synagogues, or other religious groups.

School counselors, school social workers, and teachers can be helpful when trying to cope with a dysfunctional family. Youth ministers or other clergy may be able to provide guidance and support. In a crisis situation, many police departments have social workers and specially trained officers who work only with youths. The police may be the first ones to turn to in an emergency.

Many other resources in your community are ready to offer help. Among them are Alateen, YMCA, YWCA, Boys Club, Girls Club, Big Brothers and Big Sisters, and the Salvation Army. Many communities have mental health departments, private and public hospitals, clinics, outreach centers, and similar groups. Use the phone book to find these organizations.

The most important resource that you have in your community is yourself. Once you have recognized that your family is dysfunctional and have determined that you will live a safe and healthy life, the hardest part is over. You can cope as long as you have hope.

Your Future Family

Many young people worry that their future family will be dysfunctional like the one in which they are growing up. Statistics show that people who were abused as children are more likely to abuse their own children. The children of addicts are more likely than average to become addicts themselves. However, these are averages that you can beat.

People tend to follow the model that their parents have set for them unless they think about their lives carefully and take control. Knowledge is very powerful. Once you understand the factors that contribute to your family's remaining dysfunctional, you are well on your way to safeguarding your own future children.

Your life is your own. The kind of adult that you become is up to you. Your future family will be healthy and safe as long as you take steps to keep it that way. You may need counseling, encouragement, and support along the way. But someday you can have a functioning family in which all members love, accept, listen to, and communicate with one another.

Glossary

addiction A psychological condition that causes someone constantly to desire a potentially harmful substance or action.

alcoholism The state of being addicted to alcohol.

antagonist A person who opposes someone else's wishes or actions.

anxiety A feeling or state of fear.

bipolar disorder A psychological condition in which a person experiences dramatic mood shifts between states of severe depression and incredible joy or excitement.

codependent A person who enables another to behave in an unhealthy way because he or she fears that stopping the behavior will harm that person or their relationship.

compulsive disorder A psychological condition in which a person performs certain actions repeatedly or without his or her control.

conform To act in the same way that others do or to act as they expect you to act.

cult A religious group that requires followers to obey without question.

dependency Condition in which a person continually relies on something or someone for support.

depression A deep sadness or gloominess.

dysfunctional Not working properly.

emotional abuse Treatment that intentionally hurts someone's feelings.

fanaticism An extreme belief in a religious or political idea or group.

incest Sexual intercourse between people who are closely related.

incompetent Unable to function properly or to accomplish a task.

isolation Mental or physical separation from other people.

mentor Someone who provides support, knowledge, or advice.

neglect Failure to provide for someone's basic needs such as food, clothing, shelter, and medical care.

obsession An uncontrollable preoccupation with a person, object, or idea.

overprotection Practice of defending someone from all sources of harm or grief. This can negatively affect that person's ability to handle everyday problems.

passive Tending not to take an active approach to life.

perfectionism Unrealistic demands or expectations that something or someone be perfect.

phobia A strong, usually irrational and excessive, fear of something.

psychosis A severe mental disorder in which a person loses contact with reality.

schizophrenia A psychological disorder in which a person losses contact with everyday reality and often acts in a bizarre or withdrawn manner.

self-esteem Feelings of confidence and self-worth.

situational depression An overwhelming sadness caused by a terrible event or loss.

trauma A shocking experience that has a long-term negative effect on a person.

unconditional Absolute and without question.

workaholic A person whose work is more important than anything else in life, including other people.

Where to Go for Help

Hotlines

Generally, you can find telephone numbers of organizations in your community that can help you in the front pages of the phone book or in the Yellow Pages under "Crisis Intervention." If you are unable to find help locally, the following national organizations may be able to provide you with referrals or information. The 800 prefixes are toll-free anywhere in the United States.

If you are in a crisis situation or feel suicidal, call 911 or your local police immediately.

Al-Anon Family Group
(800) 356-9996

Cocaine Hotline
(800) COCAINE

National Alliance for the Mentally Ill
(800) 950-NAMI

National Center for Missing and Exploited Children
(800) 843-5678

National Child Abuse Hotline
(800) 4-A-CHILD

National Council on Compulsive Gambling
(800) 522-4700

National Crisis Prevention Institute
(800) 558-8976

National Runaway Switchboard
(800) 621-4000
Stepfamily Association of America
(800) 735-0329

In Canada
YouthLink
(416) 922-3335

Other Resources

Alcoholics Anonymous (AA)
P.O. Box 459
Grand Central Station
New York, NY 10163
(212) 870-3400
Web site: http://www.alcoholics-anonymous.org
e-mail: 76245-2153@compuserve.com

Center for Substance Abuse Prevention (CSAP)
5600 Fishers Lane
Suite 800, Rockwall II Building
Rockville, MD 20857
(301) 443-0365
Web site: http://www.samhsa.gov/csap/index.htm

Children of Alcoholics Foundation
Box 4185
Grand Central Station
New York, NY 10163
(800) 488-3784

Children's Advocacy
200 Westside Square
Huntsville, AL 35801
(205) 534-6868
Web site: http://fly.highway.net/ncacdm
e-mail: ncacdm@highway.net

Cocaine Anonymous (CA)
3740 Overland Avenue, Suite G
Los Angeles, CA 90034-6337
(800) 347-8998
Web site: http://www.ca.org/

Gamblers Anonymous
International Service Office
P.O. Box 17173
Los Angeles, CA 90017
Web site: http://www.gamblersanonymous.org
e-mail: isomain@gamblersanonymous.org

Narcotics Anonymous (NA)
World Service Office
19737 Nordhoff Place
Chatsworth, CA 91311
(818) 773-9999
e-mail: wso@aol.com

National Domestic Violence Hotline
3616 Far West Boulevard, Suite 101-297
Austin, TX 78731-3074
(800) 799-7233
Web site: http://www.inetport.com/~ndvh

National Network for Youth
1319 F Street NW, Suite 401
Washington, DC 20004
(202) 783-7949
Web site: http://www.nn4youth.org
e-mail: nn4youth@worldnet.att.net

In Canada
Addictions Foundation of Manitoba
1031 Portage Avenue
Winnipeg, MB R3G 0R8
(204) 944-6200

Alcoholics Anonymous
#202 Intergroup Office
234 Ellington Avenue E.
Toronto, ON M4P 1K5
(416) 487-5591

For Further Reading

Berger, Gilda. *Violence and the Family.* New York: Franklin
    Watts, 1990.
Bratman, Fred. *Everything You Need to Know When a Parent
    Dies.* Rev. ed. New York: Rosen Publishing Group, 1995.
Clayton, Lawrence. *Coping with a Drug-Abusing Parent.* Rev.
    ed. New York: Rosen Publishing Group, 1995.
Clayton, Lawrence, and Smith, Betty Sharon. *Coping with
    Depression.* Rev. ed. New York: Rosen Publishing Group,
    1995.
Cooney, Judith. *Coping with Sexual Abuse.* Rev. ed. New York:
    Rosen Publishing Group, 1991.
Flanders, Stephen A. *Suicide.* New York: Facts on File, 1991.
Glassman, Bruce. *Everything You Need to Know about
    Stepfamilies.* Rev. ed. New York: Rosen Publishing Group,
    1994.
Grosshandler, Janet. *Coping When a Parent Dies.* Rev. ed.
    New York: Rosen Publishing Group, 1995.
—.*Coping with Alcohol Abuse.* New York: Rosen Publishing
    Group, 1990.
Hill, Margaret. *Coping with Family Expectations.* New York:
    Rosen Publishing Group, 1990.
Jamiolkowski, Raymond M. *Coping with an Emotionally
    Distant Father.* New York: Rosen Publishing Group, 1995.
—.*Drugs and Domestic Violence.* New York: Rosen Publishing
    Group, 1996.
Kaplan, Leslie S. *Coping with Stepfamilies.* New York: Rosen
    Publishing Group, 1991.
Kreiner, Anna. *Everything You Need to Know about Creating
    Your Own Support System.* New York: Rosen Publishing
    Group, 1996.

Kurland, Morton L. *Coping with Family Violence.* Rev. ed. New York: Rosen Publishing Group, 1990.

LaMar, Donna F. *Transcending Turmoil: Survivors of Dysfunctional Families.* New York: Plenum Press, 1992.

Lee, Mary Price, and Lee, Richard S. *Drugs and Codependency.* New York: Rosen Publishing Group, 1995.

Levine, Beth. *Divorce: Young People Caught in the Middle.* Springfield, NJ: Enslow Publishers, Inc., 1995.

Love, Pat, and Robinson, Jo. *The Emotional Incest Syndrome: What to Do When a Parent's Love Rules Your Life.* New York: Bantam Books, 1990.

Marcus, Eric. *Why Suicide: Answers to 200 of the Most Frequently Asked Questions about Suicide, Attempted Suicide, and Assisted Suicide.* San Francisco: HarperCollins Publishers, 1996.

Miller, Deborah A., and Kelly, Pat. *Coping with Incest.* Rev. ed. New York: Rosen Publishing Group, 1995.

Miller, Maryann. *Coping with Cults.* New York: Rosen Publishing Group, 1990.

Mufson, Susan. *Straight Talk about Child Abuse.* New York: Facts on File, 1991.

Porterfield, Kay Marie. *Coping with an Alcoholic Parent.* Rev. ed. New York: Rosen Publishing Group, 1990.

—.*Coping with Codependency.* Rev. ed. New York: Rosen Publishing Group, 1994.

Ratto, Linda Lee. *Coping with a Physically Challenged Brother or Sister.* New York: Rosen Publishing Group, 1992.

Smith, Judie. *Coping with Suicide.* Rev. ed. New York: Rosen Publishing Group, 1990.

Stark, Evan. *Everything You Need to Know about Family Violence.* Rev. ed. New York: Rosen Publishing Group, 1997.

Wagonseller, Bill R. *Coping in a Single-Parent Home.* Rev. ed. New York: Rosen Publishing Group, 1997.

Index